READING OTHER-WISE

Society of Biblical Literature

Semeia Studies

Gale A. Yee, General Editor

Number 62

READING OTHER-WISE
Socially Engaged Biblical Scholars
Reading with Their Local Communities

READING OTHER-WISE
Socially Engaged Biblical Scholars
Reading with Their Local Communities

Edited by

Gerald O. West

Society of Biblical Literature
Atlanta

READING OTHER-WISE
Socially Engaged Biblical Scholars
Reading with Their Local Communities

Library of Congress Cataloging-in-Publication Data

Reading other-wise : socially engaged biblical scholars reading with their local communities / edited by Gerald O. West.
     p. cm. — (Society of Biblical Literature Semeia studies ; no. 62)
     Includes bibliographical references.
     ISBN-13: 978-1-58983-273-2 (paper binding : alk. paper)
     1. Bible—Criticism, interpretation, etc. 2. Theology. I. West, Gerald O.
     BS511.3.R425 2007
     220.6—dc22   2007015208

CONTENTS

RESPONSES

Abbreviations

AThR	*Anglican Theological Review*
ATLA	American Theological Library Association
EstBíb	*Estudios bíblicos*
JBL	*Journal of Biblical Studies*
JTSA	*Journal of Theology for Southern Africa*
LTQ	*Lexington Theological Quarterly*
Neot	*Neotestamentica*
OTE	*Old Testament Essays*
SemeiaSt	Semeia Studies
SNTSMS	Society for New Testament Studies Monograph Series

Reading Other-wise: Socially Engaged Biblical Scholars Reading with Their Local Communities: An Introduction

Gerald O. West

This volume joins the discourse initiated ten years ago by *Semeia* 73 (West and Dube 1996b), which Musa Dube and I edited. In that volume we explored the kind of biblical scholarship characterized by an explicit collaboration between the biblical scholar and ordinary, nonscholarly, readers of the Bible. A secondary concern in that volume was to privilege African voices in this regard. In this follow-up volume I return to the topic, but from within a wider perspective, inviting scholars from other parts of the world to participate who share similar commitments to do their scholarship in the interface between the academy and the community.

A great deal has changed in these ten years, among them the attitude of the *Semeia* Board (now the Semeia Studies Board) to the project. Then Musa Dube and I had considerable difficulty in convincing certain Board members that what we were doing was a worthwhile "academic" project. We were told that "the accent" (and I am quoting) of the volume was too strong, and consequently there was worry that scholars in the United States of America might not understand. Fortunately, the Editor at that time, Daniel Patte, and enough members of the Board believed in the project, and so the reluctance of some was overcome. But the tussle was instructive. We learned that though we saw ourselves as contributing to a common project—biblical scholarship, in broad terms—we were perceived by some "at the center" to be on the periphery, on the margins. The primary problem, it seemed, was that we had blurred the boundary between biblical interpretation in local communities and biblical interpretation in the academy.

When this follow-up project was proposed, the reaction was quite different. The *Semeia*/Semeia Studies Board eagerly embraced the idea and even suggested I invite "an ordinary reader" to be one of the respondents to the volume. I was delighted by the response, and I have tried very hard to implement their suggestion. My failure to find "an ordinary reader" to do a response is also instructive. Allow me to explain more fully.

As I have indicated, repeatedly, my use of the term "ordinary reader" has both a general and specific designation. Generally it designates the "nonscholar," to use the phrase used by the Nigerian biblical scholar, Teresa Okure (1993). However, because I come from South Africa I am reluctant to use "non" language, for its sets the "non-non" as the norm, as in "non-white." Part of the substantive claim I am making in differentiating between the scholar and nonscholar/ordinary reader is that there is a difference in the way each of these sectors read biblical texts. This difference, I have argued (West 1996; 2003), is significant, and recognition of this difference can lead to creative and socially transformative collaboration between the different sets of interpretive resources these different sectors bring to a collaborative reading project. So, in the general sense of "ordinary reader" I am focusing on the kind of interpretive training different sectors have received. The ordinary reader has been "trained" by his or her primary (for example, the family) and secondary (for example, the church and school) communities, whereas the scholarly reader has been trained (very overtly, so I drop the quotation marks) by a tertiary community, the academy (Meyer 2002).

But I also use the term "ordinary reader" in a specific sense. I am not interested in all "ordinary" readers. My commitment to the liberation struggle in South Africa and to the subsequent reconstruction and development of our liberated country leads me to take sides with particular social sectors, especially the poor, the working class, and the marginalized (including, for example, women and those living with HIV and AIDS). In South Africa this means that most of the "ordinary" readers I work with are black South Africans.

This brief clarification of the term "ordinary reader," and I am not wedded to the term, helps to explain why it has proved difficult to find an ordinary reader to respond to the essays in this volume. First, the collaborative acts that constitute the readings of the Ujamaa Centre for Community Development and Research, the social location for most of my own work over the past seventeen years (West 2006a), are acts of collaboration, not "education." We are not educating the community to read the Bible in our "trained" way. We are sharing the resources of biblical scholarship in particular social sites where there are already substantial local interpretive resources. Moreover, we quite deliberately share these interpretive resources in ways that do not foreground their academic framework. Our experience is that these additional reading resources are potentially empowering in enabling familiar texts to be read in unfamiliar ways and in enabling unfamiliar texts or literary units to be read, and in so doing to provide alternative lines of connection between local community contexts and biblical texts (West 2006a). However, there is usually little interest in local communities to engage with the broader academic context from which these resources come.

Second, the kind of collaborative biblical interpretation I am here speaking about is primarily an act of engagement with contextual realities rather than an interpretive experiment or scholarly research (West 2006a:148). What is written about these primary acts is second-order reflection on practice, and its primary purpose is to complete the action-reflection cycle that is praxis. In other words, within a liberation paradigm praxis involves ongoing action and reflection, with reflection being a requisite component of emancipatory action. Within the praxis of the Ujamaa Centre, contextual Bible study is about community-based action. The reflection on the reading process that forms a constituent part of the action is a secondary moment and is largely confined to the staff of the Ujamaa Centre. The community has other priorities. They invite us to work with the Bible with them around a common project, and in order to serve them as fully as we can we do reflection on the Bible-reading process. Their own focus is on community-identified issues they are struggling with, to which the collaborative contextual Bible study might make a contribution.

Third, while the communities we work with are eager to have socially engaged scholars work with them, they are not really interested in conversing with the academy. So when I asked, very tentatively, if they would like to read what biblical scholars were saying about this kind of collaborative work, they expressed polite interest and some real interest in particular aspects of my oral summaries but declined to actually read any of the essays. If there had been an essay that partially represented their participation in an actual Bible study, their response may have been different. In other cases where I have shared published work with communities with whom I have worked, first having secured their approval to be represented, there has been considerable interest in picking through the written words for "their voices," represented though they are. They enjoy holding the text and noting their presence in it (see, for example, West and Zengele 2004; 2006), but there is seldom in-depth engagement with the essay, even in such cases.

To be honest, I did not try too hard to get an "ordinary reader" to be a respondent. I worried that I would be setting them up. The academy is not always an appropriate place for different "accents."

But I am delighted with the two scholarly reader respondents this volume does have. Naveen Rao is someone whom I met in Chennai, India, when I was invited to do some contextual Bible-study workshops there. He has become a comrade and collaborator and has recently visited the Ujamaa Centre to work with us in our context. Werner Kahl comes from the German tradition of biblical scholarship, wherein he now teaches, but has worked for several years in Ghana. He has had a long and sustained interest in African biblical scholarship, particularly in the way it is partially constituted by ordinary African "readers" of the Bible. These two respondents bring two quite different forms of engagement to the essays in this volume. They speak for themselves.

The contributions that form the core of this volume are quite diverse and yet share a common commitment to a place for real ordinary "readers" in their biblical scholarship. Eric Anum's essay keeps the connection with *Semeia* 73 and with Africa, offering as it does his reflections on the earlier volume. The essay by Mogomme Alpheus Masoga is also, in a way, an engagement with the earlier volume, for it is the kind of essay that might have been included in that volume had it been written then. What Masoga brings to this current volume is the voice of a black biblical scholar in dialogue with popular African culture, which is often saturated with allusions to the Bible. My own essay too is part of this "African" opening section. In response to a presentation I gave at Emmanuel College, Toronto, in 2002, Gerald Sheppard made the comment that he had reservations about my use of the term "ordinary 'readers,'" for, he said, all ordinary readers are actually "extraordinary" readers. I agree with him and thank him for reminding me of this reality, a reality that impacts me every time I do contextual Bible with local communities of the poor, working class, and marginalized. With Sheppard's reminder in mind, I have identified three particular ordinary "readers" as the focus of my essay, attempting to give voice to the remarkable extraordinariness of their interpretations and contributions. Shifting into the African diaspora, Stephen Jennings, from Jamaica, provides a detailed historical and hermeneutical reflection of a range of "extraordinary" Jamaican interpreters of the Bible and goes on to show the relevance of such work for socially engaged biblical scholars.

The essay by Nicole Simopoulos moves the volume away from Africa, but does so by showing how a methodology developed in South Africa might be useful in a range of other contexts. She does contextual Bible study on the same text, the story of Sarah and Hagar, with three different communities of women, including women in South Africa and the United States of America. Janet Lees's essay makes a similar move, taking the contextual Bible methodology and working with it among participants with communication difficulties and in inner-city churches in the United Kingdom. Up the coast from where Simopoulos has done some of her engaged readings, Bob Ekblad works with inmates of the Skagit County Jail, reading the story of Moses' call dialogically with them.

One of the sites that has been especially significant in pioneering an engagement between socially engaged biblical scholars and communities of the poor, working class, and marginalized has been Brazil. The essay by Monika Ottermann demonstrates clearly how socially engaged biblical scholars are receptive to learning "from below" and how this can lead to new scholarly questions, in service of ordinary women "readers" in this case. Valmor da Silva shows in his essay the diversity of local contexts that forms of socially engaged Bible reading impact. The early days of liberation theology and its associated forms of biblical interpretation are having to respond to a wider set of social realities, both in Brazil and elsewhere (as Masoga's essay also demonstrates). The essay by Kari Latvus shows how Latin American forms of biblical interpretation have impacted on Britain, particularly in urban theology projects, but goes on to suggest that other forms of communal Bible reading, such as bibliodrama, need to be developed if grassroots communities are to be engaged.

These essays offer a rich array of insights and challenges. Each of them in its own way recognizes and provides a place for the other, who is not a biblical scholar, in their practice of biblical interpretation. We all believe that biblical scholarship has resources to offer to those for whom the Bible is a significant text in the many struggles of our time; what we share in these essays is our various attempts to construct and participate in collaborative acts of reading for the purposes of particular projects of transformation and life. We are all trying to read the Bible other-wise.

YE MA WO MO! AFRICAN HERMENEUTS, YOU HAVE SPOKEN AT LAST: REFLECTIONS ON *SEMEIA* 73 (1996)

Eric Anum

INTRODUCTION

The articles in this volume can be classified into three groups. First, there are articles that are specifically directed toward scholarly readers, concerning the way forward in developing hermeneutical models in Africa. John Pobee's article is one such article in the volume, in which he argues that African traditional religion and culture are themselves "hermeneutic" and therefore should be considered as such by biblical scholars in their exegetical endeavors. Teresa Hinga agrees with Pobee's point that there should be "a "passover of language," a shifting of epistemological centers so that biblical scholarship is done in a language that makes context, in all its variety, hermeneutically relevant (Hinga 1996:279). These comments were specifically directed toward scholarly readers working in Africa, who are being asked to shift from Eurocentric to Afrocentric hermeneutical approaches to biblical interpretation.

Second, there are essays that reflect the quantitative and qualitative research carried out by scholarly readers among ordinary readers. Examples of these are Jonathan Draper's research among selected Anglican congregations in South Africa and Megan Walker's research among South African Roman Catholic women in the township of Mpophomeni, KwaZulu-Natal, as they interpret Marian texts. There is also Musa Dube's research among Batswana African Independent Church (AIC) women in Botswana.

Third, there are articles in the volume that "attempt to practice hermeneutical principles of reading the Bible" (Hinga 1996:279) within specific African contexts. For example, there is the article of Gerald West, which attempts to put forward principles for "reading with" marginalized people in the province of KwaZulu-Natal, South Africa, which he refers to as Contextual Bible Study. In addition, the article of Justin Ukpong puts forward inculturation hermeneutical principles for reading the parable of the shrewd manager in Luke 16 from the context of poor and exploited peasant farmers in Nigeria, West Africa.

ORDINARY READERS

In some senses, all the articles in the volume deal with both general and particular descriptions of the ordinary reader. According to West and Dube in their introduction to the volume, "The general usage includes all readers who read the Bible pre-critically. But we also use the term 'ordinary' to designate a particular sector of pre-critical readers, those who are poor and marginalized" (West and Dube 1996a:7). However, a review of the articles in the volume indicates that certain characteristics are associated with ordinary readers.

First, poor and marginalized groups are identified as ordinary readers. West identifies ordinary readers in the South African context with "ordinary people from poor and marginalized communities" (West 1996:23). Musa Dube and Itumeleng Mosala make a similar identification in their articles in the volume. However, Hinga responds to the characterization of the poor and oppressed as "ordinary readers" and scholars as "critical readers" by asking, "Does material poverty reflect intellectual poverty?" (Hinga 1996:284). In other words, why should the scholar describe her/himself as "critical" and the poor as "ordinary." Perhaps this characterization is generalized from the social locations and the harsh economic realities that are associated with some African contexts. These often determine that the poor and oppressed usually possess little or no education and therefore lack the critical reading skills normally associated with classroom education, even though they might not necessarily be deficient in argumentative and critical discursive competence.

Second, residual oral cultures and grassroots groups are identified as ordinary readers. Jonathan Draper identifies the ordinary readers that his team of researchers worked with as residually illiterate and therefore they employ what he calls a residual oral hermeneutic in their readings. Draper reports that his team of research assistants took part in revival meetings with the groups they were working with in order to collect additional data for their research because they discovered that their textual approach was inadequate among such groups. Thus, for Draper, "Transcriptions of the revivals present more interesting data than do the textual studies. They seem to confirm my suspicion that the black communities we were working with in our research are still operating with a residual oral culture" (Draper 1996:69). Draper further observes that these particular readers also utilized nontextual strategies, which were situational and not abstract. Dube and Walker also agree with using residual oral reading methods with the ordinary readers they were dealing with by proposing the development of hermeneutical models along lines that take issues of orality seriously into consideration. Likewise, Ukpong's article identified the context of peasant farmers from grass root locations in Nigeria as the subject of his exegesis of the parable of the shrewd farmer in Luke 16 who also live in predominantly oral cultures.

Third, those described as "real contextual readers" are identified as ordinary readers. In Bernard Lategan's response to the articles in the volume, where, in citing George Steiner's identification of scholarly readers as "critics" and ordinary readers as "readers," he quotes with favor Robert Fowler's explanation that, "the critic steps back from the text to strike a magisterial pose of critical, objectifying distance, whereas the reader tries to eliminate the distance between himself and the text to allow the merging of his being with the text" (Fowler 1992:27). Thus, in this context, the ordinary reader is identified as the real subjective reader who reads the text directly from her/his social context or location while the scholarly reader is identified as the one who stands back and acts as an objective critic. Tim Long also explored these distinctions in his article and attempted to employ it in his reading of the Book of Revelation.

Fourth, ordinary readers are identified as spontaneous and sub-conscious readers. In Daniel Patte's response to the articles in the volume, he observes that as the ordinary reader makes "epistemological judgments" from her/his readings as well as "value judgments" that are relative and significant for her/his context (Patte 1996:271). Due however to lack of time and critical resources, the ordinary reader reads the text sub-consciously and spontaneously for direct use in her/his social location. This, in a sense, is similar to the views of West and Dube stated in the introduction to the volume, that the ordinary reader is the one who reads the text precritically. Patte bases his description of ordinary readers as being spontaneous and sub-conscious, on examples drawn from within the volume, arguing the presence of a context-derived epistemology that is not European (although, as readers, they can be brought into dialogue) (Patte 1996:272–73).

SCHOLARLY READERS

In the volume, the scholarly reader, whether explicitly or implicitly, is identified as a Western educated, middle-class person. Judging from the contexts from which the contributors write one can deduce that scholarly readers in the specific contexts that they describe are not only people that possess composite skills for reading biblical texts, but also people who belong to the middle or elite class in their contexts. Most of those classified as scholarly readers are urban dwellers influenced by Western education and values. West for instance, identifies himself as a white middle-class male (West and Dube 1996a:9). Dube also how estranged she feels, (through the acquisition of Western education) from her traditional and rural people in the AICs.

Second, the scholarly reader is identified as an academic, literate and textual reader. This comes to the fore in the research of Dube, who declares that she is an academic scholar whose biblical interpretation is informed by "Western academic interpretative communities" (Dube 1996:127), which is associated with textuality.

Dube also admits that she shares a commonality with her ordinary readers in that they are both dominated by imperialistic and patriarchal modes of reading. Hence, what Dube does as an academic is to search for "modes of reading that are subversive to imperialistic and patriarchal domination" (Dube 1996:127). Ukpong's reading is another example of an academic who works for the social sector among whom he is located, that is the peasant farmers of Nigeria. They provide a reading of the parable of the shrewd manager in Luke 16, which not only takes the context of the oppressed and exploited peasant farmers as its starting point, but also forms the subject in his interpretative work.

The scholarly reader is also identified as literate. This description of the scholarly reader is vividly articulated in Draper's article. He identifies academic readers in the African context as those "readers who have internalized textuality and whose consciousness has been structured by textuality" (Draper 1996:59). The academic readers identified here are those who work mainly from a textual approach.

Third, scholarly readers are identified as objective/critical readers. Biblical studies are considered an academic discipline in the humanities. Thus, the Bible, being one of the main resources for biblical studies has "been the focus of scholarly attention as academics seek to present the Bible in its own terms by seeking to analyze the Bible as literature (literary criticism) and as history (historical criticism)" (Hinga 1996:277). The scholarly reader is identified as being involved in what Lategan calls "critical activity." Lategan states that, "The very critical activity which is the core business of the critic depends on an (ongoing) act of reading, and everything said about the text, its origin, background, and history" (Lategan 1996:243–44). Thus, some biblical scholars such as Steiner and Fowler identify the scholarly reader as the "critic" and the ordinary reader as "reader." Long's article identifies the dangers of the distanciation of the scholarly reader from the readings they produce. This is because the scholarly reader is understood to engage in an objective and universal reading of texts. Traditionally therefore, the scholarly reader has been given designations such as, the informed reader, the competent reader and the expert reader (Long 1996:86–87) but not the subjective reader. Long challenges this notion, contending that the scholarly reader is a real contextual reader.

Fourth, the scholarly reader is identified as a facilitator or enabler to ordinary readers. In this particular volume, it is proposed that the role of the scholarly reader ought to be as a facilitator or enabler to ordinary readers. It is suggested that scholarly readers should see themselves as those who are to be made use of by ordinary readers and not those who would "make use of" (Nolan 1996:217) ordinary readers in the reading process. This comes from the argument that readings originate from ordinary readers and their contexts. Patte, reflecting on the essays of John Pobee, Albert Nolan, and Gunther Wittenberg, argues that the first and last word with respect to readings lies with ordinary readers. For Patte, scholarly readers are to facilitate the process of reading by providing critical understandings to the epistemological judgments and values that ordinary readers cannot possibly achieve on their own (Patte 1996:268, 273). This idea of facilitation by scholarly readers is also emphasized by Wittenberg who advocates for a theology "from below," and by Nolan's privileging of a "workers theology" which must be constructed by workers themselves. In the proposed theologies of both Nolan and Wittenberg, the role of the scholarly reader is to make her/him available as an enabler or facilitator to ordinary readers.

Ordinary and Scholarly Together

Importantly, there exist commonalities between ordinary readers and scholarly readers in the volume, who together we can classify as members of the community of readers. I borrow the phrase "members of a community of readers" from the article by John Riches in the volume. Riches argues that both ordinary and scholarly readers belong to "a community of readers" (Riches 1996:180). This is because, firstly, both ordinary readers and scholarly readers are involved in the activity of reading texts (even if they do this differently). They possess the common objective of reading biblical texts. Secondly, there is only one starting point for the reading of texts, namely, to begin as an ordinary reader. This means that scholarly readers begin their reading activities as ordinary readers. Lategan argues that biblical scholars have become more and more identified as part of the community of "real" readers by the "shift of attention to the interaction between text and reader, away from the relationship between author and text" (Lategan 1996:243). Lategan further argues that:

> The world of the reader forms the inescapable context—also for the historical critic. He or she is part of it. The very critical activity which is the core business of the critic depends on an (ongoing) act of reading, and everything said about the text, its origin, background, and history, is reader and reading mediated. (Lategan 1996: 243–44)

John Riches also challenges the sharp distinction made between biblical scholars and ordinary people with respect to biblical interpretation. He argues that:

> Those who are academics do not cease thereby to be members of a community of readers, just as those who are not academics are not wholly untutored in readerly skills or indeed in the techniques of biblical interpretation. (Riches 1996:186)

This implies that both the scholarly reader and the ordinary reader are involved in the act of reading and thus, constitute a community of readers within their particular sociocultural realm, even if they work from different standpoints and perspectives.

The volume also indicates that both ordinary and scholarly readers are involved in sociocultural readings. South African biblical scholars such as West, Mosala, Nolan and Wittenberg do their readings from the sociocultural perspective of a society that has a sociocultural history of race and class discrimination, where oppression and marginalization of poor black people is the focus and hence they exercise a hermeneutical option for the poor and oppressed. Ukpong also operates in the sociocultural context of the exploited peasant farmers in Nigeria and the unjust world economic order that affects most post-independent West African countries. He therefore adopts an inculturation biblical hermeneutic that gives preference to the sociocultural context of the reader who is exploited in the West African market place as the subject of biblical interpretation and not the object. What these academic readers have done is to read from their sociocultural contexts; an approach that is not dissimilar to that of ordinary readers. Even though scholarly readers may use different reading models and focus on different questions in their readings, they still select to read from the same sociocultural context that ordinary readers in their community do. According to Riches, this sociocultural commonality between ordinary readers and scholarly readers became clear to him during the Glasgow consultation that he reported on in the volume: "What the consultation brought home to me, more than anything, was the realization that there is no sharp division between cultural readings of the Bible and "purely historical" readings, or indeed any kind of readings" (Riches 1996:186). Long also believes that the scholarly reader is not merely reconstructing biblical texts to produce objective and universal biblical interpretations. For him, the academic scholar who embarks on a reading activity does so from a particular sociocultural standpoint and therefore is an "actual reader" just as the ordinary reader. Long further identifies himself as an actual reader with respect to his reading of Revelation:

> My interpretative stance has the aspect of self-disclosure, in which is revealed the complex, often contradictory, web of social relations in which I find myself (like everyone) embedded.... These contradictions especially are painful to acknowledge to myself, let alone share with anyone else, but they will have definite effects on the way I enter the text and my engagement with it. (Long 1996:91–92)

Long's argument reveals that both the ordinary and scholarly reader is influenced by their sociocultural context and therefore cannot dissociate or disengage from it in their interpretative activities. Thus, when they as critics or as ordinary readers, get involved in providing a sociocultural reading of a text, their own sociocultural context inevitably affect their entry point into the text, as well as the meaning that they seek from the text for their own specific purposes. Interestingly, the same person can play both roles in a particular sociocultural context, because, as Lategan claims, the contrast between ordinary readers and scholarly readers is more a function of their role within a particular context, than of their person (Lategan 1996:244).

The Relationship between Ordinary and Scholarly Readers

The question that African hermeneutics grapples with in this volume is the relationship between ordinary and scholarly readers. In Lategan's response to the articles in the volume, he expressed concern about the possibility of assuming that the relationship between the ordinary and the scholarly reader is simple and that all scholarly readers have to do as facilitators of the reading process is to make themselves available for ordinary readers. Lategan, however, identifies a range of "other contrasts" that inhabit this interface, such as, "theoretical/empirical," "dominant/dominated," "male/female," "text-centered/oral culture," "exegesis/ theology," "North/South" (Lategan 1996:244). I agree with Lategan, and in this section will discuss a range of factors that need to be considered when developing a hermeneutical model interfacing ordinary and scholarly readers.

First, there are functional factors that need to be considered. As has been noted above, both the ordinary and scholarly reader is involved in the cultural reading of texts. However, ordinary readings and scholarly readings perform different functions within the sociocultural contexts from where they are done. As has been noted earlier, most of the contributors to the volume understand scholarly readers as being facilitators or enablers in "reading with" ordinary readers. Gerald West is a strong advocate of the idea of scholarly readers being facilitators whenever they engage in reading with ordinary readers. Also, the main objective of both ordinary and scholarly readers is to make meaning out of biblical texts. However, the way meaning is sought and used depends largely on the function that meaning is put to, by the readers of the text. For example, the ordinary reader is said to be the one who diligently reads the Bible "seeking the word of God for themselves and their circumstances" (Hinga 1996:277), while the scholarly reader "seeks to present the Bible in its own terms by seeking to analyze the Bible as literature (literary criticism) and as history (historical criticism)" (277). The function of the Bible for the ordinary reader seems to be driven by the desire to make direct links between the text and the social location of the ordinary reader. This is because of their perception that the purpose of reading a text is for practical use in a sociocultural context. However, the scholarly reader reads the text primarily to contribute to the academic progress in scholarly biblical interpretation, even if she or he does it from her/his sociocultural context. This is because intellectual culture influences the way academics in general perceive the function of biblical interpretation. This scholarly culture also affects the way hermeneutical models are developed by scholars and the way they are presented, which is primarily to satisfy the standards and dictates of the academy.

What is unique about this volume is that it advocates that scholarly readers should reflect more on how the Bible is perceived by ordinary readers in Africa in their hermeneutical work. Pobee, for example, points out that most ordinary readers in Africa perceive the Bible as a magical book, while scholarly readers would see it more as a literary document. This also affects the purposes to which the Bible is put by the academic reader and the ordinary reader. Most African ordinary readers would see the Bible as functioning as a powerful book for dealing with problems, while scholarly readers would see the Bible as containing texts that are interpreted and analyzed on their own terms.

Perhaps the most important outcome of the "reading with" models of interpretation is, as West indicates, that at the end of the reading practice the subjectivities of both the ordinary reader and the scholarly reader are enlarged (West 1996:37–38). In other words, the interchange between the ordinary and scholarly reader influences the understanding of the text in different ways, which also affects the way the Bible functions in each respective context.

Riches develops this point, arguing that such co-operative readings might go a long way to bring about a paradigm shift in biblical studies within the academy (Riches 1996:186). I would also add that it might improve the critical consciousness of the ordinary reader with respect to their critical engagement within her/his context.

Second, there is the factor of power relationships that cannot be overlooked in this venture of ordinary and scholarly readers reading together. Lategan cites Steiner's use of the term "critic" (scholar) and "reader" (ordinary) with regard to the power relationships that exist between them. Steiner points out that, from the start, the one operates from the position of oppression and subjugation while the other operates from the position of authority and power. According to Steiner's distinction between the "critic" and the "reader," "the critic is judge and master of the text" while "the reader is servant to the text" (Steiner 1979:449). Hence, "the critic steps back from the text to strike a magisterial pose of critical, objectifying distance, whereas the reader tries to eliminate the distance between himself [sic] and the text to allow the merging of his being with that of the text" (Fowler 1992:27). Most of the contributors to this volume express concern about the position of power from where the scholarly reader operates. Not only do some scholarly readers regard their readings as superior and therefore worthy of being listened to by ordinary readers, but some less-opinionated scholarly readers, influenced by the ideological perspectives from which they operate, (whether as the functionaries of liberal theology or particular denominational biases or of their social class), create postures of which ordinary readers become very conscious and suspicious whenever they engage one another. Sometimes, the ordinary reader will voice her/his misgivings in the reading process, but most times will simply keep silent.

A very subtle case of protest, vocalized by ordinary readers against domination by scholarly readings can be deduced from Dube's attempt to read Matt 15:21–28 with Batswana AIC women in Botswana. She states that as the discussion progressed, the respondents frequently pointed out that, "Remember, we are discussing issues of the spirit" (Dube 1996:124). I suspect that as Dube read the text with the Batswana women, when they sensed her attempting to dominate the discussion they would use the above protest or caution to free them from her reading.

The challenge facing the scholarly reader is how to address the imbalances between the scholarly and ordinary reader. The ideal solution would be to level the ground and thereby create an atmosphere of equal participation and discussion. It is necessary therefore, to reflect on the practical out-workings of "reading with" hermeneutical models in sociocultural contexts where there is clearly an imbalance of power.

Thirdly, there are various resources available in the joint reading enterprise between ordinary and scholarly readers. The contributors to this volume mention several. Pobee argues that resources such as proverbs, art, music, liturgy, poetry and stories, as found within African religions and sociocultural contexts, must be taken "as the 'hermeneutic' which provides the legitimate epistemology for African readings" (Pobee 1996:165; see also Patte 1996:272–73). Music, liturgy, proverbs, stories are indeed resources which are already being used by ordinary readers in their readings in most parts of Africa. Draper's article gave an example of the resources that ordinary readers use in reading the Bible. For instance, in the Markan reading that he cites, Draper reports that after reading Mark 5:21–23 aloud "the women responded with their own poem, song and role-play" (Draper 1996:73). Albert Nolan's essay emphasizes the point that there is the need for a workers theology that cannot be formulated by the biblical scholar who has not had first hand experience of such a life. Nolan therefore argues that:

What the worker does have is experience of work, and what the Christian worker also has is faith. Out of this, and by simply hearing the stories of the Bible, an elementary, perhaps somewhat superficial theology, can be constructed. (Nolan 1996:217)

What Nolan is saying is that the reading that may emerge out of the economic exploitation and working experience of the ordinary working-class reader is the main resource from which a workers' theology can be constructed.

With respect to the scholarly readers, they too have resources. They have textual skills and resources, which most ordinary readers do not possess. Most ordinary readers in Africa are described as illiterate; hence, oral or residually oral models of interpretation drive their interpretative models. On the other hand, the scholarly reader possesses textual skills of interpretation; these however do not make her/him a more competent reader, but only a different kind of reader. Such resources may be of use to ordinary readers, indeed, even the ability to read may be a resource, assisting ordinary readers in their biblical interpretation. For example, with respect to the Mark 5:21–43 reading mentioned by Draper, he reports that after the story had been read aloud by the trained reader, he then requested the women to identify key words in the story, which the women did without any difficulty at all (Draper 1996:73).

Fourthly, the scholarly reader is described by some of the contributors to his volume as an "expert" reader. This is due to the assumption that through her/his training, the biblical scholar has acquired certain skills and knowledge in dealing with biblical texts, which the ordinary reader does not have. Nolan therefore argues for the construction of a workers theology, which in order to "have any real depth and consistency" must "make use of the expertise and technical knowledge of academics" (Nolan 1996:217). The only condition here is that this skill should only be made available to the ordinary reader, rather than being used to dominate ordinary readers, a situation that often results due to the tendency of scholarly readers to think that they are the more competent readers.

Another resource that the scholarly reader ought to possess (according to some contributors to this volume) is facilitation skills. These skills are rare among scholarly readers. This is because scholarly readers find it easier to "teach" or pass on information, than to "instruct" others, and therefore engage in dialogue with them. Facilitation does something different; it is aimed at empowering other people to reconstruct their own ideas and views through a discursive or dialogical methodology.

THE TASK AHEAD

One may ask why I am saying "*Ye ma wo mo!* African Hermeneuts." I am commending those African hermeneuts who have contributed to the volume because it is a landmark in the development of hermeneutics in Africa specifically, and a significant contribution to biblical interpretation generally, the world over. In this regard, the volume is an attempt to point to possibilities that are inclusive of both scholarly and ordinary readers in various African contexts. The writers have identified areas where they as scholars are inter-connected with ordinary readers. The contributors have also identified areas where scholarly readers differ from ordinary readers. However, the most striking point that I have recognized from this volume is the challenge that all the contributors put to scholarly readers in Africa to offer themselves as hermeneutical servants to the specific sociocultural contexts in which they do their readings.

Another factor that comes out of this volume is the concern expressed by contributors that universalist hermeneutical approaches, so common in the academy, do not respond effectively or fully to the contextual and sociocultural hermeneutical needs of the African contexts. This volume therefore calls for the adaptation of hermeneutical models and practices by scholarly readers in African contexts. The development of hermeneutical models that respond to residually oral/illiterate and oppressed groups are some of the realities that need to be considered by scholarly readers in Africa. In other words, African religious and sociocultural concepts, as well as the economic, political and missionary heritages of diverse African contexts must be taken into consideration in the adaptation of hermeneutical models in Africa. To obtain information concerning these issues, the scholarly reader needs to work hand in hand with the ordinary reader. The question to ask therefore is how can scholarly readers create an effective interchange between themselves and ordinary readers in their respective contexts?

Among others, I have identified the following issues that scholarly readers have to consider in preparing to undertake readings "with" ordinary readers.

First, the scholarly reader ought to be socially committed to the sociocultural context of the ordinary people that s/he wants to read with. As described by some of the contributors to this volume, the scholarly reader must be a socially engaged reader in order to be able to read with the ordinary reader.

Second, West argues that the scholarly reader must be, or must somehow be linked with, what Antonio Gramsci describes as an "organic intellectual," namely, one who is "the thinking and organizing element of a particular fundamental social class" (Gramsci 1971:1). This means that the scholarly reader must possess specialized critical skills in order to function, not so much as one with knowledge or understanding, but rather, as one who is able to assist in organizing and shaping the ideas of a social group.

Third, the scholar must be prepared to engage in a boundary crossing exercise. It is important to recognize, that due to the different spheres and perspectives from which the scholarly readers and ordinary readers operate, there is a real need for scholars to cross boundaries so that they can begin to read effectively with ordinary readers. Any attempt by scholarly readers to interact with ordinary readers starts with inhibitions, suspicions and unease operating on both sides, even if the initiative comes from the ordinary readers. According to Gramsci, the interaction between organic intellectuals and ordinary oppressed people "is double and appears contradictory" (Gramsci 1971:14). This is because the oppressed and marginalized person "respects the social position of the intellectual…but affects contempt for it, which means that his admiration is mingled with instinctive elements of envy and impassioned anger" (14).

According to West and other scholarly readers such as Dube, Walker, and Draper, there exists a "hidden transcript" among ordinary poor and marginalized groups in Africa. Scholarly readers are needed who will cross the boundary between their class and the under-classes. The purpose of such boundary crossing is to create a forum where subversive readings can take place as well as processes for enabling the possibility of action in the public realm. According to West, for the scholarly reader to be able to cross class (and other) boundaries, s/he must choose to be partially constituted by ordinary readers. Only when the ordinary reader is convinced that a scholarly reader is genuinely committed to her/his cause will they have the freedom to reveal portions of the "hidden transcript" in their interaction with scholarly readers. My own research shows that it is not easy for trained readers to get to the point where ordinary readers see them as having crossed social boundaries. The hidden transcript does not come out that easily. Ordinary readers typically take refuge in "dogmatically correct" readings, using the "public transcript" to portray their acceptance of the official stance, which is thrown at them by their churches and scholarly readers.

Fourth, the process of reading "with" is a mutual one. For those who participate in this reading practice, whether the scholar or ordinary reader, the process and its products are mutual, although what each takes from the reading encounter may well be different. As has been indicated by John Riches, when scholarly readers read with ordinary readers, there is the potential for a paradigm shift in the academy. This is because, according to Riches, new questions and issues may be introduced into the academy through the interchange between scholarly readers and ordinary readers. What ordinary readers take from the process is often more elusive, given that their contexts are often more constrained and so the impact of the process on them is less easy to determine. However, the impact they have on the academy, may well serve them in the longer term, in that the questions and realities they bring to the reading process could generate scholarly work that in turn serves their interests and concerns.

Conclusion

In conclusion, this volume calls for more investigation into the sociocultural contexts of both ordinary and scholarly readers in Africa. First, as all readings are cultural readings, better understandings are required of the cultural contexts from which proposals for particular models of biblical interpretation emanate.

Second, one needs to evaluate the epistemological judgments and values that come out of the various sociocultural contexts in Africa. This means a closer look at the epistemological categories with which ordinary readers work in their respective contexts in Africa. This will include the general usage of the Bible by ordinary readers in their daily lives, their selective readings and the choices that they make.

Third, what are the models employed by ordinary readers in reading the Bible in various African contexts? *Semeia* 73 suggests a model of "reading with," and although this model shows promise, we need to examine how this model works in practice and how it interfaces with other interpretative models. The African scholars in this volume have spoken, *Ya ma wo mo! Aye koo!*

Finally, the way forward is the practical outworking of this process. For instance, in order to adapt the model for particular contexts in Africa, there is the need to explore further the roles that both ordinary readers and scholarly readers play in this exercise. What we learn, must be formalized, publicized, and made widely available and accessible to others. This will ensure the sustainability and usability of these models in our contexts.

"Dear God! Give Us Our Daily Leftovers and We Will be Able to Forgive Those Who Trouble Our Souls": Some Perspectives on Conversational Biblical Hermeneutics and Theologies

Mogomme Alpheus Masoga

Introduction

I begin this essay by citing the conversation between Dabula, Mzimama, and MmaDlamini, the main characters in the short story entitled *Weeping City—Our Story* (Masoga 2000:4–11). This is how they converse around Luke 2:4–7:

> "Was it like this in those days in Bethlehem, the town of David, where Joseph the father of Jesus went to from the town of Nazareth in Galilee?" asked Dabula. "Was there rape, unemployment, diseases, homelessness, crime, illiteracy, prostitution, drug-trafficking, HIVAIDS, abuse of women and Children? I wonder *madoda*," concluded the poor Dabula.
> Mzimama then protested, "But you do not tell the whole story; Sunday School tells me another story. A story told by Luke the evangelist is that Joseph, the father of Jesus went there to register with Mary, who was pledged to be married to him and was expecting a child. While they were there, the time came for the baby to be born and Mary gave birth to her first-born, a son. She wrapped him in cloths and placed him in a manger, because there was no room for them in the inn."
> Agitated and with some emphasis MmaDlamini cleared her throat to share her insight. "Mmm … clearly there was a problem in that town called Bethlehem.

---

* This paper was originally presented at the Institute for the Study of the Bible and Worker Ministry Project of the University of Natal, School of Theology, Pietermaritzburg, Workshop held 25–27 September 2001, under the theme "Equipping the Church and Communities with Biblical and Theological Resources in the 21st Century." Another version of this essay was published in the *Journal of African Christian Thought* 8/1 (2005): 22–25.

Why were Mary and Joseph not offered a place to rest? Why was the child placed only in a manger?"

Dabula emphatically enquired, "But there is still a problem. I repeat: what was wrong with Bethlehem? Could there really have been no room for accommodating Jesus? Even on a door step with open door? Come on *mense* ... I fail to grasp this one?"

Now yawning a bit, speaks Mzimama, "Surely, that manger gives us the gift of solidarity. Perhaps even at that time there were wastebaskets to be emptied, leaking and stinking sewages, a colorless bar ... *bara majita* with all sorts of bottles, prostitutes, male and female for male or female, people pursued by all consuming drives, drug lords and mistresses, sniffers and addicts, Hotel 224 with red light business, the world of odd rush hours, swingers, and hardcore sex. No place or room for the birth of a child. Haven within a weeping city. *Dis waar Modimo* ... had a plan by having his only begotten son born in a manger in the downtown of Bethlehem. What do you think my well-informed MmaDlamini?

The basic focus of this presentation is on alternative readings or, to be precise, what I call the various conversations of the Bible. These readings are aimed at transformation, empowerment and deliverance from the strangling situation (Buthelezi 1973:103). My essay uses a number of examples, including the popular music of Solly Moholo (the contemporary Zionist Christian Church [ZCC] gospel singer) and short stories taken from the booklet: *Weeping City, Shanty Town Jesus: Introduction to Conversational Theology* (Masoga 2000). The overall aim of this essay is to show how peripheral readers engage, *dis*-engage, voice, and *de*-voice the biblical texts. The essay analyses the notions of center and periphery, particularly those readers of the Bible who are located in these sites: the "trained readers" (West 1993; Draper 1994; Botha 1994) at the center, representing readers from institutions of learning with regard to biblical tools, and those from the periphery, who are the focus of my essay (Masoga 2000:133).

"My Bible and I/We Will Travel Together/ The Book without Measure": A Tricky Affair!

The Bible is here to stay, as the lines of the popular song I have used in my subheading attest! This very same document that was used many years ago still remains with us. The old guards of the apartheid ideology have come and passed, but not the Bible. It (the Bible) has acquired permanent status in Black and White Africa, in particular South Africa. The immanent location of the text prevails despite the pains and sufferings most black South Africans experience. These pains comprise of many genres ranging from inadequate housing, lottery gambling that exploits rather that multiplies their money for paraffin and daily bread, cash loan sharks, HIV/AIDS, landlessness, to death at the hands of farm bosses and other forms of dehumanization at the hands of factory employers. The forces of evil have taken new shapes, forms, and sizes. Even in these situations of pain, hopelessness and suffering, most South African Black Christians continue to converse around this tricky text. Some are buried with the Bible in their graves, carry the Bible in trains traveling from home to their places of work, sing with the Bible, recite their praises around some major themes of the Bible, are landless with the Bible, die from AIDS with the Bible, have HIV with the Bible, are retrenched with the Bible, and heal and divine with the Bible in their hands. The business of reading and interpreting the Bible in South Africa is a tricky one! The Bible is everywhere and in the hands of many, including the pain inflictors.

The former stance *scriptura sacra ipsius interpres* (Ramm 1970:107) has no basis at all (Yorke 1995:1–2). Gosnell Yorke rightly observes that:

> In some Christian theological circles, it is now a truism that God may have made us in God's own image (Gen. 1:26) but that in our theologizing about who God is, we inevitably end up, to varying degrees, making God in our image as well—be it consciously or subconsciously. (1995:3)

Furthermore, Yorke argues that "Our presuppositions, pre-understandings, and biases of whatever kind invariably impose limits on us—limits that no amount of formal education or life experience seems able to eradicate entirely" (1995:4).

Itumeleng Mosala takes us a step further when he points out the ambiguity of this presence of the Bible in South Africa: "The Bible is there in every aspect of South African life in curious and often contradictory ways" (1991:44). In terms of my analysis, this very same text, which is a terrain of "fierce struggles" (Mosala 1991:44; Mofokeng 1988), exists within the corridors of conversation (Masoga 2001:133). Echoing Mosala, I would argue that in order to confront the fundamental question of the nature of the biblical text displaced Bible reading discourses have to occupy their space and have to converse with centralized discourses.

It is in this light that I argue that "conversational" biblical hermeneutics and theologies be considered as a way of narrowing the gap that exists between the two discourses of the center and the periphery (West 1995b). Conversation allows openness, presence, life and honest critique. Ideally, "trained readers" need to converse and walk with peripheral readers, and in so doing to learn anew, having their "truths" continually challenged and changed by their conversations with peripheral readers (Masoga 2000:i). In what follows I allow some of this conversation from the periphery to enter the center via my essay.

The Bible as *Mukhukhu*

This section looks at the concept or rather philosophy of *mukhukhu*. *Mukhukhu* when sounded audibly is capable of delivering two distinct messages and meanings, in particular to someone coming from the Pretoria (Tshwane) surrounding region. The first meaning has to do with a gathering of male worshipers of the

Zion Christian Church (ZCC), whose center is located outside Polokwane, in the Limpopo Province, at the place popularly known as Moria (embodying as it does a number of biblical connotations). The *mukhukhu* gathering, characterized by chorus and dance, brings together a group of males. Usually families who are members of the ZCC decide, depending on their financial strength, to *go bitsa mukhukhu* (that is, to call for a *mukhukhu* gathering). This gathering starts late in the evening. Males sit in a circle and have their leader to facilitate the entire gathering. The *mukhukhu* gathering helps young members to learn the Bible by means of chorus and dance (*re bina mukhukhu*, that is, we dance and sing *mukhukhu*; or *ba bina mukhukhu*, that is, they sing and dance *mukhukhu*). Here is a peripheral reading the Bible.

For the purposes of this essay, I have decided to focus on some of the works of Solly Moholo as an example of this form of reading. The story around Moholo, which I will not elaborate, is that he started as a member of the ZCC and was later excommunicated on the basis of internal matters of the church. I do not intend to embroil myself in the internal matters of ZCC politics; rather I will look at some of the songs by Moholo in the context of the *mukhukhu* discourse.

The second meaning that *mukhukhu* conveys to a hearer is that of a corrugated iron building. Conditions in this kind of *mukhukhu* are such that it becomes very cold in winter and very warm in summer. This typical housing structure is common in South Africa. They are usually around most cities and towns and are occupied by people from a low or non-existent income class. A good example of such a housing structure is the Kanana Village, at times called *kua mekhukhung* (that is, where shanty houses are situated). What follows below are critical reflections on these two meanings of *"mukhukhu"*. I begin with the latter.

Reading the Story of the Little Girl

The following are excerpts adapted from Masoga's *Weeping City, Shanty Town Jesus* (2000), in which a young girl prays to Jesus:

> "Lord Jesus who sits on the clouds where helicopters fly, fly over my house tonight. I live at number 3 *mukhukhu*, plot 455, Winterveldt. My name is Dineo. I am a girl of 12 years. Will you come to my house?" (12)

> "Our home has two rooms. The first room is a bedroom for mum and dad, while the other is a kitchen and bedroom for Junior and me. We both sleep on the floor. *Mukhukhu* is very, very cold in winter and warm in summer. We do not have a television." (12)

> "I like that story of the boy who had fish and bread. He was clever you know. I want to be like him. He was little but did miracles for everyone. What do you think of him? Was he not a cute young boy? Mrs Mbatha wants us to act like him. To do good and act good. Again Mrs Mbatha tells us about you. She says that you love children. Do you really love children? Do you love Junior and

me? Do you love my friend Magdeline? Do you love Sipho? Sipho troubles us at School. Sometimes he is fine."

"Next week will be Christmas. I will act the role of Mary in the play we are preparing. I like the part of Mary. This will be the second time that I will be playing the part of Mary. We are given verses to read. This year I will read the following:

"And she gave birth to her first born. She wrapped him in cloths, and placed him in a manger, because there was no room for them in the inn.

Mary treasured up all these things and pondered them in her heart – So the shepherds returned, glorifying and praising God for all the things they had heard and seen, which were just as they had been told."

"My brother will play the part of the angel. He is good. I wish you could see him acting this part, especially reading this portion:

"Do not be afraid, I bring you good news of great joy that will be for the people. Today in the Town of David a Savior has been born to you: he is Christ the Lord. This will be a sign to you: You will find a baby wrapped in cloths and lying in a manger."

I love Christmas time. We eat sweets. We drink *gemmer*. Mum is a good cook. Will you be present in Christmas? Please come. We invite you. Bye Bye." (14–15).

The above prayer discourse by the little girl opens up an interesting reading of the Bible from the shanty-context (*mukhukhu*). It is often taken for granted that the current reflections on God and the Bible are the same to all and everyone. The shanty perspective of God reflects on the real "happenings" within the shanty-context. They deviate from what might be regarded as the "norm." This reading, however, releases voices from the periphery. Dineo, the little girl speaking to Jesus, in the context of the above prayer discourse, shouts to the God who should be able to understand and respond to the shanty context. In this context, the words and phrases, including the blending of languages, are appropriate given the unique life and philosophy of the shanty context. It has to be understood that this type of reading finds its space and time within its location. It is a reading that deals with realities as opposed to un-realities and vague *lingua*. The reading deals with life, and for that matter, real life. Images are dominant in this type of reading. The little girl (in this case Dineo) reflects seriously on life and about life. Experience in this case becomes the tools and skills used to evoke God.

Inherent in this *mukhukhu* reading is a level of criticality that we should not lose sight of. In conversing with God, Dineo uses "forward questioning methods" to indicate her skills in terms of critical thinking. The following example from the same prayer discourse illustrates this technique. Dineo hears voices in conflict outside their corrugated iron shack and then the sounds of gunfire:

I was scared, Mum embraced me in her arms and made a short prayer. "Lord Jesus Christ of Bethlehem, help us. Amen." It was a short prayer which called upon your name. "Did you hear her? She looked in the skies when she prayed to you. There was fear on her face. I could see that she was scared too. I was happy that I was with her. Her arms made me feel protected." (Masoga 2000:13)

Traditional critical biblical scholarship may not detect the kinds of criticality operating here. However, when one looks closely at the extracts one is confronted by a deep sense of criticality. Implicit in Dineo's discourses is an interrogation of both God and the biblical texts she quotes and/or alludes to. This is a form of what I call a *deep hermeneutical discourse,* a discourse deeply shaped by life experience and reflections of this experience.

The next section of my essay considers another brief example of this *deep-hermeneutical discourse* by reflecting on and conversing with the works of Solly Moholo.

Listening and Conversing with Solly Moholo (Ba Mmitsa Tsotsi): The Bible as *Mukhukhu*

The work of Solly Moholo provides a vivid description of both deep hermeneutical and conversational discourses. Both the name of the cassette and the particular track I will focus on bear the same name: *Ba Mmitsa Tsotsi.*

Ba Mmitsa Tsotsi

Ba Mmitsa Tsotsi
Kganthe ba ra Jesu
Kgosi ya rona

Ba e bitsa tsotsi
Kganthe ba ra Jesu
Kgosi ya rona

Bomme le bontate
Somelang Morena
Kgosi ya rena e leng kgotso

Kgotso a e ate
Ahee ...
Kgosi ya rona e leng kgotso

Baruti kopanang khutlong tse nne tsa lefatshe
Le rapedise kgotso
Moya wa kagiso
Lefatsheng la Congo

Bajuda ba motshwara
Bajuda ba mmofa
Ba moisa go Pilato
Jesu ba motshwara
Jesu ba mmofa
Ba moisa go Pilato
Kgosi Pilato a hlapa diatla
A itatola
A re ga go na molato (Moholo 2000)

Translation of the Sotho into English

They call him a thug
They refer that to Jesus
Our King

They call it (King) a thug
They refer that to Jesus
Our King

Mothers and Fathers
Work for the King
Our King of peace

Let there be peace
Indeed …
Our King of peace

Pastors/ministers of religion unite from all corners of the world
Pray for peace
The (spirit?) of peace
In Congo
Jews seized him
Jews tied him up
They took him to Pilate
Jesus was seized
Jesus was tied up
They took him to Pilate
King Pilate dismissed the case
He declared unlawful

CLOSE REFLECTIONS

The song opens with a bold statement: *Ba mmitsa tsotsi*. The performer or artist makes a quick contrast between Jesus and a thug. For Moholo, and probably taken from his "general" knowledge of the Bible and his "reading of the Bible,"

Jesus is the King and is not to be regarded as a thug. One has to pause for a while and reflect on the thug discourse. It becomes clear that Moholo uses the Pretoria (Tshwane) *lingua* and cultural space (*polelo ya kasi and toropo*). There is also strong intertextual referencing going on here, with clear allusions to the images of thuggery that Moholo has conjured with in another of his tracks *Dambsi wa lengangele* (Dambsi, the stubborn). In the latter track, Moholo contextualises events around South Africa's loss in their bid to host the 2006 soccer World Cup. The particular backdrop of this particular track the listener is reminded of that notorious Mr. Dumpsey (note that Moholo uses the Dambsi *nomen* for critical and subversive reasons) who withheld his vote, preferring to abstain during the voting process, which action seriously affected the South African chances of hosting the 2006 World Cup. In the end Germany was announced as the winner and host of the 2006 World Cup. Alluding to all this, all of which would have been fresh in the memories of his listeners, Moholo uses local notions of thuggery (*botsotsi*) to depict how "rude and malicious" Dambsi was because *o tshabile voutu ya South Africa* (he ran away with the South African vote). In this particular track (*Dambsi wa lengangele*) the word *lelainara* (the one who lines up) runs through the entire song. Lelainara in this context refers to thieves who queue with people, for instance at bank ATM queues, with the intention of robbing them. In this regard, the Jesus of Moholo is different from *lelainara*.

Returning now to the song quoted above, the second stanza continues to reinforce the idea that Jesus is different from a thug, but is rather a King (*Kgoši ya rona*). The third stanza attempts to exhort mothers and fathers, irrespective of color, race, religion etc., to work with this *kgosi* and for peace.

The fourth stanza deals at length with the theme of peace (*kgotso*). This too is a subtle play on words and could be appropriated from two perspectives, the first being the common greeting formula by members of the ZCC. The ZCC members reciprocate their greetings around the word *kgotso*. The first interlocutor would call out: *kgotso*, while the respondents would in turn call out: *A e ate* (let it increase). A second, more general, perspective draws too on a greeting discourse, in this case the greeting pattern used by the majority of Basotho-speaking people: *khotso! khotso!* For Moholo, peace can only be achieved through the king of peace (*kgoši ya kgotso*). It should be noted that for Moholo, the call for peace does not imply passive resistance but instead is a bold call for peace in a situation of suffering full of political ills. The present government is seriously challenged to take up the situation of hopelessness faced by many South Africans.

The fifth stanza appeals to priests/pastors from "all corners of the world" to unite and work as a joint team for peace. The Democratic Republic of Congo (DRC) is specifically cited because of its volatile political reality. Also in this instance the prince of peace is said to be the only answer to both continental and world problems.

The above close reflections should be viewed within the context of *mukhukhu* performance. Moholo reads the Bible in performance. This reading challenges the dominant and central reading of biblical texts: It is not fixed text oriented, but creatively introduces other forms of reading. In this regard, the text is read in the context of a performance (*go bina mukhukhu*). One is therefore introduced to the "dancing," performing text within the context of a performance.

Conclusion

Reading the Bible can take a number of forms. This essay has taken a preliminary look at another perspective on the biblical text, that is, reading the Bible from the periphery, specifically, a conversational context. I have called this form of conversational, performance driven, interpretation *mukhukhu* hermeneutics. As Piet Naude concludes:

It is clear: our work to be second-order oral theologians has just begun....if we expand our understanding of oppression, broaden our hermeneutical perspectives and leave our comfortable desks to listen to theology, exciting prospects open. Our advantaged location amidst oral communities in South Africa, a new openness after the apartheid era, growing interest from African and local theologians, set the scene for a creative hearing-theology in the South African context. The voice of the hitherto marginalized voicings must be heard. (1996:29–30)

(Ac)claiming the (Extra)ordinary African "Reader" of the Bible

Gerald O. West

Introduction

Ordinary African "readers" (of varying levels of literacy or none) of the Bible have intruded on African biblical scholarship since its inception (whether from the time of Clement of Alexandria or more recently in the 1930s [Ukpong 2000b:11]). The most apparent reasons for this is that the predominant religio-cultural interests of African biblical scholarship north of South Africa have provided an organic and ongoing link between the scholar's work and the life world of African streets. Similarly, the predominant socio-political interests of black African biblical scholarship in South (and perhaps southern) Africa have played a similar role, binding both the scholar and the non-scholar (to use Teresa Okure's distinction [Okure 1993:77]). While many, if not most, African scholars have been inducted into the modern scholarly guild by the hands of western trained whites, whether in Europe, the United States of America, or Africa, a significant proportion of these have (re)turned (either geographically or ideologically) to use the resources they have acquired to engage with African realities.

The imperialist projects of Euro-American colonialism (including apartheid as a form of colonialism of a special kind [de Kock 1993:65]) during the 1600–1900s and their more recent manifestations in the form of neo-liberal global capitalism (for the latter, see Terreblanche 2002) have demanded a response from Africans. So to have less clearly authored crises, the most notable of which is the HIV/AIDS pandemic currently ravaging Africa's peoples.

That all African readers of the Bible, whether scholars or not, share, substantially, similar life interests and social concerns (in Stephen Fowl's sense [Fowl 1998:56–60]) has forged an alliance between the African biblical scholar and the ordinary African "reader" of the Bible. Much of my own work over the past eighteen years has been an attempt to understand this alliance (see, for example, West 2003a), but my focus in this essay has a more historical hermeneutical concern.

The larger question which frames this essay (and much of my current work) is: What constitutes "ordinary" African biblical interpretation? Because African biblical scholarship is a direct product of the colonial encounter, it is understandable that its primary attention has been on asking this same question of African biblical scholarship. Only part of the answer—though an important part—has had to do with the presence and resources of ordinary African biblical interpreters. The bulk of the answer has had to do with a post-colonial religio-cultural and socio-political interpretive paradigm in which historical-critical and sociological methodological tools are favored (West 2004b; 2005). But because ordinary African interpreters do partially constitute African biblical scholarship, work has and is being done on their interpretive practices. The pioneering work of Takatso Mofokeng and Itumeleng Mosala made passing, but important, reference to how ordinary black South Africans adopted a variety of strategies in dealing with an ambiguous Bible, including rejecting it (Mofokeng 1988:40) and strategically appropriating it as a site of struggle (Mofokeng 1988:41; Mosala 1986:184), though neither Mofokeng nor Mosala provide the kind of detail their analysis promises (West 2003a:72–73). More detail is available from the fieldwork study conducted by Justin Ukpong in Port Harcourt, Nigeria, between 1991–1994, in which he investigates the attitude of ordinary Nigerian people to the Bible, including how they interpret and apply the Bible to their daily lives, and what the differences are between how the Bible is used in mainline churches and African Instituted Churches (Ukpong 2000c). In their essay on "How Should Africans Interpret the Bible," Zablon Nthamburi and Douglas Waruta end their essay with some significant analysis of how African Christians actually do read the Bible (Nthamburi and Waruta 1997). Adopting a more descriptive mode, Nahashon Ndung'u identifies and analyses the role of the Bible in the rise of the Akurinu Church among the Gikuyu of Kenya and in their worship (Ndung'u 1997; 2000). Also taking up the descriptive task is David Tuesday Adamo's work on the use of Psalms among the Aladura churches in Nigeria (Adamo 1999; 2000). Anthony Nkwoka's work in Nigeria gives a more general systematic analysis of the role of the Bible in Igbo Christianity (Nkwoka 2000). In his analysis of the use of the Bible in contemporary Tanzanian hymns, Fergus King (King 2000) gives us a sustained description of ordinary African hermeneutics, as does the late Hilary Mijoga in his extended analysis of the use of the Bible in preaching within the African Instituted Churches of southern Malawi (Mijoga 2000; 2001). Musa Dube provides considerable descriptive detail of how ordinary Batswana women in African Independent Churches interpret and use (or do not use) the Bible, and how the Bible is interpreted in the corporate cyclical sermons of their churches (Dube 1996; 2000:184–92). A recent volume of the South African journal *Scriptura* (78 [2001]) includes a number of articles that like Dube, use empirical fieldwork in order to analyze the reading processes of a range of South African interpretive communities. My own attempts at describing ordinary African biblical hermeneutics analyze particular encounters with the Bible and reflect on and conjure with concepts that elucidate the way in which ordinary black South Africans "read" the Bible (see, for example, West 1995a:174–200; 2002; 2003a:78–82); I also do some preliminary analysis of how black Christians "view" the Bible as an iconic object (West 2000:47–49). A more thorough reflection on the latter can be found in the work of Hezekiel Mafu on the use of the Bible in traditional rain-making institutions in western Zimbabwe (Mafu 2000).

While analysis of African biblical scholarship attempts to cover the entire historical period, from the 1930s to the present (Ukpong 2000a), analysis of ordinary African biblical hermeneutics tends to focus on the present. However, there is a growing body of work that is going further back, investigating the shift from an indigenous African hermeneutics to a neo-indigenous African hermeneutic (Draper 2003; 2004; Smit 2004; West 2002; 2003b; 2004a; 2004b). My interest in a more historical perspective has been prompted both by the work of Vincent Wimbush, who has argued that the early encounters with the Bible among African Americans are foundational for all subsequent biblical interpretation (Wimbush 1991; 1993), and the work of Tinyiko Maluleke, who has argued that African Christianity should perhaps be reconceptualized as a form of African Religion (Maluleke 2004). In this conceptualization, African agency is placed at the center, and while the ravages and damages of missionary Christianity and colonialism are neither ignored nor minimized, African transactions with Christianity and colonialism are given new weight.

HISTORICAL HERMENEUTICS

Historical and theoretical support for such a shift in perspective is found in a recent study by J. D.Y. Peel on the encounter of the Yoruba people of Nigeria with Christianity. Commenting on the insightful work of Robin Horton on African conversion (Horton 1971; 1975), J. D. Y. Peel argues that the appeal of Horton's theory is that it places what is really recent religious change, "attributed all too easily just to external forces, in the long span of African history" (Peel 2000:3). There are, as Peel acknowledges, limits to this analysis. As H. J. Fisher has pointed out with respect to Islam (but the point holds for Christianity too) (Fisher 1973; 1985), Horton's account "ignores the distinct cultural dynamics of the world religions themselves, which produce real effects even where their initial adoption has a strongly local rationale." "Moreover," argues Peel picking up Fisher's concerns, "the theory embraces little sense of the uneven power relations and the bitter conflicts that have often attended on religious change, which arise from the fact that religions are not just ways of explaining and modifying experience but are formative of communities and the power structures within them" (Peel 2000:4).

Agreement with the latter, amply supported by the work of V. Y. Mudimbe (Mudimbe 1988) and Jean and John Comaroff (1991; 1997) on the missionary-colonial enterprise, should not, however, cause us to neglect the former, equally clearly supported by the work of Horton and Peel, as well as by the work of Terence Ranger (1986), Lamin Sanneh (1989; 1990), Kwame Bediako (1995), and Tinyiko Maluleke, all of whom have given emphasis (though with important different nuances) to the continuity between African Religion and African Christianity.

The three (extra)ordinary interpreters of the Bible who form the focus of this essay bear testimony both to the devastating impact of colonialism (including apartheid as a special form) and to the agency of indigenous Africans and the continuity that exists between their forms of African Christianity and African Religion. Their lives span two hundred years of biblical interpretation in South Africa and are more or less equidistant from each other. Mmahutu of the Tlhaping first encountered the Bible in the early 1800s, Isaiah Shembe in the late 1800s, and Trevor Makhoba in the late 1900s. They are "ordinary" African interpreters in that they have had no formal training from biblical scholarship. They are extraordinary in that there is nothing "ordinary" about them![1]

Mmahutu

Mmahutu, senior wife of Mothibi, chief of the BaTlhaping people (who now form part of the Tswana) probably first encountered the Bible directly when she went to pay an official visit to the missionary John Campbell and his companions who had arrived in her city, Dithakong, in June 1813. Dithakong was then a hundred miles north of the nearest mission station, Klaarwater, and outside of the borders of the Cape Colony. Campbell and his associates had become frustrated by the absence of Mmahutu's husband, chief Mothibi, from Dithakong, and the refusal of the Tlhaping leadership to allow them to "instruct the people." While they waited for Mothibi's return, they proposed to visit a large village further to the north. Learning of this, Mmahutu visited their tent and said that she "was averse" to their "going any where

Fig 1. Portrait of Mmahutu as drawn by William Burchell on 31 July 1812 (Burchell 1824:494)

---

1. I dedicate this essay to the late Gerald T. Sheppard, who reminded me that all ordinary readers are extraordinary readers.

till Mateebe came," and that at the very least they should leave part of their wagons and party behind if they did go, being fully aware that they would be too fearful to venture forth without their full complement. Entering into a process of negotiation, and using her reluctance to have them leave as a lever, the missionaries tell her that they would never have thought of leaving Dithakong "even for a day before Mateebe's return" had they "been permitted to instruct the people; but that having nothing to do," they wished to visit that village and hunt. However, being in control of their immediate situation, Mmahutu insisted they remain. Having been persuaded by Mmahutu, the missionaries then "endeavored to convey some information" to her (Campbell 1815:199).

What follows is a remarkable exchange, albeit represented as it is from the missionary perspective, signifying as it does a range of possible appropriations of the Bible:

> We explained to her the nature of a letter, by means of which a person could convey his thoughts to a friend at a distance. Mr. A. shewed her one he had received from his wife, by which he knew every thing that had happened at Klaar Water for two days after he left it. This information highly entertained her, especially when told that A. Kok, who brought it, knew nothing of what it contained, which we explained by telling her the use of sealing wax. The Bible being on the table gave occasion to explain the nature and use of a book, particularly of that book—how it informed us of God, who made all things; and of the beginning of all things, which seemed to astonish her, and many a look was directed towards the Bible. (199)

Here the missionaries draw Mmahutu's attention to the power of the letter as text in at least two respects. First, text can re-present "every thing" that happened in a place in a person's absence. Second, text can be made to hide its message from the bearer and reveal its contents only to the intended receiver. Turning from the letter, to a quite different genre of text (from the perspective of the missionaries), the Bible, but here conflated with the letter (from the perspective of the Mmahutu), the missionaries use the interest generated in their exposition of the letter to return to their preoccupation with the contents of the Bible, particularly the matter of origins: "The Bible being on the table gave occasion to explain the nature and use of a book, particularly of that book—how it informed us of God, who made all things; and of the beginning of all things, which seemed to astonish her, and many a look was directed towards the Bible" (199).

Mmahutu is astonished, but what she is astonished at may not be what the missionaries imagine. Clearly, from her perspective these objects (texts) have power, with some appearing to have more power than others, hence "many a look" at the Bible. Text can reveal and text can hide; text can be manipulated by the people who transact with it. Clearly too, text contains knowledge and power; its contents, for those who have the power to make it speak, has to do with matters of importance to a community. This becomes clearer in a letter written by Campbell to a friend, Mr. David Langton, some days later (27 July) in which he elaborates on this episode. Immediately following the final sentence in the quotation above, the following is added: "Mr Reads eye caught a verse very suitable to our situation in the page that was lying open, viz. Matt. 4–16" (J. Campbell, Klaar Water, 27 July 1813 [CWM. Africa. South Africa. Incoming correspondence. Box 5-2-D]). If this text was read, and the literary context suggests it would have been, Mmahutu would have heard this: "The people which sat in darkness saw great light; and to them which sat in the region and shadow of death light is sprung up." This then makes some sense of Mmahutu's questions, recorded in the next paragraph of the journal entry: "Will people who are dead, rise up again?' "Is God under the earth, or where is he?" (Campbell 1815:199). But only some sense, for her questions do not seem to deal directly with the passage read. The passage clearly makes sense to the missionaries, being made to bear the full weight of English missionary images of Africa (see Comaroff and Comaroff 1991:86–125). However, such allusions are probably absent from Mmahutu's hearing of this sentence from the Bible. Whatever she hears, and it may be the word "death," prompts here to bring her own questions to the text/missionaries, disturbed as she and others have become by talk of people rising from the dead, worrying especially that their slain enemies might arise (see also Comaroff and Comaroff 1997:342; Moffat 1842:403–5).

Already we see emerging evidence from this very early encounter of a recognition that the Bible is power and knowledge, that as power and knowledge it can be manipulated by those that control it. Further, we see signs that it is beginning to be prized from the hands of the missionaries by indigenous questions. Finally, there is even a suggestion that the bearer of the Bible, like the bearer of the letter, might not fully know the power and knowledge it contains. Perhaps the missionaries are not fully in control of this object of strange power—the Bible—they carry; perhaps others—the Tlhaping—might access its mysterious power?

Having "answered her [Mmahutu's] questions," though we are given no hint of how her questions were answered, and having heard and accepted her concerns that they not leave the city until Mothibi's return, the missionaries show her (and her companions) a watch, "which both astonished and terrified them." Commenting on this reaction to the watch, Campbell says, "On observing the work in motion, they concluded that it must be alive, and on offering to put it to their ears, to hear it sound, they held up their hands to drive it away as if it had been a serpent" (Campbell 1815:200). Their interpreter also comments on this encounter with the watch, in the vernacular, saying "something to them which made them laugh immoderately." But what he actually said was probably hidden from the hearing of the missionaries and so from us, for when translated, the missionaries "found he had said, that before he went to Klaar water [*sic*], he was as ignorant as they were, but there he had been taught many good things, which they also would be taught if Mateebe permitted missionaries to settle among them" (200). How this could have caused Mmahutu and her companions to "laugh immoderately" is difficult to imagine! But the missionaries did not bother to probe any further, for they had heard what they wanted to hear.

The multiple layers of language and translation clearly offered fertile ground not only for accidental misunderstandings but calculated misunderstandings, as the theoretical work of the Comaroffs (1991:13–39) and James Scott (Scott 1990) on hegemony, ideology, and resistance amply demonstrate. Language in these early encounters was an obvious site for "infrapolitical" exchanges, "a politics of disguise and anonymity that takes place in public view but is designed to have a double meaning or to shield the identity [and/or ideology] of the actors" (Scott 1990:19). Here we find, unlike the missionaries, "a tactical choice born of a prudent awareness of the balance of power" (183) in which what was said was intended to communicate one thing to those in the know and another to outsiders (184). Such misunderstandings are a very early "foundational" (201) form of infrapolitics, a form that was soon to be joined by a host of others as the contours of colonization became ever clearer. Misunderstanding and misconceptions, as elementary forms of infrapolitics, are aptly appropriated by the Comaroffs as major metaphors of the "long conversation," "a dialogue at once poetic and pragmatic" (Comaroff and Comaroff 1991:171) a dialogue, in the words of William Burchell, an English explorer who had visited the Tlhaping a year earlier, with "each party using his own language and comprehending very little of what was said by the other; and talking probably on subjects widely different" (Burchell 1824:433).

Here, then, is "a discernible Tswana commentary … spoken less in narrative form than in the symbolism of gesture, action, and reaction, and in the expressive play of language itself" (Comaroff and Comaroff 1991:171). Quite what this commentary (on commentary) says is difficult to determine, but perhaps the reaction to the watch (the first layer of commentary) is not unrelated to the reaction to the Bible, given their proximity in the missionaries tent (and narrative). Here, perhaps, are two "devices capable of working transformations" (Comaroff and Comaroff 1991:185), "indispensable tools" in navigating, charting, incorporating, and so transforming that which was other (186)—if we add the Bible to the Comaroffs' inventory of devices such as looking glass, clocks, telescopes, and compasses. Juxtaposed in text and tent, the Bible and watch comment on each other, each occupying a particular place in the missionaries' scheme of things, but just how they are commented on by Mmahutu and her translator must remain somewhat obscure, deliberately so for the missionaries, but also, perhaps, somewhat inchoate and incipient for the indigenous commentators themselves as they observed for all they were worth in an attempt perhaps to find a place for these "goods of strange power" (182)—including the Bible—in their rapidly changing world.

However, and this must be stressed, the incident which Campbell and now I recount occurred in a time and place under Mmahutu's control. The Bible arrives among Africans, specifically among the Tlhaping, at a moment when they are in control—if not fully, then at least substantially. Although re-presented by the texts of European others, the context was controlled by the Tlhaping. When the missionaries (like the explorers before them [Burchell 1824]) entered Dithakong on the 24 June 1813 they encountered a world substantially under the agency of the Tlhaping. Of this the missionary record is absolutely clear!

In the long history of Mmahutu and her people, the Bible is just one more feature of their changing context that they have to deal with. "Colonialism" is still some way off. It will be many years before the pressures of colonial expansion will force Mothibi to move his settlement towards the missionary location on the banks of the Kuruman river (to which he had banished them). Even then, Mothibi takes the initiative to align his people with the missionaries for his own purposes. During all this time the Tlhaping will dictate how they will transact with the Bible, and different sectors of their community will make different decisions, this much is clear from the very earliest encounters (West 2004a).

Mmahutu may well be the first of a long line of many millions of African women in South Africa who found in and forged from the Bible life-giving resources.

Isaiah Shembe

Not too far from Mmahutu's part of the country, but nearly a hundred of years later, another (extra)ordinary "reader" of the Bible heard God's call (which he describes in his own words in Gunner 2002:56–63). Born into a Zulu polygamous family in the late 1800s, Isaiah Shembe spent his early years in Harrismith district, where his family may have been labor tenants (17). While living and working there, probably attending the Wesleyan mission church for Africans, Shembe met the Reverend William Leshega, an indigenous African Baptist minister who became "a mentor to the young Shembe" (18). Leshega baptized Shembe on the 22 July 1906 and later returned to the region to baptize "those to whom Shembe had

Fig 2. Portrait of Isaiah Shembe on cover of Hexham (1994)

preached and in many cases healed" (20). During this visit, Leshega "laid hands on Shembe and ordained him as a minister, authorizing him to 'preach to the nations and to baptize in the name of the Father and of the Son and of the Holy Spirit' (Dube, 1936:28–29)" (Gunner 2002:20).

In the turbulent times following the Bambatha Rebellion of 1906 and the formation of the Union of South Africa, Isaiah Shembe "returned" to KwaZulu-Natal from Harrismith in the Free State province.

> Initially an itinerant healer and preacher, he sought to reconstitute a sense of community and collective identity among the African people in the region at a critical moment in its history. He emerged in the early 1900s, after a century of social transformation, domination, and fragmentation of the African people through intertribal warfare, colonization, European and American missionization, increased industrialization, and environmental factors of drought and disease.
>
> While Isaiah Shembe did not initially intend to build a religious empire, his growing following of women, young girls, and orphans persuaded him to provide a space of sanctuary for them. He purchased the first piece of land in 1915 or 1916 using money given to him by those he had healed. On this site, called Ekuphakameni, Isaiah Shembe established what became the headquarters of a large and powerful religious community [numbering more than a million members]. Combining his deep knowledge of the mission Bible with his respect for Nguni traditional ways, and with some knowledge of commodity capitalism, he constituted a new and hybrid regime of religious truth (Foucault 1980) in competition with ideologies of the state and the Christian mission (Muller 1999:19).

While "what had been culturally significant pre-colonial Nguni cultural forms—song, dream, dance, and narrative … became the mechanisms for claiming cultural truth" (Muller 1999:20), the Bible and biblical interpretation became the mechanisms for claiming religious truth.

That Shembe was familiar with the Bible is plainly apparent to anyone who listens to or reads his hymns and teachings. Esther Roberts records that though Shembe had "little mission education," he was reported "to have been able to cite biblical references by chapter and verse, outwitting most European missionaries" (cited in Muller 1999:48; Roberts 1936). What makes this more remarkable is that there is no clarity on whether or to what extent Shembe was literate. Carol Muller claims that "Though illiterate in his early life, he learned to read and write in order to both read the Bible and write down his visions" (Muller 1999:48, but see Muller 2003:96). Bengt Sundkler makes a similar claim, but restricts his comments to Shembe's writing, stating that Shembe taught himself to write in order to record the hymns that were given to him, often in dreams (see also Gunner 1986:182; Sundkler 1976:187). Drawing on Shembe's own characterization of his literacy, Elizabeth Gunner provides a more circumspect picture, quoting Shembe as he speaks before the Native Economic Commission in Pietermaritzburg in April 1931: "No, I have not been taught to read and write, but I am able to read the Bible a bit, and that came to me by revelation and not by learning. It came to me by miracle" (Gunner 1986:187).

Shembe's own characterization of his education and reading ability may indicate that he had what Sam Tshehla calls "Bible literacy." This form of literacy is characterized by functionally non literate people who "spell-read" the Bible.

"They combine their knowledge of biblical tradition, collected over the years from sermons and/or public readings of the Bible, with patient identification of each letter and syllable until each word, phrase, or sentence rings familiar" (Tshehla 2003:184). Suggesting that this form of literacy may characterize Shembe's literacy, Tshehla goes on to say, "Many elderly oral-aural readers of the Bible from my context who possess this ability cannot tell precisely when it began. These nonliterate believers then read the Bible without whatever else attends the acquisition of literacy; that is, they read the Bible orally" (184).

As both Jonathan Draper and Gunner note, Shembe's "literary credentials" do not come from the missionary schools of his time, "so that his biblical literacy remains rooted within the discourse patterns of Zulu oral culture" (see also Brown 1998:119–63; Draper 2002:311). In a deliberate allusion to Matt 11:25 and perhaps 1 Cor 3:18–19, Shembe says of himself, "If you had educated him in your schools you would have taken pride in him. But that God may demonstrate his wisdom, he sent Shembe, a child, so that he may speak like the wise and the educated" (Gunner 1986:182). Whatever his levels of literary (see below) and however he acquired it, it is clear that he knew his Bible.

Shembe would have had access to both a Sotho Bible (published in 1881 and distributed in 1883) and a Zulu Bible (published in 1883 and revised in 1893), and it is the latter that is still favored by the AmaNazaretha (Hermanson 2002:15; and personal communication). While almost every one of the many commentators on Isaiah Shembe remark on his extensive knowledge and use of the Bible, there is hardly any detailed analyze of his biblical interpretation, and yet Shembe remains a quite remarkable (extra)ordinary "reader" of the Bible.

Among the teachings which he had scribed—for "Writing, and the act of recording through written word, have … been a key part of the church's making of itself" (Gunner 2002:15)—are extensive teachings on adultery, one of Shembe's major concerns. An analysis of one of these teachings will provide a glimpse of Shembe as biblical interpreter at work. This teaching is found in a handwritten notebook of "Histories and Laws," a collection that is particularly significant in that "their range gives a sense of the debates and preoccupations of Shembe himself, and of the church and the wider African community in the 1920s and first half of the 1930s." Furthermore, as Gunner goes on to state, "They provide a sense of a leader attempting to set in place church organizations, constantly in dispute with other authorities—chiefs, state officials, magistrates—as well as with his own ministers. They also provide a record of Shembe speaking to his own congregations" (35).

The sections of "Histories and Laws" which deal with adultery follow immediately after an account of Shembe's early life, with which "Histories and Laws" begins.

> The period dealing with the progression from the early paranormal visions that set Shembe apart as a prophet, to his place as a revered and perhaps feared public

figure in the racially stratified world of Natal in the 1920s and early 1930s, is compressed into the early pages of "Histories/*Imilando.*" Immediately after the accounts of Shembe's early visions comes the entry on laws and marriages. This underlines his status as leader and shows his incessant wrestling with the organization of his community as one that existed both within and without the other co-existent legal structures of his era. (Gunner 2002:35)

Gunner is right when she states that "The voice that speaks immediately after the recounting of 'My First Vision from the Almighty' (Gunner 2002:60–63) … is utterly different from the previous entry" (Gunner 2002:35). It is indeed, "the speech of authority, of a leader and law-maker" (Gunner 2002:35). It is the voice of a leader who stands (rhetorically) in the tradition of Moses and Paul (and even Jesus).

I say "rhetorically" for two reasons. First, I use this term because there can be no doubt that in these teachings Shembe adopts the rhetoric of Moses the law-giver addressing the people of "Israel" (in the Pentateuch) and Paul the apostle addressing his churches (in the Epistles). He even situates himself as Jesus speaking to his disciples, delivering his very own Sermon on the Mount (see "The words of counsel of Shembe at Ekuphakameni, March 4, 1932" [Gunner 2002:99] and compare with Matt 5). Secondly, I use this term to assure my biblical studies colleagues that I am not making a historical claim here concerning the authors of the biblical texts Shembe alludes to and "cites." Shembe, I am sure, was not particularly interested in the historical debates of his time (on other continents), if indeed he was ever aware of them, concerning the authorship of the Pentateuch and/or Pauline Epistles. What is clear is that he locates himself within the rhetoric of these biblical texts.

Among the many biblical texts that are "cited" and alluded to in "Histories and Laws," the most frequently referred to Old Testament text is Deuteronomy and the most frequently referred to New Testament texts are the epistles, with the Pauline (including the Deutero-Pauline Pastoral epistles) being by far the most frequent. Clearly the direct form of address that these texts adopt, often incorporating a first person subject, lend themselves to Shembe as he instructs his followers and constructs his church.

The phrase "referred to" above is more accurate than "cites," which is why I have placed the latter in inverted commas. Biblical texts are explicitly cited in "Histories and Laws," but in most cases the biblical text is not actually quoted. In fact, I found very few actual quotations, and when Bible texts are quoted it is only a few words of the verse/s cited. In the extracts from the notebook Gunner has translated, cited biblical texts provide a broad orientation to the issue at hand rather than a specific proof-text. This is particularly the case in Shembe's instructions on adultery.

Instructions on adultery occur with regularity in "Histories and Laws" (Gunner 2002:65, 71, 83, 87, 105). In "Pertaining to laws" (65–67), the first of these teachings and the only one I will examine here, Shembe gives his "pronouncement concerning marriage as it affects both married men and women" (65). He begins immediately by stating the responsibilities of the man, namely, that "A man must not desert his wife and only death may separate them" (65). Though not sustained, Shembe is alluding here to Rom 7:1–3, picking up on part of Paul's argument concerning the temporal scope of the law and his example of how the law of marriage is binding on a woman until, but not beyond, the death of her husband. However, as can be seen in more detail in the next extract, "The law," where he again alludes to Rom 7, Shembe immediately goes on to use this allusion for his own purposes (and not Paul's), stating that "A married woman must not leave her husband when he is in good health and even if he comes on hard times she must try to alleviate his troubles" (65). However, he then qualifies his instructions to the married woman by saying that "If [*uma* (Gunner 2002:64)] it becomes unbearable, she may part from the man by acting as follows: she should take the matter to the elders for them to discuss. If the decision goes against the man then the woman may leave him" (65). Then follow "the conditions of her going" (65). These include that neither the woman nor the man should marry again while the other is alive. However:

> If the man leaves his wife because he is caught red-handed in adultery with two or three witnesses, the elders can release the man and allow him to take another wife if he has subsequently separated from his wife for that reason. And a woman may leave an adulterous husband, and may marry again. If the man is married, then she must not live in that house. [The sense of this sentence in Zulu is not entirely clear. (Gunner's parenthesis)] If a man commits adultery, he must depart and leave his wife in the house. (65)

The reference to "two or three witnesses" is another biblical allusion, this time to a number of Shembe's favorite texts, Deuteronomy (17:6; 19:15), Matthew (18:16), 1 Timothy (5:19), as well as to another Pauline text, 2 Cor 13:1. There is also a reference to "two or three witnesses" in Heb 10:28. Though none of these texts deals explicitly with adultery, they are all (except the Hebrews text) designed to protect the accused from a false accusation. Remarkably, though the demand for "two or three witnesses" may seem to protect the man, so far in Shembe's teaching there is no blame whatsoever on the woman.

Shembe's pronouncement continues, turning now to how re-marriage affects inheritance. In discussing the question of inheritance in such circumstances Shembe says, "The inheritance in such cases will go to the first-born son but he will use it as his mother wills. If this woman re-marries, the second man need not pay *lobolo* as the woman has access to her son's inheritance from his father" (Gunner 2002:65). "If the man has been adulterous and the couple have separated and there is no child, the inheritance will go to the wife; the man should leave with only his clothes (Deut. 22 v 22)" (Gunner 2002:65). Recognizing, I would suggest, that what he is here saying goes against the patriarchal grain of both the Bible and local African culture, Shembe continues immediately to ask: "You are surprised that if a man loses a case of adultery and he and his wife are childless, that he is to leave with nothing but his clothes, and the inheritance is the wife's even if she marries again? Even if the man has a farm, he takes nothing" (65).

Shembe's position here is remarkable, as I have said, declaring as he does the man to be the one most likely to commit adultery and adopting a theological position that is not found in the Bible (nor in local African culture). Indeed, to deal with the first of these observations, Shembe thus far in this instruction says nothing about the woman committing adultery. But he does in the very next sentence cover this, albeit briefly, by saying, "You are surprised that if a wife commits adultery and she has children she should leave them with her husband and only go with the child at her breast?" (65) So Shembe does recognize that women do commit adultery, but clearly it is not at all common, in his view. It is the man who has the adulterous nature!

Returning to my second observation in the paragraph above, Shembe adopts in this instruction a position that goes against the general orientation of the Bible. His citation of Deut 22:22 at this point allows us to analyze how he uses the Bible more closely (in this instance and more generally) and to note how willing and able he is to use its authority while modifying its import. First, Deut 22:22 says the following: "If a man is caught lying with the wife of another man, both of them shall die, the man who lay with the woman as well as the woman. So you shall purge the evil from Israel" (NRSV). Clearly, Shembe is not quoting this text. As with many other texts, Shembe is alluding to the general textual context of the text, in this case a text dealing with instructions/laws on marriage (beginning at 22:13 and ending at 22:30 or perhaps 23:2). Second, however, while the general thrust of the Deuteronomy pericope lays the blame for divorce and adultery at the door of the woman, Shembe shifts the emphasis to the man. In fact, whereas "Pertaining to laws" begins with the woman experiencing problems with the man, and so seeking a divorce, Deuteronomy is exactly the opposite, beginning with the man finding fault with the woman he has married (22:13). What Shembe retains from this text is the rhetorical mode of instruction, the general topic (marriage, divorce, adultery) and the communal context in which these matters are to be decided.

Shembe's instructions in this extract, "Pertaining to laws," continues with the issue of a man marrying a second wife. The way in which Shembe begins this instruction is significant, echoing as it does the hortatory tone of the (in particular, Pauline) epistles: "This is the law I set out for believers who wish to marry. If a man asks his wife permission to take a second wife..." (Gunner 2002:65–67). Though there is no more discussion about adultery here, except by implication—perhaps Shembe's point is that by taking a second wife the man is less likely to commit adultery—I conclude my analysis of this instruction by drawing attention once again to the rhetorical tradition in which Shembe locates himself. The first person form and the hortatory tone are especially reminiscent of the so-called Pastoral Epistles, whose influence recurs again and again in Shembe's teachings.

Here, then, is an (extra)ordinary "reader" of the Bible who interprets the Bible in a complex matrix of the following elements: continuity with his cultural heritage, contestation with the state controlled domains of the political and economic, and local (rather than missionary) appropriation of the Bible's rhetorical patterns and themes (for a fuller discussion see West 2006b).

TREVOR MAKHOBA

I do not have a picture of Trevor Makhoba, but I do have one of his pictures, for he is an artist, and his biblical interpretation is found in his art. Biblical themes and theological trajectories run through many of Trevor Makhoba's works. Even a casual glance at his art recognizes religious themes in work after work, while in-depth analysis of his work by almost every commentator draws attention to the profound impact of both African (Traditional) Religion and Christianity on Makhoba (Leeb-du Toit 1993:20). Indeed, not only is Makhoba clearly aware of "The Mixing of Religions," the title of one of his early works in which Christianity and traditional African Religion and culture form an integrated reality, Makhoba is conscious too of the contestation that takes place within Christianity, as is evident in his work "Mr A.C." (ca. 1998), in which the antichrist is depicted as a skeletal priest on a horse (probably

Fig 3. "It gives sufficient time for repentance: God wants his people." A linocut by Trevor Makhoba, 2000. This image is used with the permission of Mrs. G. Makhoba

inspired by the dreadful horses of Revelation 6) among, and looking down on, ordinary Christian women, in their church uniforms, with their church building in the background (see also Leeb-du Toit 2003:232). Both the mixing of religions and theological contestation, I will argue in this essay, are integral to Makhoba's linocut, "GOD WANTS HIS PEOPLE" (2000/01).

That this work of Makhoba's, produced as part of the HIV/AIDS Billboard and Print Portfolio Exhibition for the Artists for Human Rights Exhibition, is to be read theologically is clear; what is less clear is how this work is to be read theologically. The words included in the frame, "IT GIVES SUFFICEINT TIME

FOR REPENTANCE"—the uppercase and spelling are Makhoba's—are clearly theological and their message seems self-evident (alluding perhaps to 1 Pet 4:1–3 and/or 2 Cor. 12:9). The words handwritten below the frame, "GOD WANTS HIS PEOPLE," are also theological, though less obvious in their theological thrust.

At first glance the work presents the prevailing theological position on HIV/AIDS in South Africa (and further north), which is that this disease is a punishment from God. What we know of Makhoba's Christian and cultural commitments (Leeb-du Toit 2003; Leigh 2002) would predispose him to some form of theology of retribution, and this particular work of Makhoba's seems to support this view. The mouth of some great beast is waiting (or perhaps advancing) to devour those who do not repent with its twin gapping jaws: HIV (the upper jaw) and AIDS (the lower jaw). Tombstone and coffin-like teeth are posed to crush. Yet Makhoba's theology provides some hope: there is time, he proclaims, for repentance. The jaws have not yet closed, they remain open. "IT GIVES SUFFICEINT TIME." The "IT" he refers to is unclear, but probably refers to this beast, whose millennial nostrils provide an overt date. The darkness, he seems to be saying, of the new millennium and its heraldic disease are almost upon us, but there is still time to repent.

Here Makhoba aligns himself with a long line of biblical prophets who read "the signs of the times" and speak accordingly to the people of God. "GOD WANTS HIS PEOPLE" Makhoba proclaims, along with Moses, Elijah, Isaiah, Jeremiah, Amos, John the Baptist and the many others Makhoba has encountered in his well-used Bible. The implication of this prophetic call is that God's people have gone astray, that they must repent and return to God and that if they do not God will punish them. From some of Makhoba's other works, particularly "Satan's Victim" (ca. 1990), Makhoba shows both that he is adept as reading the signs of his times and that sexual sin is one of most significant and damaging to his community. Here it is apparent that he sees abortion as a satanic rite, rejected by both the Bible and African Traditional Religion: "the woman is a murderer and the child the victim of so-called liberal legislation" (Leeb-du Toit 2003:231). Indeed, sexual abuse is a dominant element in his work, with picture after picture—see, for example, "Great Temptation in the Garden" (1995), "It's Dad, Mum" (1995), "Dogs on Duty" (1995), "Summer Friday Night with the Taxi-Driver" (1996), and "In the Eyes of a Pedophile" (1996)—cataloguing forms of sexual abuse. Significantly, Makhoba does not restrict himself to analyzing the sexual abuse of women and children, though these images do predominate, he also explores the sexual abuse of men ("Great Temptation in the Garden" [1995]) by white madams. In this instance, he shows us, racial, economic and sexual abuse mutually coalesce and sustain each other.

Another evident element in Makhoba's portrayals of sexual "sin" is his shifting perspective in terms of whom he situates as victim and whom as perpetrator. As I have already indicated, though women are usually the victims, they too can be the perpetrators of sexual "sin." At a more complex level, while the woman is clearly the victim of Satan in "Satan's Victim," she is, at a secondary level, also the perpetrator of the abortion and so the "sin." Perhaps female agency in general is something of a problem for Makhoba, both theologically and culturally, for in "A Hard Blow in Beijing" (1996), the largely white male audience of a boxing match laugh with approval as a buxom, bare-breasted black women flattens a black male, supported, it would seem by a white, bare-breasted white female referee. It is only the traditionally clad women, sitting at ring-side, and perhaps the black males sitting further back, and perhaps the artist himself (despite the attempt by Paul Sibisi to read this work of Makhoba's in a more inclusive light [Sibisi 1996:11]), who express dismay.

I mention this shift in perspective because while Makhoba is almost always the prophetic commentator, pointing and proclaiming, there are signs in his work of an even more radical shift in perspective. While his predominant role is that of prophet, there are indications that at times he stands with the bewildered people, lamenting, waiting in hope to receive the prophetic oracle. Such, I will argue, is the case with respect to this linocut.

However, before I come to this, it must be emphasized that Makhoba locates himself, primarily, as social commentator and religious prophet. In his images generally, Juliette Leeb-du Toit argues, Makhoba "broaches tradition within the context of current realities in response to crises, both personal and national, upholding communal ideals, a return to the values of the past and the mores of Christianity as a counter to such problems" (Leeb-du Toit 2003:230). Similarly, Valerie Leigh argues at length that Makhoba's Zulu heritage and Christian beliefs provide him with the moral framework from within which he takes on the role of evangelical Christian and African cultural commentator (Leigh 2002:125–47).

The linocut which is the focus of this section fits the prophetic pattern well. The horror of the punishment that awaits those who refuse God's call is vividly portrayed. But the prophet's voice/text is equally clear: God wants his people, and there is therefore sufficient time to repent. This work of Makhoba's also fits the disciplinary parameters of the Deuteronomistic theology of retribution (which pervades the books of Deuteronomy, Judges, Samuel and Kings): the people of God have forsaken their God, so God has therefore given them over to the consequences of their sinfulness, but when they cry out to God and/or the ancestors (as Makhoba's pictures do), God hears, raises up a prophetic leader, and restores the people (Jobling 1995; 1998).

But is this all we can read in Makhoba's work? I think not. Makhoba's theology is more complex, I would suggest, and this is clearest in the work under discussion. HIV/AIDS demands a more complex theology.

Fortunately, there are biblical theological trajectories (Brueggemann 1993) that interrupt the dominant theology of retribution, and there are signs of these in this work of Makhoba's. The clearest clue to the presence of other theological voices is the identity of Makhoba's beast. It seems that this beast most closely resembles the hippopotamus, though it may also exhibit some of the features of the crocodile. While I could find no sustained mythological signification to either the hippopotamus or crocodile in southern African cultures, crocodiles do feature in at least one other of Makhoba's works, "African Beat" (1991). In this work, Leigh suggests, "the crocodiles stand for obstacles the people experience in finding jobs" (Leigh 2002:132). Here, in "GOD WANTS HIS PEOPLE," the beast is a more ultimate, terminal obstacle, and the blurring of the characteristics of the crocodile and hippopotamus signals, in my view, something more sinister and significant.

These beasts, the crocodile and the hippopotamus, share significant features. They are both beasts that lurk beneath the surface of life, seemingly still and disinterested in human activity, and yet they can be roused with ferocious force and devastating effects. While the real beasts reside in rural communities, they are present in other forms in urban township life, or so Makhoba seems to be saying.

Makhoba's beast is, I think, also found in the Bible, in the book of Job. For it is in this book that we encounter Behemoth, sometimes translated as "hippopotamus," as it is in the both the old and new Zulu translations (*imvubu*) (Job 40:15–24) and Leviathan, sometimes translated as "crocodile," as it is in the new Zulu translation (*ingwenya*) (Job 41:1–34). In these two concluding chapters of the book of Job we come to two strange and wonderful beasts, beasts over which human beings clearly have no control (which is God's point in these chapters), but beasts over which even God does not have complete control (which is perhaps the poet's point in these chapters) (Perdue 1991). Might part of Makhoba's theology be found here, with Behemoth (the hippopotamus) and Leviathan (the crocodile) in the book of Job? "Look at Behemoth," says God, "It is the first of the great acts of God—only its Maker can approach it with the sword" (Job 40:15 and 19, NSRV). As for Leviathan, says God:

> were not even the gods overwhelmed at the sight of it?
> No one is so fierce as to dare to stir it up.
> Who can stand before it?
> Who can confront it and be safe?
> —under the whole heaven, who? (Job 41:9b–11)

Like the Job of the poetry Makhoba too struggles, I would suggest, with how to speak of God in the context of HIV/AIDS. His beast, like Behemoth and Leviathan, poses the profound theological question of whether God is fully in control. While his beast derives, I think, from or resonates with Behemoth and Leviathan in Job 40–41, the darkened human forms and the night's sky behind the beast's gapping mouth and crushing teeth may derive from or resonate with Job 3. Like Job, I hear Makhoba in this work lamenting the day of his birth and calling for the day to become night. As prophet, Makhoba stands outside the picture, proclaiming the words of the frame to others. As fellow-sufferer, Makhoba stands inside the picture, with the darkened figures, with the devouring beast in the darkness of the night.

In this work more than any other of his that I have seen, Makhoba inhabits the creative, honest and tensive space between subject and object. His care for his culture, faith and community and his prophetic calling make him the subject, identifying the signs of the times, warning his people of coming calamity, and offering words of hope. His human integrity and his awareness of his own "sinfulness" place him as the object, lamenting as he wonders and waits for a word of comfort and hope, and perhaps, a more relevant theology. Is the HIV/AIDS beast God's punisher, like the accuser (the satan) in the book of Job (2:1–7), or is the HIV/AIDS beast more like Behemoth and Leviathan, creatures that even God himself struggles to control? The answers are not easy, as Job found, but he and Makhoba are commended by God (Job 42:7) for asking the hard questions in face of conventional theology and even of God.

CONCLUSION

Why bother with this kind of description and analysis of ordinary—even (extra)ordinary—biblical interpreters? Because, I believe, African biblical scholarship needs to take up a less prescriptive tone to the task of biblical scholarship. In my opinion, it is time to bracket—but not abandon—the prescriptive/interventionist paradigm; it is time to listen rather than to proclaim. As Tinyiko Maluleke has said so aptly, the time has come "*to observe and analyze* the manner in which African Christians 'read' and view the Bible" (Maluleke 1996:15, emphasis added). Maluleke's distinction here captures the two sides of the Bible's presence in Africa: as an opened "read" text and as a closed icon of power. Both dimensions are worthy of our analytical attention.

Fortunately, just as there are signs of an emerging new paradigm in African theology with African agency at its core (Maluleke 2000), so too there are signs of a more descriptive paradigm with respect to African biblical interpretation. I see this study as a contribution to this paradigm, but also as a plea for a more historical perspective. Simply to speak of the post-colonial is imprecise, for in Africa (and elsewhere) the encounters with the Bible began when African were substantially in control of their contexts, continued into a period when Africans contested for control in contexts of increasingly colonial domination, continued into a further period when Africans resisted colonial control, and has recently (in South Africa) entered a period when Africans are once again substantially in control of the contexts in which biblical interpretation takes place. To lump these (and I am sure, other) moments together as either "colonial" and/or "postcolonial" is sloppy and unhelpful. A more detailed historical hermeneutical analysis of particular communities' biblical interpretation will not only help us to understand the genealogy of our present Bible reading realities more clearly, it will also assist us to become more precise about the analytical categories we employ.

Furthermore, this is more than an exercise in cultural studies, for by paying attention to these African interpreters we may discern more clearly the contours of our task as African biblical scholars.

"Ordinary" Reading in "Extraordinary" Times: A Jamaican Love Story

Stephen C. A. Jennings

Introduction

Gerald West, in his seminal works *Biblical Hermeneutics of Liberation* and *The Academy of the Poor*, has popularized in (Western) biblical scholarship, the term "'ordinary' 'reader.'" By that he means at least four overlapping things: (1) interpretations of biblical material, textual or otherwise, by (2) persons who are from politically, socially, and economically poorer groupings, who (3) are often not (very) literate in the official languages of their societies, and who (4) are often not theologically trained and therefore precritical in their interpretation of scripture(s) (see West 1995a; 1999). Though the term is not without its problems, not the least because it tends to elide various categories of persons who are not necessarily the same, and whose interpretations could radically differ from one another, it is connotatively powerful in conveying the sense that one's social location influences one's interpretation and application of anything, the Bible included.

Consequently, the term ought to be accepted as valid, and as West intends, can provide a useful guide eliciting the interpretations and applications of the majority of persons in the world through time and in space, the "poor, [needy] and oppressed" (West 1995a; 1999) whose voices and views tend to be ignored and/or neglected by the power brokers of the world and their agents in academies, even biblical ones.

My aim is simply to tell the story of some Jamaican "'ordinary' 'readers,'" whose histories, stories, and readings, have affected my own. While I am not an "ordinary" reader of the Bible, at least in some of the ways in which the West outlines it, I nevertheless intend to update that story, even while locating my own story, with its present concerns, within it. After all, story telling tells more about the storyteller than about than about the story itself.

In Miserable Slavery (1494–1834)

Jamaica, as a geographical territory, has existed for millennia, and has been populated for almost as long. It started its "modern" history when it became part of the itinerary of Christopher Columbus's second journey to the New World in 1494. That mercantilist adventure, which led to the genocide of the Taino "Amerindian" people, also eventually led to the arrival of enslaved Africans to provide the labor for first the feudal, then the capitalist project that was plantation society. The Trans-Atlantic Slave Trade brought an estimated 10,000,000 Africans over a 300-year period, with many others perishing along the way. Of that number, Jamaica received nearly a million in the same period, importing 469,893 slaves between 1703 and 1775 alone.[1]

Of further significance is the fact that Christianity came as a part of this modernist/mercantilist/plantation slavery project, for the most part providing for its justification. Such an influence came literarily through various Iberian Catholic catechetical material in the Spanish period, but was increasingly replaced by the Common Book of Prayer and the King James (1611, Authorized) version of the Bible in the period after the British (Protestant) takeover in 1655. Although this Bible was primarily used to teach the enslaved Africans both English and subordination—both necessary to maintain the status quo in plantation society—some of these socially and theologically "ordinary" ones quickly grasped not only its psycho-spiritual benefits but its sociopolitical implications for oppression and liberation as well. It is to that story, one fueled by Jamaican people's love for freedom, to which we now turn.[2]

George Liele and Moses Baker

George Liele (also spelled Lisle or Lyle) was an "ordinary" reader of the Bible. Born into slavery in about 1750 in Virginia in pre-independent United States of America, Liele came to the Caribbean as a consequence of the American War of Independence. He had previously bought his freedom from his pro-British master to carry out pastoral duties among his fellow enslaved ones, and not wanting to be re-enslaved by some anticolonial Caucasian-Americans who had stated this as their policy for ex-slaves in Independent America, he headed for Jamaica,

---

1. The works on Jamaica are voluminous. For a general introduction to some of the themes mentioned here see, Curtin 1990; Sherlock and Bennett 1998; Wavlin 1997; Segal 1995; Shepherd et al 1995.

2. A useful summary of the Christian religious influences in Spanish and British colonial Jamaica is to be found in Lampe 2001. For the use of the Bible to "teach English and subordination," see Roberts 1997.

a British-held territory with which he, like many of the African-American Diaspora, was familiar.

Though coming as a transport-for-hire operator, Liele soon went back to his ways of pastoring, and helped to start a movement in 1783, which he termed Members of the Ethiopian Baptist Churches of Jamaica. It was the first mass-based movement for people of color in Jamaica, and was the foundation for all others to follow. It also started the end of miserable chattel slavery, not only in Jamaica, but also in the entire British Empire.[3]

Much of Liele's "readings" of the Scriptures have not survived in print. There are, however, two versions of his church covenant extant. In them, every article is supported by a number of biblical texts as justification for the positions taken. Enough remains to show that for Liele, the Scriptures were to be equated with the word of God and, as a consequence, ought to be obeyed. In fact, one article, number 18, stated categorically "If any one of this Religion should transgress and walk disorderly, and not according to the Commands which we have received in this covenant, he will be censured according to the word of God. Luke 12:47, 48" (Gayle 1983:45).

That covenant was not to remain unchanged, however. For it was re-read by Moses Baker, an associate of Liele. Baker was also an African-American émigré artisan to Jamaica, a barber by trade. Though nominally a Christian in his native New York, he became more committed while in Jamaica, and was baptized by Liele in 1786. He later was commissioned by Liele to start work in the north-western end of the island, with the coastal towns of Montego Bay and Falmouth being mission centers. Baker's work was fruitful and by 1814, there were 500 converts.

Baker, we are told, was a man of the Spirit. By that it seems that it was meant that he placed a premium on direct, non-human mediated experiences of the Divine, which enabled him to become a seer, a see-er into the deeper mysteries of life. Thus it is recorded that on one occasion, he spoke in tongues (thought to be divinely-inspired utterances), while at other times he went into "trances" for days. Small wonder that Baker found aspects of Liele's covenant problematic; for in its received form he felt it was too ambiguous. Consequently, Baker's version of the covenant reflected significant changes. He left out, for instance, article 15 and its supporting texts 1 Pet 2:13–16 and 1 Thess 3:13. That article had read in one rendering: "We do not permit any to join our company without a few lines from their owners towards them and religion," while in another it reads, "We permit not slaves to join the church without first having a few lines from their owners of their good behavior." Whatever the original was, it is clear that Baker felt that that article made too many concessions to the status quo, and therefore should be omitted.[4]

---

3. Much of this is based on the pioneering work by Clement Gayle 1983.

4. See Russell 1993:9–14, who seeks to nuance Gayle's sketch of Liele and Baker at a number of points.

The rereading of Liele's covenant by his associate Moses Baker shows the sophistication that "ordinary" readers of Scriptures can bring to their task and that "ordinary" and "sophistication" need not be opposed, but rather can in fact be juxtaposed. It also raises the interesting notion that for some "ordinary" readers at least, the literal or more precisely, the letter of the text is subordinate to the inspiration of God. At any rate, what this divergent set of "readings" indicates is that, as Vincent Wimbush and others have noted, literalism was not a standard feature of the readings of "ordinary" African and African-diasporic religious practitioners, at least not in those early years (Wimbush as cited by West 1999:81–86).

Samuel Sharpe

One of those who benefited from Baker's brand of hermeneutics was Samuel Sharpe.[5] Sharpe was a deacon in one of the Baker-founded congregations, Burchell Baptist in Montego Bay, and actually a pastor or "daddy" in his own right, since he was a leader of a set of underground congregations of "Native Baptist Churches," as they were called. Sharpe's significance in Jamaican history was that he organized and led a forceful, non-violent work strike in 1831 which, through its wide-spread appeal and subsequent violent suppression, led to a speeding up of the Abolition of the State of Slavery throughout Jamaica and the rest of the then British Empire. This abolition partially took place in 1834, with "full free" taking place in 1838. Sam Sharpe's hermeneutics informed and was informed by praxis vis-à-vis slavery, colonialism and imperialism that was both assertive and subversive. Sharpe received his mandate to assert/subvert from his reading of the following biblical texts: Gal 3:28 "There is neither Jew nor Greek, there is neither bond nor free, there is neither male nor female; for ye are all one in Christ"; Gal 5:1 "Stand fast therefore in the liberty wherewith Christ has made us free, and be not entangled again with the yoke of bondage"; Matt 6:24 "No man can serve two masters: for either he will hate the one, and love the other; or else he will hold to the one, and despise the other. Ye cannot serve God and mammon"; and 1 Cor 7:23 "Ye are bought with a price: be ye not servants of men."

But it was words from Jesus in John's Gospel that seem to have special appeal for Sharpe. Two favorite texts were: John 8:32, "And ye shall know the truth, and the truth shall make you free" and John 8:36, "If the son therefore shall make you free, you shall be free indeed."

These latter references come from a biblical book that emphasizes the Word, and that in fact describes Jesus of Nazareth as the Son, the Truth and the Word (of God). Sharpe, who obviously knew this, intellectually and experientially, drew

---

5. Much of the following is based on the pioneering work of Reid 1988 and Brathwaite 1982.

the clear inference that it was incompatible to be truly a follower of Jesus Christ, and to be enslaved and to enslave. So, if people, particularly those who called themselves Christians, (as some members of the Jamaican plantocracy claimed to be), wanted others to do work for them, they must pay them. Indeed, some of his colleagues reported in the aftermath of the uprising that Sharpe had said that he organized the protest in the name of "the natural equality of man [sic], Scripture, and simple justice."

For Sharpe then, it was a matter of letting the word (in at least three senses of that word), become flesh. He and others were acting out what John's Gospel said about God's purpose for sending Jesus and Jesus' disciples into the world (John 1:1–18, especially v. 14; 14:12–14).

What we are seeing here is not merely a "local" expression but rather a "glocal" one.[6] For such hermeneutics as was found in Sharpe's movement was also to be found in other parts of the enslaved African Diaspora especially in the North American continent and in the African continent itself at around the same time. (See, Wimbush 2000; West and Dube 2000). It was also later to be present in the Indian sub-continent and still later in Latin America. As it was, these slavery-subverting (biblical) wordinterpretations were transnational for a good reason: they were meant to counter another set of transnational hermeneutics supporting slavery which were present in precisely these places and which had their genesis and initial development and sustenance in the Euro-western colonial project. Citations such as "slaves, obey your masters..." (see Eph 6:5; Col 3:22; 1 Tim 6:1–8; 1 Pet 2:18–25), along with the racist use of the cursing-by-Noah-of-Ham story (Gen 9:25), had come to form the staple diet of the plantocracy and later of mercantile and industrial capitalism. So Sharpe and his collaborators, as persons into whom the word had come, had to express through and because of that word, their cry for justice, freedom and respect. Their legacy to future generations was how they enfleshed that word (see also Felder 1989a; 1989b).

In Domineering Colonialism (1834–1962)

Chattel slavery ended in Jamaica in 1834, domineering colonialism did not. Thus political biblical hermeneutics was again brought into service, coming as it did from the struggles of "ordinary "readers. In fact, the period was marked by some of the richest readings of Scripture by "ordinary" readers the world has ever seen.

---

6. "Glocal" is a derivative of "glocalization," a neologism coined by Japanese entrepreneurs in the 1980s to describe the impact of global conditions had on local contexts. It was popularized in English and in Western scholarship by sociologist Roland Robertson. See his essays, "Globalization and the Future of "Traditional Religion" in Stackhouse et. al. 2000 and "Social Theory, Cultural Relativity and the Problem of Globality" in King 1997. For a further explication of Robertson's use of these terms, see Tomlinson 1999.

Starting off the period would be the "readings" of Paul Bogle and Alexander Bedward. Both are significant for this story, as not did they both, at separate times, lead widespread movements subversive of aspects of colonialism, but did so from explicit platforms of political biblical hermeneutics as "ordinary" readers of the Bible. Both set the basis for subsequent movements of a similar ilk, such as Garveyism and Rastafari, themselves significant anti-colonial movements with clear hermeneutical under- and over tones.

BOGLE

Bogle's movement (1860–66) had as its aim the more equitable distribution of land and resources to the peasantry from the plantocracy, and the concomitant subversion of the race-based, shade-mediated, classicism that was present in much of colonial Jamaica. Its immediate flashpoint though, was the failure of the congregation-based movement to gain justice in the courts. The presiding judge in that case, Baron von Kettleholt, was also the highest holder of political office, chief property holder, and the most prominent lay churchman in that parish of Jamaica. When Bogle's group challenged the decision, they were fired upon by the court militia, which in turn brought its own response. The result was became known as the Morant Bay Uprising (or Rebellion), which led not only to the judicial execution of Bogle and several others as part of an increased colonial dominance and presence, but to the displacement and dispersement of many to other parts of Jamaica and the world (see Hutton 1992; Holt 1992; Heuman 1994; Schiller 2000).

Of immediate interest to us are the readings of Scripture that underlay Bogle's movement. Most of these came from the book of the Psalms, and equated members of the landed gentry and the emerging merchant class with the "oppressors" of the texts. On the other hand, members of the peasantry in general and the Bogle movement in particular were seen as "the poor and the needy" of the passages, who were crying to God for help, and whose invocation would soon be answered with justice, judgment, and vengeance. Thus texts such as Pss 3:1, 5, 11; 11:2, 6, 7; 115:16; 121:2, 4, 6, 8; 139:8; 143:3, 12 were all read contemporaneously, a feature of all "ordinary" reading of the Bible in Jamaican experience, then, before, and since.

BEDWARD

Bedwardism (1890s–1920s) was one of the urban-based political-biblical movements that emerged out of the dispersion brought on by the Morant Bay Uprising.[7]

---

7. Much of our information on Bedward and Bedwardism is based on Patrick Bryan's 1991 work. The quotations that follow are taken from Bryan 1991:38–45.

His was the "largest and most sustained, Creole religious movement , with a colonial-wide organization." While "the evidence does not really point to Alexander Bedward as leader of a political movement," the "statements attributed to him do suggest a perception of a relationship between religion, political power and the question of race in Jamaican society." As Patrick Bryan states: "It is striking ... that Bedward's movement saw an association between white rule and misery" (Bryan 1991:45).

Bedward's words, uttered in 1895, thirty years after Morant Bay, shows that for him, at least, there was clear continuity between his movement and that of Bogle's. He stated:

> It is time for the black wall to knock down the white wall.... I am master of the black ... and master of the white.... The Pharisees and Sadducees are the white men; we are the true people.... Brethren, hell will be your portion if you do not rise up, and crush the white man.... The Government passes laws that oppress the black people, rob them of their bread.... Let them remember the Morant War.... The Constables and the Inspectors are Scoundrels. (Bryan 1991:44–45)

The comparison of "the white men" that is, the plantocracy and mercantile class, with the "Pharisees and Sadducees," members of the ruling elite of Jesus' day, speaks for itself. For it indicated and illustrated a long-standing feature of African diasporian hermeneutics, namely, an identification of Jesus with the African diasporian "readers" themselves, through the common experience of political oppression. But the reference to "the black wall" knocking down "the white wall," an allusion and a subversion of the stone not made of hands in Nebuchadnezzar's dream (in Dan 2), showed that since conditions had not changed but had in fact worsened, from the perspective of the displaced peasant-turned-proletariat, the political-biblical hermeneutics had to remain the same also, becoming more strident and deeper if anything.

Those threatened by such "ordinary readings," predictably, "Put [Bedward] away in the lunatic asylum which was the destination of many Afro-Jamaicans who were certified "insane through revivalism, obeah or other religious excitement'" (Bryan 1991:44).[8]

GARVEYISM

Bedward, as Rupert Lewis has noted, was one of Marcus Garvey's forerunners (Lewis 1987a:36–40).[9] That allusion, itself a rereading of a biblical rereading, implicitly makes the statement that Garvey was/is to be seen as a messianic figure.

---

8. For more on Bedwardism, see also Pierson 1969.

9. Lewis is a noted Garvey scholar. Among his published works on Garvey are Lewis 1987b; Lewis and Bryan 1988; Lewis and Warner 1994. For more on the life, times, and work of Marcus

That this is not far-fetched is seen in the fact that Marcus was often referred to, and referred to himself as "the Black Moses," noting that his very middle name—Mosiah—was an indication of this, which was termed his "destiny."

Garvey's beginnings in Jamaica were modest enough. But the context of domineering colonialism was pervasive and formative enough to make him both seek to escape and to find it elsewhere. As a result, his subsequent formation of the United Negro Improvement Association, which became the biggest and most transnational Pan-African movement in modern history, was grounded in serious acquaintance with and solid experience of racist and classicist oppression in Jamaica.

Garvey's political biblical hermeneutics are complex, and given the fact that many clergy persons and trained theologians were part of the movement, it is difficult to say with precision whether the reading which emerged from the group can be classed as "ordinary" in every instance. Nevertheless, allowing for wide-ranging and obvious intelligence, it would be fair to say that Marcus Garvey himself would qualify as an "ordinary reader," since he was not formally theologically trained.[10]

Two biblical texts were central to Garveyism, namely, Ps 68:31 and Acts 17:26. The former, "Princes shall come from Egypt; Ethiopia shall soon stretch forth her hand to God," was quoted at almost every meeting of the UNIA. This text had a long history of use in African diasporic hermeneutics, having been cited by church leaders from at least the eighteenth century. It was unanimously held as a proof text to show that God had a special concern from African/black people, contrary to what the "white" slave system said. What Garveyites did was to apply it to the aims, aspirations, agendas and activities of their movement. Thus in the Universal Negro Catechism, produced by the movement for its followers, neophytes and enquirers, the following explication typically occurs:

> Q. What prediction made in the 68th Psalm and the 31st verse is now being fulfilled?
> A. "Princes shall soon come out of Egypt, Ethiopia shall soon stretch forth her hands unto God.
> Q. What does this verse prove?
> A. That Negroes will set up their own government in Africa, with rulers of their own race (Cited by Burkett 1978:34).[11]

According to Renford Maddix, such an interpretation and application was given new fillip by the then ongoing European colonial portioning of the African con-

---

Garvey in the wider context of Caribbean Radicalism in early twentieth-century America, see James 1998.

10. See Burkett 1978 and Maddix 1987 for more on Garvey as an "ordinary" theologian.

11. For a later critique of African diasporic use of Ps 68:31, see Chambers 1993.

tinent, heightened racism, and a emergent spirit of nationalism, including that of Zionism (Maddix 1987:34).

The latter text, "God created of one blood all nations of man to dwell upon the face of the earth," was present on every official letterhead of UNIA stationary. Thus while Garveyism clearly espoused racial pride, even centricity, it did so in a quest for equality and solidarity with other "races," some of whom were denying the common humanity of all.

As Randall Burkett says: "To be sure, Garveyites were unabashed in proclaiming the goals of their particular organization as being the uplift of one particular racial group, but it was always in the context of a demand for respect of the rights of all mankind [sic] and a commitment finally to the brotherhood of man [sic] and the Fatherhood [sic] of God" (Burkitt 1978:34). Such "ordinary rereading" of Scripture is still needed in our post–September 11 (2001) world.

RASTAFARI

Rastafari (erroneously called by some Rastafarianism) emerged as a direct consequence of Garveyism. Again it was those who had been dispersed who came back to help others from the same situation from which they originally sprung, and who based their message on a certain political "reading" of the Scripture. Again too, it was the rural-turned-urban peasant-proletariats who found such "readings" appealing, and who took them the most seriously. After all, these urban poor were "ordinary" people themselves.[12]

Rastafari's point of hermeneutical departure was the crowning of the Emperor of Ethiopia, His Imperial Majesty (HIM.), Haile Selassie I, in 1930. Two bits of Scripture were re-read to interpret, that is, to explain the significance of, the epoch making event. One was the notion of Jesus (the) Christ, returning in power, majesty, dominion, and rule. Based on Rev 5:5, Selassie was seen as the "Lion of Judah," who "broke every chain," and was seen as "the King of Kings and Lord of Lords" of Rev 19:16. These interpretations were easier to believe as valid, since Ras Tafari (Selassie's precoronation name) himself apparently took these names as part of his accession titles, and wore them accordingly across his body. For these "ordinary" readers, without necessarily knowing the Latin, Emperor Haile Selassie was Jesus Christ *revividus*, the returning and reigning Christ prophesied and longed for.

This leads to a second major re-reading of Scripture by these "ordinary," original followers of Rastafari, namely an alleged prophecy of Marcus Garvey, who was slated to have said "Whenever you see a black king being crowned, lift

---

12. For a useful introduction to Rastafari and its hermeneutics, see, Chevannes 1994; Murrell et al. 1998. Murrell et al. also has one of the latest and most exhaustive bibliographical guide on writings by and/or about Rastafari.

up your hearts, for redemption draweth nigh." Whatever the factual basis of the prophecy (apart from Luke 21:28), what is beyond doubt was what it represented, a mandate for expecting (messianic) deliverance from the oppression of colonialism by a heaven-sent earthly source. It is no surprise, therefore, that many persons of the lower classes sympathized with the message of Rastafari.

The subsequent history, though of note, is beyond the scope of the essay. What is of importance to know here is that while, under the weight of (de) colonizing harassment, it became a distinct and somewhat (counter) distinctive religious expression, its political biblical readings, derived from and dependent on the "ordinary reader," never waned. Thus Rastafari re-read the biblical Christian paradigm of Incarnation in their own image and stated categorically: "Almighty God is a living man." That man was Selassie and any other man who came to "livity" (conscious knowledge of that fact in him). Furthermore, as an outgrowth of development of Jamaican peasant contextual readings of the Scriptures, they saw Jamaica and the Western world as "Babylon" and longed to go back to Ethiopia/Africa à la Garvey and Liele, which they saw as "Zion." The legacy of these insights from "ordinary readers," continues to be a crucial part of Jamaican political-biblical hermeneutics until today.

In "Independent" Jamaica (1962–Present)

When Jamaica became independent in 1962, it was a signal moment. It was now probable that the majority of Jamaicans would come into the better and greater economic, social and cultural benefits that were expected to accompany political independence. In the political-biblical hermeneutics of the day, Jamaicans, like the ancient Israelites, would be entering the Promised Land.

But that dream did not hold much sway for long for a number of Jamaican "ordinary" biblical "readers." For by the mid to late sixties, some began to think that their situations had not changed in comparison to pre-independent Jamaica. Again, "rereadings" of the Scriptures, this time of a more aural and oral nature, came into play. A popular song of the day gives an idea of what the thinking was:

> Get up every morning slavery for bread, suh [sir]
> So that every mouth can be fed,
> Poor me Israelite…,
> Shut [Shirt] dem a tear up, trousers a go,
> Don't want end up like Bonnie and Clyde,
> Poor me Israelitas…[13]

---

13. As recorded on the project *Tougher than Tough: The Story of Jamaican Music* 1993, Disc 2. For more on the song in particular and Jamaican music in general, see the above-mentioned project's liner notes and also Chang and Chen 1998; Barrow and Dalton 1997.

The comparison, indeed, the virtual convergence, of the socially "ordinary" Jamaican with ancient Israelites in Egypt is instructive: the fear, even threat, of increasing poverty (as epitomized by the wearing items of clothing) leading to a life of crime (as seen in the allusion to the legendary U.S. robbers) even more so.

Such thinking emerged among the urban youth, who called themselves "rude bways [boys]" and on whom the culture of Rastafari had had a profound influence. The evolving musical sound of these urban youth, called "reggae" by the late 1960s-early 1970s, became the vehicle of the Jamaican discontented; those of the urban youth, of Rastafari, and of the disillusioned lower middle class and the Black Power influenced middle class. The many songs of the period "'fighting' against 'Babylon'" attest to such discontent, which was directed against the post-colonial condition as symptomatically embodied and expressed in Jamaican society.

When the government of the mid-1970s became democratic socialist and a leader in Third World affairs, again "ordinary readers" had their "readings" pressed into service. "Babylon" became (again) a code name for the entire Western dominated post-/neo-colonial order, as it was in the earlier period of Rastafari. Many of the classic anthems (such as *Exodus*) and icons (such as Bob Marley), come from this time and ethos. For even though reggae and Marley himself predated this era, the merging of Third Worldism with the Pan-Africanism of previous generations gave wider currency to the political biblical hermeneutics emanating from these sources. Suddenly, the "ordinary" readings of Scripture by ordinary reading Jamaicans became the voice of the damned of the earth (to translate Franz Fanon's famous term more precisely): "Stepping out a [of] Babylon, into Jerusalem, in Mount Zion."[14]

The 1980s brought on a sea change. With the ascendancy of middle and more right of center thinkers in positions of power in various parts of the world, such as Margaret Thatcher of the UK, Ronald Reagan of the USA and Edward Seaga of Jamaica, those kinds of vocalizations ceased, or at least were submerged. Instead, biblical, indeed plural-scriptural rereadings of health, wealth and prosperity as signs of, and not just means to, salvation, became the norm. The interesting thing here was that such readings did not come from "ordinary" Jamaicans, but often from "extraordinary" American televangelists, via newly acquired satellite dishes, VCRs, and color television sets. Often individualized and privatized in emphases, such messages were gladly received by a number of "ordinary" Jamaicans who were beginning to lose the benefits of state subsidized benefits of one sort or another as a consequence of the International Monetary Fund, World Bank

---

14. See Chang and Chen 1998:176 for the story behind this song, as told by its writer and singer, Marcia Griffiths, a member of Bob Marley's back-up group, the I-Threes.

induced, "structural adjustment" programs the government of the day, though center-right, had to put into effect.[15]

Such readings of Scripture and their effects formed a large part of the diet of many Jamaicans by the time neo-liberalism was fully introduced by the former democratic socialist, now turned to a middle to right of center party, which became the Government in1989. This about turn was made complete by the ideological (and other forms of) eclipse of the Soviet Union and its allies, which spelt the end of the socialist dreams of many. That year, 1990, also symbolically saw the end of white domination in the entire African continent, signaled by the release of Nelson Mandela from prison. This fulfilled an explicit aim of the Pan-African, Third World ideology which Jamaican popular voices had consistently campaigned for. In being fulfilled however, it also deprived those same persons of another major ideological plank in their struggle for space, respect, and justice.

Thus from the beginning of the 1990s, Jamaicans have been in an ideological vacuum, or more accurately, have had nothing to choose from ideologically but neo-liberalism.[16] No wonder that not a few "ordinary" readers of the Scriptures, some of whom do not know the word neo-liberalism but who nevertheless are feeling both the good and bad of its effects, are interpreting the era as "the end of time," again highlighting their creative use of the Bible to make sense of their situations.[17]

"ORDINARY" READERS, TRAINED SCHOLARS: JAMAICANS ENGAGING (IN) AN INCREASINGLY GLOBALIZED WORLD

With the advent of the forced acceptance of the neoliberal project of "globalization" by Jamaican society, there has been the tendency for people's lives, identities, relationships, and institutions to be dominated through the economic and ideological mechanisms of the market system. Put differently, the forced (greater) integration of Jamaican society into the "global economy" has prompted a necessary reconfiguration of Jamaican polity, economy, society and identity. Specifically, it has produced an economic, social and political marginalization and (further) subordination of the public, private and civil sectors, generated an identity crisis, created an ideological eclipse, and exacerbated a state and sense of implosion and intermestic violence.

---

15. For more on this story from the perspective of international relations see Henke 2000. For more on the "health and wealth" gospel and its 1990s cousin "dominion theology," see Barron 1986; 1992.

16. For the ideological changes in the wider context of the Caribbean in the late 1980s into the 1990s see Klak 1998; Meeks et al. 2001.

17. Based on surveys carried out by the writer of this article in urban and rural Jamaica in 1992 and 1995.

In sum, the forced acceptance of the neo-liberal project of "globalization," though not without its merits, has undermined human agency and potential, disempowering many for the benefit of a relative few. Such has been the Jamaican experience of "globalization" as I see it.[18]

In light of this, I believe with Michael Peter Smith (Smith 2001:158) that there is the need "to imagine new forms of grassroots political agencies," that are both local and global. More precisely, there is the need to enable more Jamaican people to become empowered to resist and counter the economic, social, political and especially ideological effects brought on by the neo-liberal globalization project. What is needed is a perspective, and ultimately a movement that will give (back) persons a sense of identity, provide a basis for an ideology to combat/engage that of neo-liberalism, and to deal with the sense and state of implosion and the concomitant intermestic violence. Such a task could itself become a unifying mission to bring cohesion of persons living together in the same geographical space who are now becoming increasingly fragmented as a result of this latest expression of world capitalism.

Such a perspective can better emerge when there is greater collaboration between "ordinary" readers and trained scholars of the Bible. At least three urgent needs present themselves. First, there is the need for trained scholars to do more systematic gleaning of the reflections of "ordinary" readers, along the lines of the Institute of the Study of the Bible in South Africa or the *Centro de Estudos Biblicos* in Brazil (see also West 1995a:216ff.). "Ordinary" readers here would include not just the churched—though in a country that is reputed to have more churches per square mile/kilometer than any other, the majority are—but also the many who do not identify with Christianity, Rastsfari, or any other "faith" or "religion." "Ordinary" readings would also need to be looked for and found in popular cultural artifacts; including songs, rituals, and practices, as well as in more direct references and commentaries on and from the biblical texts. For example in the context of Jamaica, it would be helpful to see just how many persons believe that for Jamaicans and Jamaica, it is the "end of time," for what reasons, and what biblical texts they use/cite to justify their views.

Second, there is the need to for "ordinary" readers to engage more with the varieties of biblical scholarship present in the "academy of the elite" (to invert, but not subvert, West's felicitous and accurate phrase). For not all that comes out of elite institutions are meant to keep elites and elitism in place. Thus in the context of Jamaica, persons from "elitist" seminaries who would have known about and contributed to Caribbean and Third World biblical hermeneutics ought not to be regarded in the same way as those who have been content to receive and privilege Euro-western theological readings of the Scriptures. Most ordinary

---

18. For some of the implications of the "globalization" project and paradigm on Jamaica see Klak 1998; Meeks et al. 2001; Serbin 1998; Benn and Hall 2000a; 2000b.

readers of the Scriptures do not know the differences, although they sense these through differing denominational emphases. So more contextual readings would become accessible to "ordinary" readers, if *trained and socially engaged scholars* were willing to share their message and resources through a channel such as the Institute for Contextual Theology, also in South Africa (West 1995a:216ff.). Thus for Jamaica today, for example, there is a need to look at "end time prophecies" in their original contexts, and to look at the connections between this work and the current scenario. Perennial theological themes in Jamaican readings of the Scriptures such as Exodus and Exile could also be more explicitly treated and applied from a variety of helpful perspectives.

Third, there is a need for a more systematic engagement by both "ordinary" and trained readers of the Scriptures of the issues affecting the wider society, such as is attempted by the Biblical Institute for Social Change, based in Washington, D.C., U.S.A.[19] Such study would naturally, along with socialized spiritual formation, lead to informed, sustained and sustainable activism, which could responsibly challenge the powers that be into shaping society in more wholesome ways for the multitude, many of whom are "ordinary" and suffering Bible "readers."

In the context of present day Jamaica, such engagement would have to tackle head-on the good and bad effects of "globalization," in an effort to engage "globalization" itself. Thus, to round out the example, trained and socially engaged scholars and "ordinary" readers of the Scriptures might agree that it is "the end of (a) time," the ending of an era, and as some (not necessarily biblically) trained scholars have opined and argued, the ending of the Third World Bandung project and period.[20]

As every end holds within it the possibility of a new beginning, such collaboration might yield within it the emergence of the perspectives, ideological and otherwise, of a new and different future, which could come with human help. Because of this possibility, collaboration between "ordinary" biblical readers and trained biblical scholars is not just desirable but necessary. I am hopeful that such a collaboration will take place, since many "ordinary" Jamaican readers can dialogue regularly with trained and engaged scholars, who are often pastors of their congregations and in their communities, and since many trained and engaged scholars, who are often pastors, are already in a position to engage with "ordinary" readers who are often their congregants and/or their fellow community members. I am hopeful that together we will engage our society and wider world, since we both are inheritors of a rich heritage of fruitful political-biblical engagement. I commit myself to such collaboration. *A luta continua.*

---

19. For an example of the work it does, see Felder 1989b.
20. Such scholars include Scott (1999) and Amin (1997).

Who Was Hagar? Mistress, Divorcee, Exile, or Exploited Worker: An Analysis of Contemporary Grassroots Readings of Genesis 16 by Caucasian, Latina, and Black South African Women

Nicole M. Simopoulos

Introduction

Adultery. Divorce. Political Exile. Worker Exploitation. As Norman Gottwald has noted, no reader comes to the text "naked" (Gottwald 1995). Rather, every individual—ordinary, untrained readers[1] and biblical scholars armed with scientific theories and techniques alike—are "outfitted with pre-understandings and pretexts that shape what we see and what we emphasize in the bible" (Gottwald 1995:257). Every individual has a social location from which she or he interprets the biblical text. According to this logic, no interpretation is disinterested. All interpretations are, rather, reflections of the lenses through which we see and experience ourselves, the world and God.

In what follows, you will hear three distinct—and, as I will argue, valid—interpretations of the story of Hagar and Sarah as found in Gen 16, by three groups of ordinary, untrained readers: white, middle-to-upper-class Catholic and Protestant women living in Northern California; Latina Presbyterian immigrants and refugees from Mexico and Central America living in Northern California; and black South African Protestant women from both rural and urban South

---

1. In *Biblical Hermeneutics of Liberation,* Gerald West uses the term "ordinary reader" in general to designate all readers who read the Bible precritically; that is, those who "do not have access to the structured and systematic sets of resources that constitute the craft of biblical scholars." More specifically, West uses the term "ordinary reader" in the South African context to designate a particular sector of precritical readers; that is, poor and marginalized readers who are socially, politically, economically and culturally outcast or exploited (West 1995a:221–22). In my thesis, I will use the term "ordinary reader" to refer to poor and marginalized readers, specifically those women who participated in this project.

African townships enrolled in a year-long theological training program in Kwa-Zulu-Natal, South Africa.[2] Each group, influenced by their particular social location, interpreted the same text in distinct ways. The Caucasian women, the majority of whom had been divorced by adulterous husbands when they found new mistresses, identified with Sarah's jealous rage toward Hagar. They also identified during their divorces with Hagar's loneliness and desperation in the desert. The Latina women identified with Hagar as an exile from her native country of Egypt as well as an outsider and outcast living in a foreign and hostile land. The Black South African women identified with Hagar's exploitation as a slave and worker under her master's oppression.

In the end, I hope to show that each interpretation is valid, valid in the sense that the interpretations speak meaningfully to the reader's specific context. Perhaps after listening to these women's voices our perspectives of Hagar, Sarah, and even God will be called into question and possibly reevaluated.

"HAGAR, THE MISTRESS," AND "HAGAR, THE DIVORCEE": CAUCASIAN WOMEN SPEAK

The group of Caucasian women I worked with consisted of approximately fifteen women whose son(s) attended a Catholic high school in California. The women were both Catholic and Protestant, and they had been meeting weekly for approximately five years for Bible study. The women were relatively wealthy, at least compared to the other groups, and the majority of them had an annual household income ranging from U.S. $50,000–$100,000. In addition, the group was highly educated: most of the women had obtained a college degree.[3]

When I originally asked the participants of this group to be a part of my master's thesis, I hypothesized that given their status in the dominant sector (being white, educated, and relatively wealthy), their interpretation of the text might be more akin to Western or first-world interpretations of the biblical text and of God. As I became more acquainted with the women in the group, it became apparent that many of them were not part of the dominant sector; as women, especially as divorced women, they had been marginalized and stigmatized by their social, familial and religious networks. Six of the eleven women were divorced by their husbands after twenty-five to thirty years of marriage and raising anywhere from two to six children. Four of these six women stated that their husbands were having adulterous relationship(s) throughout their marriages, and in the end their husbands left them for another partner. In the Bible studies as well as in my personal conversations with several of the women, they spoke of the wreckage of

---

2. Bible studies were facilitated with each group. The Bible studies were tape-recorded with the permission of the participants.

3. This information was taken from a demographic questionnaire distributed in October 1999 by the author to the participants in this Bible study.

divorce: the division of their families; the shame, the despair, and the loneliness; the stigmas attached to divorced women; the rejection some of them experienced by their churches; their rejection by family members, friends and even their own children; and the wounds of distrust that followed years of deception, lies, betrayal, ingratitude and emotional abuse. The Caucasian women recognized that divorce was the dominant lens through which they read and interpreted the story of Hagar and Sarah.

The majority of the women in this group viewed Hagar from two different perspectives. In the first instance, the women saw Hagar from the perspective of Sarah, the privileged but barren wife. In this sense, they identified Hagar as Abraham's mistress. Hagar was seen as an accomplice in adultery who maneuvered her way into Sarah and Abraham's marriage. Because of Sarah's "inadequacy," another woman—the younger, fertile, and beautiful Hagar—took Sarah's place. Hagar's stature was elevated because she became the expectant mother of Abraham's child. The women in the Bible study, reading from their own experience of rejection when their husbands replaced them with mistresses, identified with Sarah's jealousy and rage toward this other woman. The women commented that, even though Sarah chose to give Hagar to Abraham, "the result is not something you are prepared for emotionally" (Simopoulos 2000). Reflecting on Sarah's situation, in which "her mate of presumably eighty monogamous years shares his bed with a younger, very beautiful woman," one of the women stated that she understood Sarah's jealous rage toward Hagar:

> Yes, I felt the jealousy because that's what happened in my situation. My husband chose a younger woman, and even at one point in time he probably slept with her in my own home. So, a part of me came out that I didn't know existed in me, and the rage hit! (Simopoulos 2000)

When looked at from this angle, the women noted that it is not difficult to understand Sarah's jealousy, rage and subsequent ill-treatment of Hagar. As Abraham's mistress or girlfriend, Hagar symbolized the destruction of the women's own marriages. In this light, Hagar was seen as an "opportunist" who took advantage of a situation to elevate herself (Simopoulos 1998b).

In the second instance, the women identified with Hagar as an outcast or a "divorced" woman. As divorced women themselves, the Caucasian women identified with Hagar's experience of being used and ultimately cast out. No longer desired by or of use to their husbands, these women were served with divorce papers much like Hagar was served with a satchel of water and some bread.

Both during and after their divorces, the women in the group identified with the loneliness and desperation of Hagar in the desert. As one woman said:

> It is really interesting because I totally can identify with Sarah in that place, in her jealous rage. But when Hagar was out in the desert and her eyes were closed

and she thought she was dying, that was totally me going through the divorce.
So I was very much both parts of these two women. (Simopoulos 2000)

The women noted that in the desert Hagar "had nothing left" (Simopoulos 2000).
The women described their divorces as a "really scary place to be" because you feel
"powerless, abandoned and completely alone" (Simopoulos 2000). As one woman
added, "Everything as you knew it changes and is gone. It's like Hagar going out
into the desert. She has nothing left. Divorce is about the most alone you can be"
(Simopoulos 2000). Hagar was also truly alone. After all, Hagar did venture into
the desert where no help was to be found and this, as the women argued, speaks
clearly about the fact that she had no one to whom she could turn.

Just as Hagar "was let go to kind of fend for herself," so too the women in the
Bible study were required to find a way to survive financially after their divorces
(Simopoulos 2000). After a lifetime of serving their husbands and children as
homemakers, the women found that they had to set out into the world as middle-
aged women with little or no work skills to fend for themselves. Likewise, Hagar
had to flee to another land to make a new life for herself and her son.

Redemption in this group's interpretation of the text was found in the fact that
God provided the means of survival for both Hagar and themselves. The women
in the Bible study started their own careers, and they are now teachers, interior
decorators, analysts with the state, and one of them is pursuing her master's degree
in spirituality. Likewise, Hagar and her son made a life for themselves in the wilderness of Paran, and Ishmael had many descendants according to the promise.
Many of the women in the Bible study related that they, just as Hagar, had personal
and salvific encounters with God in their deserts. As one woman responded:

> I agree with the compassionate God who was there for Hagar at the end, and
> I have found that to be true for me in my own life. I have seen actual miracles
> happen in my life, and I know God is there for me. I know it just as well as I
> know I am sitting here. (Simopoulos 2000)

As the women articulated it in the Bible study, the God who came to Hagar and
comforted her in her desperation is the same God who came to them in their
desperation and loneliness during and after their divorces. The God who opened
Hagar's eyes to the well is the same God who inspired these women to open their
eyes to what God could do in their situations. The women concluded that it is in
the desert, when one hits rock bottom that God creates a way for survival and
that new life begins (Simopoulos 2000).

"HAGAR, THE EXILE": LATINA WOMEN SPEAK

The women from the Presbyterian Church in Northern California are refugees
and immigrants from Mexico and Central America. They are marginalized in a

number of ways. One aspect of their marginalization in particular, their status as exiles living in a foreign country that has never become home to them, was the primary lens through which the Latina women interpreted Hagar's story.

The Latina women identified with Hagar's experience of exile from her native country, her experiences of homelessness and dislocation, and her final resignation to living as a wanderer in the desert. Having speculated that Hagar had to flee her native country of Egypt, the women spontaneously began to tell their stories of exile and flight from their own countries of origin. One of the women spoke about her harrowing experience crossing the United States–Mexican border "illegally" on foot out of economic desperation. Others spoke about their family members and loved ones who had been killed in Guatemala and El Salvador, their subsequent flights to the United States, and their appeals for political asylum. Whatever the case for their exile to the United States, the survival of these Latina women was threatened in their country of origin. Likewise, as the women noted, Hagar's survival must have been insecure in Egypt; as a result, they speculated that she was sold into slavery to be taken care of by a wealthy Hebrew family.

The women pointed out that Hagar, like themselves, must have felt displaced. Hagar's story mirrored their own in that Hagar lived as an unwanted foreigner in a distant land away from family, friends and all familiarity. The women shared their experiences of hostility, rejection and dislocation in their adopted country. Identifying with Hagar, they related these experiences to Hagar and Ishmael's rejection by their adopted family. For some of the immigrant women, particularly the undocumented women, there remained the constant fear of being caught by the Immigration and Naturalization Services (INS) and being immediately detained and deported. In an interview with one of the women participants, she stated:

> The big problem I start to see, all the Latino peoples have a lot of scare, miedo. They say, "Don't go this place, don't go this place, don't go!" And I am thinking, "Why? Why don't you go? If you need some doctor go to the hospital." And, well, I know the reason is because many people don't have papers, and they are afraid of *La Migra*.[4] (Simopoulos 1998c)

Like Hagar, there is the incessant fear that any wrong move will end in rejection and exile from one's adopted country or, as was the case with Hagar, from her adopted family. Most of the women admitted that they have never felt like the United States was or ever will be their home. One of the women from El Salvador spoke about her experiences of rejection and dislocation living in the United States:

---

4. *La Migra* refers to the Immigration and Naturalization Services.

The country, the language, the people. I have lived in this country for twenty-three years and I don't like it in any way! I do not like the food. I don't like the atmosphere. The people are very cold, and neighbors never talk to one another. And you don't ever have friends in this country. I don't have a friend in this country that I can say, "Oh, this is my best friend since I was small." No! I don't have a friend like that. I don't like life here. (Simopoulos 1998c)

As the women said, both they and Hagar were faced with a feeling of home-lessness—they never really found their niche in the foreign and unwelcoming situations in which they found themselves.

It is in these desperate situations that the immigrant women identified with what they perceived to be Hagar's attempt to return to Egypt. Studying a map, the women discovered that "Shur is very close to Egypt" (Simopoulos 1998c). The women concluded that when Hagar escaped she was headed home to Egypt. One of the women, a dentist from Guatemala, said that she, like Hagar, is always look-ing for an escape:

I have looked for ways to escape. I need an escape, a way to leave. Sometimes I think, "I am going! I am going! I do not want to be here." I believe that many of the Latinas we identify with Hagar when she escaped for her country. It is like our situation. We are in this country, and many of us want to forget everything and go. This has happened to me many times. I don't think about anything else. I don't think about my children. I don't think about my husband. I only want to go! Hagar went! She looked for a way out. And I think, "I will go to Guatemala. I will go to work in my clinic. I will go to see my parents. I will take with me my children." This is what Hagar did. What she did is better than staying. (Simo-poulos 1998c)

In her desperation, Hagar ran away. More importantly, as the women pointed out, she headed in the direction of Egypt, her home! By returning to Egypt and being reunited with her family, Hagar would live out their dream of returning to their countries and being reunited with their families. Amongst these Latina women, there is always the faint hope that some day in the future they will return to their country and family: "We say in the future you can go to your country; you can put your clinic again and start all over" (Simopoulos 1998c).

The women in the Bible study did note, however, that in the end Hagar did not return home to Egypt. Hagar's dream of returning home remained only a dream. Why? The women concluded that Hagar must have realized that she might not have been welcome in her own land. As a result, Hagar and Ishmael, with the aid of God, lived an autonomous existence in the desert of Paran. Exiled from her country as a young girl and exiled for a second time by her adopted family, Hagar grows old with her son wandering in the same desert that the Israelites wandered after their exodus from Egypt. Much like them, the women concluded that Hagar spent the rest of her life as a wandering exile with no place to call home. Similarly, the immigrant women were exiled from their country of origin, do not feel welcome in their adopted country, and accordingly are resigned to live as outsiders, as wanderers— physically settled in the United States but always longing in their hearts to return home. To borrow a phrase from Fernando Segovia, Hagar and the Latina women seem to inhabit "two spaces"—Egypt and the desert—Central America and the United States—yet they have "no place on which to stand" (Segovia 1995:33).

The redemption in this group's interpretation is similar to the redemption found in the Caucasian women's reading. As the Latina women commented, although God did not liberate Hagar by helping her return to her country, God at least provided the means of survival for Hagar, her son and their descendants.

"Hagar, the Exploited Worker": Black South African Women Speak

The black South African women identified solely with Hagar as an Egyptian slave or an exploited worker. Given their social location, this perspective is not surprising. As black South African women, the participants in this group were products of the dehumanizing system of Apartheid. They were the poorest of South Africa's poor; they had received grossly inferior educations, and they had few work skills. To make enough to survive, several of them sold food or other items in the informal economic sector. Others held odd jobs here and there as domestic workers, hotel maids and farm workers. Low pay and job insecurity made life often unbearable for many of them.

The black South African women identified abuse, misuse of power, corruption, sexual exploitation, economic exploitation and slavery as the main themes of the story. The women were outraged at Sarah's "cruelty" and the fact that Sarah, the one in power, "used her (Hagar) to get what she wanted without thinking of her" (Simopoulos 1998a). The women concluded that Hagar was forced to sleep with Abraham, and that it could have even been a case of child abuse since the text refers to Hagar as a slave-girl.

A conversation developed about what it means to be a slave in modern-day South Africa. Though the women identified several forms of modern-day slavery—including the custom of paying lobola[5] for one's wife, thereby ensuring that she is the property of her husband—their experiences of working for exploitative employers was most dominant. One woman likened Hagar's situation of powerlessness to that of an exploited worker's situation: "You had no way to say 'No' to your boss or ma'am. A slave has no voice. If a boss says you must do this, you have to do this because he's going to beat you" (Simopoulos 1998a). Initially, I assumed

---

5. Lobola is a Zulu custom in which cattle, or some other kind of compensation, is handed over to the father of the bride as recompense for the expense of the bride's upbringing and the loss of her services.

that the women were comparing Hagar's relationship to Sarah and Abraham with the relationship between the domestic worker (historically black) and her mistress (historically white). While the terms "boss" and "ma'am" were traditionally used to address only white employers, the women indicated that in the new South Africa these terms are used to designate employers of any race. Of significance is the fact that the women related Hagar's experiences of oppression and exploitation to their own experiences of exploitation as workers, specifically domestic workers or "house helps":

> You work, and then you end up getting food, not money. Then in another situation you are working and you end up doing lots of things that you are not being paid for. And what about overtime? If over the weekend you do not normally work but because there are visitors this weekend you've got to wash dishes, you've got to cook, you've got to clean up, you've got to wake up early in the morning, and you end up working really like 24 hours. So that makes a person tend to be a slave. And usually people won't say, "This is enough. I'm going." Only because they are getting money so they are able to assist their family back home do they still continue to work. But it's not worth it. (Simopoulos 1998a)

The black South African women's experiences of exploitation enabled them to understand the hopelessness of Hagar's situation.

What is striking about this study is not necessarily how the women identified with Hagar, but how they reacted to God as God is represented in the text when the Angel of the Lord tells Hagar to "return and submit" to her mistress. It is my contention that it is in their response to God that we see most clearly how their social location influenced their interpretation of this text. Although one woman stated that perhaps God was "saving this lady," the majority of the women evidenced a heated and passionate aversion to this oppressive image of God. They said the God of Gen 16 is "the God of the powerful and not the God of the poor." As one woman said:

> It would seem that even the Angel of the Lord was treating Hagar badly because she had received enough ill-treatment from Sarah and now the Angel says, "You go back." You know, it is like the Angel was approving of what happened there. So it was like the Angel blessed the status quo. It was O.K. for Sarah to oppress this poor African lady. (Simopoulos 1998a)

Another woman, the group's leader, described the God of Gen 16, in the following manner:

> It is the God of those who have a voice. It is not the God of the voiceless. I mean, one could assume that if she was a Christian she would have kept on praying that the situation should change. But it became worse so she ran away. So I think this God is the God who does not listen to those who are in trouble. It is the God who chooses who to listen to. (Simopoulos 1998a)

And yet another woman added, "He is the God of the rich" (Simopoulos 1998a).

What an indictment of God! The women did not, and as I have argued more fully in my thesis possibly could not, accept the idea that God, in telling Hagar to return and submit, was being protective of her. They were skeptical about God having her best interests in mind.

There are many ways of understanding or interpreting their reaction to God. The best explanation in my assessment boils down to their experiences as black women and black youth in an era of struggle, often violent struggle, against the Apartheid government. They had been socially and theologically conditioned to believe in the God of liberation: the God who supported the black liberation movement and the God who wanted black men and women in South Africa freed from the tyranny of domination. This is the message on which they were weaned—the message that had been preached from the pulpits in black churches all over South Africa. Black South Africans had waited patiently for their situation to change under the Apartheid government. The days of silence, submission and resignation were over by the time most of these women reached their teens. They grew up at the height of the liberation struggle when resistance and protest replaced submission and patient silence. It is not surprising that they understood the God of Gen 16 to be oppressive. The return-and-submit-to-your-mistress God is absolutely counter to the God of equality, dignity and freedom. The women's responses clearly critique this biblical portrayal of God as being a disguise of the God of oppression or the God of the rich. Redemption in this group's reading is found in an antagonistic reading of the text—the author of the Gen 16 story is clearly mistaken in his or her understanding of God.

CONCLUSION

In the introduction, I stated that I would argue that each of the three interpretations of the story of Hagar and Sarah are valid. I do not assume that they are valid in the sense that they stand in accordance with traditional, established historical-critical methods and conclusions. In addition, I am compelled to state that validity requires boundaries, especially if we are to safeguard against oppressive interpretations (e.g., those that attempt to subjugate whole groups of people based on their race, sexual orientation, gender, ethnicity, etc.). I do contend, however, that the distinct interpretations that have been articulated in this paper are valid simply because they are genuine—they speak meaningfully to the particular context of each group. The women have interpreted the text in such a way that a liberating and redemptive message of hope has emerged for them in the midst of their varying experiences of tragedy and suffering. The readings from each of these groups speak meaningfully to real issues of life and death. Biblical interpretation, in my estimate, is most valuable when it is relevant to life and one's search for transformation and meaning.

   This essay advocates for the articulation of the voices of ordinary readers in determining meaning in the biblical text. The Bible has historically remained in the hands of academics and the hierarchy of the church. Furthermore, the academic discipline of biblical studies has traditionally had little or no place for ordinary, untrained readers of the Bible, and it certainly has had no place for ordinary readers as Gerald West defines the term. The voices and experiences of ordinary readers have been left out of the interpretive dialogue. As biblical scholars who seek to use our biblical scholarship to serve the whole of humanity, it is our responsibility to give voice to these ordinary readers and their interpretations. I have found that this is most adequately accomplished by creating the interpretive space for ordinary readers to bring their life experiences and perspectives to the text and to articulate the meaning they find in the text in their own words. The challenge is to establish an interface between academic and ordinary readers of the Bible. As Renita Weems notes, by reading with the marginalized, "we step from behind the safety of our ivory tower desks and do our part in repairing the world where real people use the Bible as their manifesto for living, dying, fighting, dreaming, struggling, and maiming each other." Reading with marginalized readers forces us—biblical scholars—to "take responsibility for the world in which we live" as well as "to take responsibility for the world which our scholarship creates" (Weems 1996:261).

Remembering the Bible as a Critical "Pedagogy of the Oppressed"

Janet Lees

Introduction

The two small faith communities described here are in the inner city of Sheffield, a large industrial city in the north-midlands of the United Kingdom. They are situated, about three miles apart, on the northeast side of the city in two of the most economically deprived political wards. One is on a housing estate and was built in the 1930s while the other is in an area of older housing and dates back 100 years. Whilst the estate houses a predominantly "white working class" population, over forty languages are spoken in the racially and linguistically diverse area around the other church. The small congregation that meets weekly in this church number around twenty people, ranging in age from preschool children to adults over ninety years old. The first congregation reflects the make-up of the estate: families and retired people attend, all are white. At the second, there are both black and white members, including those born in the United Kingdom and those from former British colonies in the Caribbean and West Africa who have settled locally in the last fifty years. Both churches are heavily involved in community work in partnership with other local voluntary and statutory agencies, with preschool and school aged children and their families and elderly people, and for community education and skills training. This is the context for the work that is described in this essay.

The Bible in the Church

Attend worship in most United Reformed Churches in the United Kingdom and at some point in the service you would expect the Bible to be read aloud. For most of the rest of the service, participation by the congregation would be confined to formal responses in prayers and singing. If anything is said, it is usually by one person at a time, and that person has a designated leadership role, usually an ordained minister or an appointed lay leader. Discussion groups may happen from time to time, outside of the formal time for Sunday worship, on another day and in another place, usually with specific Christian education aims, but not during Sunday worship.

During worship there is an expected order, not just of what will happen but who will speak. This expected pattern of voices also extends to expected patterns of biblical interpretation. One person will do this, and a "proper" interpreter is one academically trained in biblical interpretation. It is the measure of a faith community within denominational politics that it has a trained and ordained biblical interpreter who does this task week by week on behalf of the rest of the community. In the absence of this person one or two others may have the agreement of the community to speak instead but access to this role is carefully controlled. Most people come to church week by week and say nothing. No one asks their views or opinions about the Bible. Either they are not considered to have any or the ones they have are not thought to be of any value whether it is in shedding new light on the biblical text itself or applying that text to daily life.

Attend worship in the two churches described earlier on a Sunday and you will find that the Bible is often not read out loud. Rather, the congregations will be engaged in remembering and discussing different "texts" in groups within the context of worship. What is said and done week by week is communal and con-versational, rather than as a monologue by one appointed person. This process, called "remembering the Bible" has grown up here over the last four years. How this came about, how it is done and what have, so far, been the effects of this pedagogy will be discussed in this paper.

A period of study at the Institute for the Study of the Bible in South Africa in 1994 introduced me to work by biblical scholars involved in reading the Bible with local communities (Philpott 1993; West 1996; 1999). At that time, my own United Kingdom context was as a speech and language therapist preparing for ordained ministry in the United Reformed Church. Whilst I was attracted to the notion that biblical scholars might read the Bible with local people, I also knew plenty of people, through my work in speech and language therapy, for whom "reading with" (West 1999:34–62) might never be possible. These were people with communication difficulties including reading and writing difficulties, like dyslexia, hearing impairments, learning difficulties and speech difficulties, like cerebral palsy. It is difficult to estimate how many such people there might be in the United Kingdom as a whole but the Royal College of Speech and Language Therapists suggests it is around 2.5 million people.[1] Because of my dual interest, I began a study to determine ways in which people with communication difficul-ties might interpret the Bible, using their preferred methods (Lees 1997). It soon became clear that many of my respondents with communication difficulties relied

---

1. Figures from the RCSLT annual report 1995/6. RCSLT is the professional body of speech and language therapists in the United Kingdom.

on remembered versions of the Bible for their biblical interpretation. They had usually not experienced these remembered methods being used in the churches in which they worshiped and were at first hesitant to claim them as their own. This conversation with an informant, [2] an Anglican religious woman who has dyslexia, illustrates this point.

> R: "From my point of view, the Bible stories come alive when they're being told. When you stand up and read stories from the Bible, all very dead pan or in a churchy sing-song speech or monotone, then I don't hear them…When the story is told, then I'll remember it."
>
> J: "And if I could just take us back a minute to reading the Bible. Would you say that's something you do or not?"
>
> R: "No. I'd say that there was a stage when I did, very disciplined, when I was a novice…. I think on the whole I left it behind…. I mean I've never admitted this to many people because people rely on the Bible…. Well, I mean, I wonder if I'm a Christian at all, but on the other hand, I have this terrific yearning to pray, and this journey and this yearning for God and all the rest of it."

It seemed likely that this underground, hidden, method of interpreting the Bible was used by people with communication difficulties, even if it were not officially recognized or widely used in churches. Moreover, as the study progressed with groups including those with and without formally defined communication difficulties, and more conversations were analyzed, it was also clear that using remembered versions of the Bible was something literate and verbal people could do (but usually did not do consciously) as much as illiterate and nonverbal people. Some cultural and ethnic groups place a higher value on an oral/aural culture. West noted that ordinary African interpreters "work with remembered as well as a read Bible" (West 1999:96). It seems likely that in many Bible using cultures these two methods, reading and remembering, exist side by side with reading dominating remembering in literate cultures and remembering being more prominent in groups with communication and learning difficulties. The different ethnic and cultural composition of these two congregations allows for some preliminary exploration of this issue. In the congregation with more black members it could be argued that the method has been adopted more readily as it is already a preferred part of the culture of this group. At a funeral service for the leader of the local black community I noted that most of the majority black congregation of over four hundred people shadowed most of the Bible readings by mouthing or whispering the words while they were being read out loud.

---

2. This is an edited version of a conversation that appears in my M.Th. thesis (see Lees 1997).

A call to work with the two churches described in the first paragraph lead me to suggest that we might work together this way four years ago. Aware that both groups embraced a wide range of abilities and learning styles, it was necessary to develop an inclusive educative method as far as using the Bible was concerned. Some people were highly literate and very verbal. They were sometimes the loudest, most prominent members of the groups. Others were less confident; some were less literate, had learning or communication difficulties or might be communicating across cultures. These were sometimes the quietest, least prominent members of the groups. What was needed was a method of using the Bible together that would challenge this status quo and provide a more equal way of working together. However, because of other factors to do with age profile, the general decline in church attendance in the United Kingdom, and awareness of other issues affecting adult learning like group dynamics, concentration span and attitude change, this needed to be a part of what the whole group did regularly, rather than an additional activity for the very few who might attend a discussion group. In other words, it had to be part of our worship and learning together Sunday by Sunday, if it was to have any real effect on our lives together.

Using Remembered Versions of the Bible

Thus we began using remembered versions of the Bible in our regular Sunday worship, usually of the gospel appointed from the revised common lectionary. We developed a number of ways of doing this. These include a range of methods which introduce the text to be remembered either by pictures or drama, those in which the group are invited to "finish off" something that has been started, or those which include some element of rehearsal or story telling by one or more members of the group.[3]

There are strategies that help people to join in the remembering process. These include: inviting people to share what they remember in a small group as a first stage; telling a story which has repetitive bits which gradually people can join in; asking a small group to prepare the remembering in advance; using an informal setting rather than a formal one; using clues from picture Bibles, films, musicals, plays, a cartoon, or a painting; providing an outline of the story to fill in the details; trying the process more than once even if it does not seem easy the first time.

There are ways in which the process can be helped and ways it can be hindered. It has been noted that: being comfortable in the group rather than knowing lots about the Bible makes for success in this process; children, who may not have heard as much of the Bible before as some older members, often participate more readily because story telling is something they do more often in other ways; some

---

3. These methods are described more fully in Rowland and Vincent 2001:37–39.

of the members who say little at times may have a lot more to contribute to the remembering process; the whole thing can be done nonverbally, by mime or through drawings, if many of the group members are nonverbal.

Participants[4] have identified three things that happen as a result of using remembered versions of the Bible in worship.

PEOPLE PARTICIPATE

The first and most noticeable effect of using remembered versions of the Bible in worship is that people participate. When doing this with a group for the first time there may be some who choose not to do so. Other will say "I can't remember anything." It is important for the group facilitator/s to enable the group to develop an atmosphere that encourages rather than discourages participation. In most similar churches adults have become used to passivity. A sudden change to a more active participation can be threatening to some, or even all, of the group. However, in spite of the fact that the Bible might be thought to have dropped out of British culture, people can and are able to participate in using this method. They do "have a Bible in them" and, with encouragement, are willing to share it. This makes for a rather noisy and chaotic scene as people talk to each other. There is less need for monologues and more opportunities for the group as a whole to own the interpretation process and product.

PEOPLE ARE SURPRISED HOW MUCH THEY REMEMBER

At some point in the process people begin to realize that they can and do remember something. Often their first reaction to this is surprise: "Oh, yes I do remember that one" or "I have heard of her." As the remembered version of the Bible is aired again and again, group members become more confident and more vocal. It is important that they own their remembered version and do not try to impose it on others. We all remember differently: different events in different ways. The aim is not competitive but collaborative: to explore shared memory.

THE LINE BETWEEN REMEMBERING AND INTERPRETING BECOMES BLURRED

Very soon people begin discussing what they think about the events they are remembering rather than just the events themselves. It is at this point that the group has moved beyond remembering to interpreting the Bible. The line between the two things is more blurred than when a written version is used. Then

---

4. These are participants in a wide range of "remembering the Bible" activities. Mostly from the two churches mentioned, they have also included participants in training events and workshops for worship leaders in various parts of the United Kingdom over the past four years.

it is more obvious when we are reading and when we are giving an opinion or interpretation of what we have read.

Using remembered versions of the Bible means that people get down to interpreting sooner, because interpretation has already influenced what they have remembered. Exposing remembered versions to the range of interpretations within a group allows for new interpretations to be formed and tested out.

However, there are some clear disadvantages of using remembered versions. Here are three that groups using these methods have noticed:

It Is Difficult to Remember What You Have Not Heard

The first difficulty participants expect to encounter is that they will not remember what they have not heard. Obvious enough, you might think. This does not account for why children, who have usually not heard as much as the older members of the congregation who have been listening to the Bible read out in church over many years, join in the process with as much, if not more enthusiasm, than their elders. This observation seems to be due to two different factors: the learned passivity of the church going adults referred to earlier and the contrasting approach to learning taken in British schools in respect of story telling and the development of narrative skills. Children learn how to tell stories, and so they readily participate in story telling activities. Adults have learnt to keep quiet in church, so engaging with them in such tasks is more challenging.

With less than 10 percent of the population now attending church in the United Kingdom, some adults will be new to church culture. They will not have much background in the Bible in any form. Even though biblical images still crop up in British culture they are increasingly not understood by most of the population, nearly half of which no longer knows what Easter celebrates. Indeed, the community work of the church on the housing estate has already attracted people to join the faith community who have little or no church background beyond the compulsory Christian education and worship of the state school system. However, even these adults can and have been encouraged to share their remembered versions of the Bible, to build on these and use them more often. The cyclic nature of the lectionary means things come back round again fairly soon. Participants are gradually able to exclaim "I remember that one" and thus join in more and more.

Being "Put on the Spot" May Feel Threatening

No one is comfortable in a group where "getting it wrong" feels humiliating. This is why it is important to build up the collaborative aspect of the group. There will be those who remember more than others and those who are more verbal. It is important that these do not dominate the group and over ride the less confident or less verbal ones. Sometimes small group work in which confident and verbal participants are grouped together, with less confident and less verbal people in another group is possible. An emphasis on group listening is vital, and it is important that the facilitator/s also practice this, feeding back into the groups any small contributions that might otherwise get lost or overlooked.

Stories Can Get Mixed Up as They Are Remembered

Many of the episodes in the gospels are repetitive or similar in some way: a name, a place, an action. It is not surprising that these details get mixed up: "Is it Martha or Mary? We'll go for Mary." Rather than see this as a disadvantage, it can help the group to experience something of how the written versions of the gospels came about from oral accounts and what might have happened in the process. Again, it is important that people own their remembered version. So, if it includes a detail that differs from that remembered by someone else, or even if it is the minority version in a group, then it is their version.

At this stage it is probably helpful to illustrate what a "remembered text" looks like. Obviously they are not all identical, so one example is just that. Nevertheless, here are some "remembered texts" generated by local people and used in worship at these churches.

Example One: A Woman Pours Perfume on Jesus

"The woman had a bottle of perfume, and she poured it on Jesus' head while he was having his dinner, but he didn't mind. He said she did it "cos she loved him." With these words a six-year-old girl remembers the story of Jesus being anointed with perfume by an anonymous woman. The same girl, on another occasion, concluded that the church community project was something we did "because we love Jesus," making a link between the biblical text and the praxis of the faith community.

Example Two: Two Versions of Jesus' Baptism

The sacrament of baptism is frequently celebrated. It usually begins with remembering of the baptism of Jesus. Here are two remembered versions of that episode taken from two different groups.

Version One
  "John was baptizing lots of people when Jesus appeared and then John said: 'I am not worthy to baptize you.' But Jesus said: 'Don't be stupid, we are all our Father's children.' A dove came down and a voice said: 'This is my son.'"

Version Two

John was baptizing in the Jordan. Jesus came to be baptized. John refused saying that Jesus should baptize him. Jesus insisted and hinted at the fulfillment of scripture. Those observing saw a dove descend on Jesus. A voice was heard saying: "This is my beloved son, listen to him."

The first remembered version is presented in a very direct and informal style. It led to a discussion of what it is to be "the Father's children" from shared experiences as parents and as children. Work with children and families make up a significant part of the daily work of this faith community through its community project, a further link between the biblical text and praxis. The second, with worship leaders from the group of churches, has more emphasis on scripture and authority. Its more formal style is also a contrast with the first version. This demonstrates something of the difference between the two groups: one a group with little or no formal training in biblical interpretation, the second having some training as lay leaders. The second version finishes with a plea to those gathered to listen; an obvious concern of the local worship leaders.

MARTHA, MARY, AND LAZARUS: MATTERS ARISING

Using "remembered texts" with these faith communities and others over the last four years, I have noted that similar issues tend to arise around the "who," "where," "what" and "why" of the method. A scenario I often use for "one-off" or "taster" sessions is about remembering the family at Bethany: Martha, Mary and Lazarus. This remembering is usually rich with questions and issues and silences, as are the gospel texts themselves. The following discussion of these four issues includes examples from work with several different groups using the example for the family at Bethany. The words used by the groups during discussions are given in quotation marks.

REMEMBERING WHO?

"A noisy one and a quiet one."

The first point people usually remember about this family is the two sisters: one was noisy and one was quiet. It is this stereotype which has been at the heart of most interpretations and which needs liberating. However, it does provide us with a place to start.

"I can't remember who went to prepare the dinner."

Not everyone remembers names. When people work in groups the aim is to get people to co-operate to share what they remember rather than one or two thinking they know it all and dominating the discussion.

"One of them poured oil over his feet. Martha or Mary? We'll go for Mary."
"I'm not sure which one came to the graveside. Does it matter?"

Not remembering names can lead onto not remembering who did what. The facilitator needs to let the group share the knowledge they have rather than rise to the urge to tell everyone what s/he knows. However, this kind of confusion can also provide an opportunity to discuss the reliability of the written text, where it came from and what the the role of remembering was in its original formation.

"There was another mention of Lazarus and a rich man."

There are often people with similar names in other parts of the Bible. Again, see this as an opportunity to see what else people remember and why, rather than "That is not the one we are remembering today."

REMEMBERING WHERE?

"I think the Luke 10 one is probably the one she means."

First there is the location in the written biblical text. Some people may know this, others will not. It is not necessarily important to know it and evidence from these groups suggests that not many people find it helpful. I rarely give the location of the written version unless asked or unless I am trying to point out differences between different people's versions. If the group are having difficulty coming to an agreed version it can help to know that those attributed to producing the written gospels rarely agreed on everything.

"A mile and a half down the road from the Mount of Olives."

Then there is the geographical location. This may help some people. Equally there may be some who have visited the places and will have a reflection they can add.

REMEMBERING WHAT?

"Mary said: My house is different. My brother is different. He lets me be different. He lets me learn and listen."

Not being tied to a written version allows participants to retell the story in more liberating ways. Time should be allowed for these imagined versions to be heard.

"He was useless and he went and died."

For some participants it is enough to baldly state what silences there are in the story.

"I was not a well man. My name was never mentioned because I was never there."

"Lazarus said: I've not said a lot. My sisters keep the family on an even keel. I went and died. I'm a bloke with not many choices in life."

For others those silences do become something that can be opened up and examined depending on their lived experiences. This can be tender, poignant, painful and emotional so there needs to be time and space for affirmative listening when this is happening.

"It's funny there is no mention of them [the family] at the crucifixion."

In a remembered version there are no clear boundaries for where the story begins and ends. Participants can be invited to decide for themselves and see what happens. Again this can be used in a discussion of the structure of the written version if that is relevant.

REMEMBERING WHY?

"I don't think much was said about the brother."
"Angry, angry! I think Jesus was angry in the story."
"And Jesus said a short prayer and Lazarus came to life again and everyone was gob-smacked."

These comments emerged from a session with people with learning and communication difficulties. The remembered text method is not just about reconstructing a text, although it begins there. In most groups it quickly develops into interpretation as participants consider what happened in the light of their own experiences. These participants revealed an important insight into the structure of the story that was based on their own experiences of marginalization.

Beginning	Middle	End
Silence about Lazarus	Lazarus dies	Silence about Lazarus

People often assumed to be silent could identify with the huge silences in this story about the presence and role of a key character in the story: the silent Lazarus.

NOT REMEMBERING

"I've never heard of them."
"We don't remember anything about that."

This can be true and if so it is important to handle the situation so that people do not feel they have been set up to fail. If it looks as if there may be bigger gaps in the collective memory than you hoped then I judge this by asking the whole group, "Who remembers this?" If there are those who do remember and those that do not I usually invite the groups to mix up a bit: move around so that each group contains some people who do remember and some who do not. I try not to make too many assumptions about who this will be. Hannah is seven years old and she remembers Martha, Mary and Lazarus because "Mummy is always talking about them." She was able to share the story with a group of half a dozen people of all ages quite readily. Using this strategy in an all age worship session may look risky but the ensuing chaos can be creative. Even if we remember nothing from the Bible we may have learned that we did not need to stay in the same seats all the way through the session after all.

Here is a remembered version of the story of the family from Bethany:

> In Bethany, Jesus turns up at tea-time. Martha panics. There is no food and she wants to do her best. Martha wants to do what is right and Mary winds her up. Mary gets distracted and Martha gets distracted. Martha looses her temper and there's the usual sibling rivalry stuff. Martha says to Jesus: "Don't you care." Jesus says to Martha: "Martha, Martha, you are worried about many things." Martha says to Jesus: "I knew you'd take her side."

Observe what the remembered version puts in and leaves out. Interpretation has immediately become part of the remembering as this group picks up the idea that family relationships and sibling rivalry are at the heart of what was going on here. This is a refreshing idea, because it gets us away from the old stereotypes mentioned earlier about "the noisy one and the quiet one." After all, neither of the sisters, in the traditional interpretation presents a very liberating role model. Whilst the line "Martha, Martha, you are worried…." is lifted more or less from the written text (and this does happen from time to time) the final line "Mary has chosen the better part" is omitted here.

WHAT KIND OF PEDAGOGY?

In his landmark literacy program among Brazilian peasants, Paulo Freire set out a ground-breaking pedagogy. As a result, it was no longer considered sufficient to educate "the poor." Rather, the very aims of education itself were exposed and reassembled. Literacy had grown into "an act of knowledge" in which text and context were united in order to pose the simple, yet provocative, question: "What is the relation between literacy, liberation and learning?" (Taylor 1993:31, 33) The key thing about this community education was that it could give people a means with which to challenge the status quo. For Paul Taylor this Freirian pedagogy goes on whenever pedagogues continue a dialogue between texts and contexts. He describes it as "a learning iceberg" with more out of sight than seen as it is "what cannot be seen that contradicts the obvious." For him it is "a pedagogy which places the presence of oppression before the absence of literacy but which also, against the popular logic, insists on treating the effect in order to remedy the cause" (149). It is this Freirian tradition in which the "remembering the Bible" strategy described here operates.

The two ingredients are present: oppression and an absence of literacy. There are several obvious kinds of oppression operating in the contexts that has been described. The first is one of poverty. These two faith communities exist in some of the poorest urban parts of the United Kingdom. Even in Western Europe this material poverty is accompanied by many kinds of social poverty of which education is an obvious one, hence the add-on absence of literacy. But there are other oppressions. There are silences amongst adults in the churches; a combined effect of years of poverty, classism, racism, sexism and poor education, including the eventual outcome of ineffectual Christian education which has clearly not been liberating. In itself this Christian education is partly the product of the retreat of biblical scholarship from the faith community to the academy. In removing themselves to the academy biblical scholars have ceased to engage with the people or the issues of the contemporary faith context. Furthermore, "the vast majority of biblical critics have been slow to read against the grain of the biblical texts and the institution of traditional biblical scholarship, and they have been generally content to re-enact the ideologies inscribed in their respective narratives and meta narratives" (Bible and Culture Collective 1995:15).

What these faith contexts required was a pedagogy that would engage with both oppression and literacy. From the earlier work with people with communication difficulties came the idea of using not written but remembered versions. From the work with others in marginalized communities came the idea of putting the Bible back in their hands as a tool for engaging with oppression. It was William Herzog who linked the pedagogic work of Freire and Jesus, pointing out that they both worked with the poor and oppressed and with peasants, comparing the imperial or colonialist situations in first century Palestine and twentieth century Brazil. He went on to affirm that "both Jesus and Freire knew the power of what we call religion to liberate and oppress." It was obvious to Herzog that Freire, in his visual culture, would use pictures and literacy as his tools, and that Jesus, from an oral culture, would use story telling. From here it was not very far to suggest that in a not-highly-literate culture remembered stories might be used as the basis of a curriculum that would work with the liberative side of religion to be "world-shaking" rather than "world-maintaining" (Herzog 1994:25-28).

This contrast probably underlies some of the reasons why not every Christian faith community would want to use "remembered texts." The tensions between maintaining and shaking the world of the church or the wider community exist in all of the faith communities with which I have worked. In some one will dominate the group's ethos and practice; in others, the other. Where "world-maintaining" is the dominant ethos and practice of the group then a curriculum and pedagogy that is in essence "world-shaking" will at best take longer to develop or at worst be rejected outright.

Conclusion

The work described here is ongoing. Even after using these methods for four years it is not complete. New things are challenging and changing the way the methods are used all the time. Recording some of the occasions when we have used remembered texts together has allowed us to review them, and discuss what was happening further. A visual display of groups using the methods will allow others to view what we do and determine if they would want to use them.

"Critical pedagogy" has been defined as "opening up institutional spaces for marginalized students to give voice to their experience and to develop a critical analysis of oppressive social systems in order to transform them in accordance with their interests" (Kramer-Dahl 1996:242). Whilst it is important to be aware of the shortcomings of the process described here, using remembered texts has lead to the opening up of institutional space, in this case the worship and learning space of the faith community. This method has enabled marginalized participants to give voice to their experiences as a first stage in analyzing the prevailing social system and its transformation. What kind of transformation this leads onto should be the subject of the next phase of this work.

Journeying with Moses toward True Solidarity: Shifting Social and Narrative Locations of the Oppressed and Their Liberators in Exodus 2–3

Bob Ekblad

Introduction

I often read the story of Moses' awakening and call with incarcerated Latino immigrants who attend my weekly bilingual Spanish-English Bible studies in Skagit County Jail in Washington State. People in our reading circle immediately identify with characters in the narrative of Exod 2:11–3:12, though their first-glance assumptions about each character's social location, shaped as they are by their own place in the world, leads to a prejudiced reading of the story. These biased interpretations of biblical stories are often alienating, reinforcing people's feelings of powerlessness or exclusion. I am convinced that oppressive interpretations can be subverted by careful reading of the narrative itself. This best happens when guided by facilitation that directly questions assumptions and invites unexpected identifications.

The story in Exod 2:11–3:12 opens with Moses, adopted son of Pharaoh's daughter, now grown up, going out to his people. At first glance, privileged Moses, going out from Pharaoh's household to see the people's forced labor and the Egyptian beating a Hebrew, does not resemble anyone except maybe me—the White, middle-class, educated professional's presence there in the jail "to help" the inmates. Their first impressions are of my eyes meeting each of theirs as guards usher them into the jail's multipurpose room, where we sit together for an hour or two in a circle.

The oppressed Israelites resemble the people I read Scripture with: Mexican, Chicano, White or Native American male inmates between eighteen and forty-five years old. The most visible equivalents to Israelite forced labor and beatings at the hands of Egyptians include their jail or prison sentences, court-ordered fines and probation, addictions to drugs or alcohol, minimum-wage jobs harvesting crops or processing fish or poultry. The taskmaster invites identifications with everyone, from me as representative of taskmaster religion, to judges, jail guards, probation officers, girlfriends, or Department of Social and Health Service (DSHS) social workers who require child-support payments. Other non-human forces like cocaine, anger, and jealousy are occasionally brought up as equivalents of taskmasters. Pharaoh represents the domination system or the status quo.

The story's first impressions of abused Israelites fighting with each other and distrusting their prospective liberator elicit contemporary versions of the same. Would-be liberator Moses' impulsive killing of the abusive taskmaster, denounced presumably by the very slaves whom he sought to defend, leads to his having to flee to a foreign country—a failed, paternalistic savior who is now completely absent from the scene. The Israelite slaves and their Latino immigrant equivalents remain passive objects of Pharaoh's, and now our, perpetual domination system. God is absent from the scene in the story and too often in people's lives, failing to intervene to keep things from messing up.

A first read might leave these characters and their readers' social roles intact were it not for the story's surprising turns. As the narrative unfolds and people take note of the text's rich detail, discussion deepens. New identifications become possible that are increasingly challenging to both inmates and myself as Moses journeys deeper into marginality. Can a trained reader from the domination system move from being identified and rejected as an Egyptian taskmaster or paternalistic Moses to a new place of being an effective agent of call, empower-ment and liberation? How can inmates and immigrants move from identifying themselves with subjected Israelite slaves to hearing the call of Moses to advocate for their people before the powers? The journey toward empowering solidarity requires great care on my part as the trained reader who seeks to facilitate this reading process without getting in the way.

Egyptian Taskmaster or Privileged Moses Reads Scripture with the Israelite Slaves?

My own social location among Latino immigrant inmates more closely par-allels Egyptian taskmaster status than privileged Moses stature before the Israelite slaves. My race, gender, language, nationality, and education mark me as a representative of the dominant mainstream American culture to my mostly undocumented, brown-skinned, Spanish-speaking, immigrant jail Bible study participants. My racial profile looks similar to the characteristics of most employ-ers that hire people for minimum-wage stoop labor field work or other physically demanding, low-paying jobs. Apart from the uniform, I resemble the jail guards, police agents, prosecutors and judges that arrest, detain, judge and sentence the people. Guards usher me into and out of the jail's multipurpose room, making me appear like an officially authorized benefit afforded to inmates by the powers. Yet since I am not one of the people who has power over them (like an attorney, judge, or prosecutor), I am viewed as someone neutral or even positively. But because I am Caucasian, a pastor, and known to them as the director of Tierra Nueva, I am viewed as clearly having more power then they do.

My status as pastor and expounder of the Bible also associates me with religious taskmasters of the dominant theology. As pastor I am automatically associated with God's social location, which in the minds of most inmates is far removed from theirs in the privileged, luxury utopia of heaven. God is viewed by most as hyper-sovereign—a distant judge whose powerful will has predetermined everything. While many confess that their troubles are of their own making, they simultaneously insist that God has their lives all mapped out in advance. They tend to consciously or unconsciously attribute all the negative things that happen to them as God's will. Since their theology assumes that God is just and good, people logically figure they must be bad and deserving of all the calamities that have befallen them. In Skagit County Jail, inmates often tell me, "God has me in jail, I was going down a bad road." Others say that they are there because of their own mistakes. They see God as both unwilling and maybe even unable to help them out. They expect no redemption, unless bail can be posted by a fellow drug dealer or a sympathetic family member.

People's perception of me as religious taskmaster unconsciously comes into play the moment people begin attending my Bible studies. Some of the people come to the gathering with an attitude of indifference, with no visible expectation of hearing any good news. They come for a combination of reasons, from socializing with friends from other pods to escaping the boredom of correctional facility's repetitive, predictable, military-like structure. Many people I work with both inside and outside of jail have given up on Christianity after finding that "accepting Christ as their Savior" with the Evangelicals or attending Mass for a while on a regular basis did not solve all their problems as the pastor promised. Addictions to drugs and alcohol and failures to change in other areas often beat people back into submission to the powers. The voice of Satan, the accuser and tempter, too often sounds louder and more powerful than that of the Paraclete—advocate and comforter.

Other people's attendance may at first be motivated by duty before a probation officer-like God who they consciously or unconsciously think might look at their "religious" efforts favorably, rewarding them with a lighter sentence or by bringing them back into favor with an estranged spouse. This view of God is visible in people's tendency to interpret every biblical text as calling them to behave in an obedient, morally righteous way. Inmates often reveal their assumptions about what pleases God when they apologize after a swear word slips naturally from their mouth in an uncensored moment or berate themselves as hypocrites who seek God only when they are in trouble but avoid anything religious once on the street. New inmates who do not yet know me are guarded with their language and self-disclosures. Others are looking for my affirmation regarding their efforts to approach God through Bible reading, pious talk and even fasting. I believe that underlying the most negative motivations people are thirsty for an authentic encounter. In most people there remains a buried hope that something real may yet happen between them and God. The trained reader of Scripture who facilitates Bible studies in settings such as this must be clear about their role and means in engaging people in liberating, transformational reading of Scripture.

My role involves deliberately subverting as many of the barriers to hope and empowerment as possible while at the same time inviting life-giving interpretation that replaces the old, paralyzing theology. I seek to help people directly identify and confront the dominant negative theology even before it appears in their interpretations. Identifying and countering evidence that appears to reinforce the dominant theology in the biblical stories is critical if the Bible is to be salvaged as medium of an empowering word. Salvaging apparently irrelevant or oppressive biblical stories must include helping people come to see themselves in the stories in ways that maximize the possibility of them hearing a liberating word addressed to them. Salvaging the story includes broadening the possibilities of Bible study participants' actual identification with appropriate characters in the story. This broadening of identifications is occasioned in part by means of careful examination of both the biblical characters narrative social location and participants own actual social location. As this happens, a shift in social locations up or down the hierarchical power ladder in the text and the group can transpire that makes room for people to take on new roles. Privileged, pretentious, Moses-like would-be liberators can become humble wandering fugitives awaiting new calls. Oppressed slaves and their contemporary equivalents can move toward new roles as Moses-like liberators of their people. So how can I as facilitator negotiate the barriers afforded me by my own privileged social location?

Shifting the Facilitator's Perceived Social Location

My own awareness that my social location associates me with the Egyptian taskmasters has led me to seek to distance myself from taskmasters in a number of ways. Firstly, I try to help people identify contemporary manifestations of both social and religious taskmasters. Before launching into our study of Exod 2:11–3:10, I first briefly present Genesis background that shows Jacob and his sons in Canaan being pushed to migrate to Egypt due to a famine. I then continue with a brief review of Exod 1—a separate Bible study that I have often done the previous weekly gathering before this study. I describe how God's people were hammered by a powerful pharaoh who sought to crush them through forced labor, physical abuse, and death penalties. The pharaoh's fear-based repression against the multiplying Israelite immigrant community provides fertile ground for Latino immigrants' contemporary comparisons. The Egyptian leaderships oppression of Israelites through hard labor looks a lot like U.S. government's lack of enforcement of labor laws set up to protect workers from abuse. The harsh targeting of male children for extermination invites comparisons, ranging from racial profiling of immigrant men by law enforcement, and mass incarceration for minor drug-dealing offenses to deportations and permanent bar to reentry to undocumented immigrant men—most of whom are fathers to U.S. citizen children residing in the United States. I emphasize that the redactor shows how God's promise of life cannot be stopped, but even increases with every deathblow. My facilitation style invites people to make associations that gradually lead them to see me as on *their* side. This establishes a gap between my identity as trained Bible reader, the Egyptian pharaoh, Egyptian people, and taskmasters.

Continuing in my efforts to show the Exodus writer (and myself) as on the side of the oppressed, I remind people how the Israelites resisted, refusing to comply with Pharaoh's laws. Moses was a slave baby who was saved because his family hid him, finally placing him in a basket and sending him down the river. There Pharaoh's daughter found him and had compassion on him. After unknowingly hiring Moses' very mother as his nanny, Pharaoh's daughter adopted Moses, raising him with all the royal privileges. He was an Israelite, but he may have been sheltered from the people's reality.

To help people shift in their perceptions regarding God's social location, I point out that God is not siding with oppressor Pharaoh. Rather, the story shows God visibly standing with the weakest most vulnerable ones in the story—the baby boys targeted for extermination. God blesses those who resist the forces of death through refusing to carry out Pharaoh's order and lying to him when confronted: the Hebrew midwives. Exodus depicts God as sovereign, but in a completely unexpected way. God's sovereignty is exercised not through the males identified by Pharaoh to be the greatest threat, but through mothers, a young girl and even a foreign princess. Their resistance takes the forms of covert disobedience, lying and hiding, and noncompliant adoption of the victim. The legal system cannot stop the fulfillment of God's covenant.

Yet everyone there in the jail is all too aware that the forces of death crush human lives. The principalities and powers wreak havoc on humans and on creation. In spite of God's movement in the world, people suffer: "The Israelites groaned under their slavery, and cried out." This cry did not fall on the deaf ears of an impersonal deity who wills the oppression as some kind of punishment. The text tells us: "Out of the slavery their cry for help rose up to God. God heard their groaning, and God remembered his covenant with Abraham, Isaac, and Jacob. God looked upon the Israelites, and God took notice of them" (2:23b–25).

People in my Bible studies are taken by surprise when they realize how God works in this story. Could this really be the way God works in our world today? Interest is sparked. The men are open to reading on. I recognize that it is not enough for them to know that according to the Bible God sees people's suffering. While this is encouraging, if God is in fact good and acts, people want to know how God actually responds to oppression. My visible agreement with and excitement about God's strategy partially confounds people's assumptions about my theology as one apparently associated with a sovereign punishing and/or Pharaoh and his taskmasters. Yet the narrative offers no clear character equivalents to myself as facilitator other than Pharaoh's daughter. None of these first mediators of liberation in Exod 1–2:10 are male, nor are they required to gain trust. Most importantly, the Israelites remain slaves.

Moses once again enters the scene at this point in the story and the Bible study is about to begin. I invite people to pay close attention to the story we're about to read of Moses. I invite them to look for tips about what this might mean for us. God is about to call a human being to a special task. The way God calls and the qualifications of the savior figure tell us a lot about God—and open up possibilities for us as well.

I remind the men that we know from the story that Moses had been given a special break. He'd escaped death thanks to his mother, sister, and Pharaoh's daughter. He was adopted into Pharaoh's household and benefited from special opportunities, escaping the grueling slavery of his people.

SEEING THE MISERY THROUGH CHANGING SOCIAL LOCATIONS: ME AND MOSES

The brief telling of my own story at this point invites a comparison with emerging Moses instead of with the oppressive taskmasters that can be helpful as part of the process but potentially harmfully if left there. I tell people how I too am from immigrant ancestors, though the comparisons are of limited value. My parents were both born in the United States. My grandfather on the father's side migrated from Sweden at the beginning of the twentieth century, while on my mother's side, my descendants trace back to some of the first English settlers in the eighteenth century. Unlike Moses, a child of slaves once immigrants, I grew up as a privileged member of the dominant U.S. ethnicity and benefited from many opportunities, including an undergraduate and graduate education. I now am an ordained Presbyterian pastor, jail chaplain and director of an ecumenical ministry to immigrants called Tierra Nueva (New Earth).

When leading this Bible study I often share my story of "going out to see" the people that began over twenty-four years ago with a life-changing trips to Europe, Israel, Mexico and Central America. This process has continued, including six years of work teaching sustainable farming and leading Bible studies among poor Honduran peasants during the 1980s. "Going out" now includes regular visits to farm workers in migrant labor camps and other immigrant workers in ghetto-like apartment complexes, and in weekly Spanish Bible studies in Skagit County Jail. I use great care to not express my going out to minister in heroic or victorious ways. If anything, I err on the side of confessing my weakness and ignorance in knowing how to effectively help people find healing and liberation from the most insidious forms of oppression (addictions to heroin or meth amphetamines) and my need for God's direct help in my work with people. In addition, my going out to see the inmates is brought about through the agency of uniformed jail guards who usher me through the thick steel doors into the jail's multipurpose room. The guards' releasing of the red-uniformed inmates who want to attend my study from their individual cells and pods and corralling them through two steel doors to take their places in the circle of blue plastic chairs reminds us all who actually is in the power position.

The men with whom I read more closely resemble Israelite slaves in Egypt than I embody Moses. Many are originally peasants from impoverished rural villages in Mexico. Pushed away by landlessness, drought, unemployment, government neglect, and global market forces, they, like Jacob's family, were drawn to the bounty El Norte (the U.S.A.)—modern-day Egypt. Once in the United States they find work as farm laborers or minimum-wage workers. Their willingness to work hard for low wages has made them invaluable to farmers, meat packing plants and countless other employers. Most of the people I read with have entered the United States illegally and live on the margins of American society. Many do not have valid driver's licenses or even identification and make use of counterfeit residency and social security cards. Most have partners and children to support, sometimes in Mexico and in the U.S.A. This is a near-impossible feat when making minimum wage. Some are tempted and succumb to small and larger-scale drug dealing for extra cash. Theirs is a life of constant insecurity. If ever arrested for anything, they can be assured they will be deported by the Department of Homeland Security back to Mexico immediately after doing their jail time.

Trusting God does not come naturally. Rather, people learn to lean on their own survival strategies, the "weapons of the weak." I continually struggle to determine how I, a trained reader of Scripture and professional religious worker, can best function as an agent of call or liberation. I propose reading the story of Moses' origins and first encounter with the oppressed in Exod 2–3 with this question in mind. How and who does God call as agents of liberation? How do would-be liberators gain trust?

Moses' journey toward solidarity appears to begin when he goes out and sees the oppression of his people. When I lead a Bible study with inmates, I often launch the actual study with this question. The following dialogue is actually a composite of several Bible studies but is reflective of the way I lead this study and ways inmates often answer.

> "The first thing we know about the adult Moses is a description of his awakening to the pain and struggle of the people. Let's see what happened to Moses," I suggest, inviting someone to read Exod 2 in Spanish and then English:
>
> > One day, after Moses had grown up, he went out to his people and saw their forced labor. He saw an Egyptian beating a Hebrew, one of his kinsfolk.
>
> "What did Moses see when he went out?" I ask the group.

"He saw the hard work they were doing," says Chris, a Chicano man in his early thirties fresh from ten years in a Texas prison.

"He was an Egyptian beating one of his people," says Vicente, an undocumented Mexican immigrant man in his mid twenties.

"This has happened to me too in many ways," I continue. "I came from a middle-class family where I had lots of privileges. I was sheltered from the struggles of immigrants, poor people, people in prison. If I or someone like me or Moses came into your lives, your families, or your villages in Mexico, what would they see?" I ask.

"A lot of poverty," says Vicente. "In Mexico one makes in one day what one makes in an hour here."

"Discrimination," says Chris. "Last week in court there were five of us Mexicans and twelve, maybe even fourteen gabachos (White people). Every one of the white guys were released. All of us Mexicans are still here."

"Lots of struggles," someone else adds. "In my home growing up, there was lots of fighting between my old man and old lady. Lots of drinking too."

"Drugs, addictions," says Jessie.

"So what sorts of ways do we react to injustices or hardships in our lives?" I ask the men.

"We use violence. We take out our frustration on someone," says someone.

"Some of us use drugs to blow it all away, to escape the pain," says someone else.

"Let's see how Moses responds," I suggest, inviting someone to read the next verse. A volunteer reads:

> He looked this way and that, and seeing no one he killed the Egyptian and hid him in the sand.

"Whoa, I thought Moses was a righteous dude," says Chris. "But he killed a man. He broke the commandments."

We talk about how Moses' *going out* and *seeing* change his life forever. Direct exposure to poverty, injustice, or oppression of whatever sort can lead us to react with violence. Moses' seeing clearly impacts him, as encounters with oppression always do. The next day he returns, trying his hand at conflict resolution between two Hebrew slaves.

> "How did the Hebrew slaves react to Moses when he tried to break up their fight? Did he prove himself in their eyes by taking a courageous stand against the bad guys?" I ask.

> "They didn't respect him," insists Julio, a confident Chicano man in his late twenties. "They saw him as a violent man, acting the same as the Egyptians."

> "I thought that being a bad-ass dude, defending yourself when you're dissed, doing a drive-by on a rival gang got you respect. Isn't that true?" I ask, half teasingly.

> "Well it does in a way, but not real respect that lasts," someone responds.

> "What about being a tough, strict parent. Isn't that a good thing? How many of you were harshly punished by your parents when you were children?" I ask. Over half the group raises their hands immediately.

> "So did it make you respect your parents more or less?" I continue.

> "Way less. Punishment didn't work," someone blurts out.

> "It just made me more angry," says another man.

> "And how about the police or the court system. Do the harsh sentences to enforce the laws make you respect them more?"

Heads are all nodding no.

> "Yeah, like George Bush beating up on the Iraqis. He just used his power. That didn't gain him no respect," adds Roberto, a thin Chicano guy who hadn't said anything until now.

> "So what would he have he had to do to win their respect?" I ask, trying to get the men to place themselves in the Hebrew slaves' shoes.

"He'd have to show respect and be more humble," says Julio.

We talk together about how seeing can lead us to reflect and act in many different ways. I point out that Moses' mother saw that Moses was a beautiful baby boy and she hid him. When Pharaoh's daughter saw baby Moses crying, she had compassion on him, adopting him as her own even though she knew he was a condemned Hebrew baby (Exod 2:6).

We wonder together how people thought Pharaoh found out that Moses was the killer. Did the Hebrew slaves need to denounce him in order to avoid being blamed for the crime? Did the slaves feel more secure with the known system the taskmaster represented than they did with unknown Moses? What would it take for the Hebrew slaves to trust Moses as their liberator? The text is silent regarding all these questions, leaving the reader surmising that Moses' heroic act likely was inadequate to earn him the allegiance of the Hebrew slaves, who chose to act in their own security interests.

One thing is certain: Moses' murder of the taskmaster forces him to become a fugitive. Rejected by his people, his crime exposed, Moses is now on the other side of the law. His law breaking in solidarity with the oppressed has made him an enemy of the Egyptian State. His adopted father Pharaoh now pursues him in order to kill him, showing that dominators cannot be trusted. A warrant issued by Pharaoh himself, Moses flees for his life (reactive, like many offenders).

Now he's in exile, wanted for murder, a failed liberator/reactionary—unappreciated by his people, a sojourner in a foreign land, shepherding for a living. At the same time Moses' crime, exile and location in the desert significantly broaden the possibilities for others to identify with this character.

"When people in Mexico commit a crime and are being hunted by the police, where do they go?" I ask the group.

"Al Norte" (to north—U.S.A.), they responded.

I have met many men who came to the Skagit Valley precisely to escape troubles at home. Many end up in jail or prison for new crimes committed in North America. Others work in the fields, picking strawberries, raspberries, blueberries, cucumbers, or working in meat-packing plants. Some sell drugs.

"So where was Moses when God met him?" I ask the guys in my study. "Was he in Mass or in some church? What was he doing? Was he praying, studying the Bible, looking for God?"

The men look surprised and slightly uncomfortable with the obvious answer. They're not used to looking at narrative gaps—at what the text doesn't say. Might there be good news there too?

"Moses was in the desert. He was working, shepherding his sheep," they observe.

"But he must have done something good, he must have been a holy person, he must have known God, otherwise God would not have met him," I insist, inviting them to look closer at the text. "What do we know about Moses?"

Occasionally people have stated here that Moses was chosen because he grew up in Pharaoh's court and had the knowledge and social class background to be a liberator. This assumption is visible in ancient Jewish and Christian exegesis too, which seeks to make sense of God's choice of Moses for such a key leadership role and to respond to the contradiction and even offense of Moses' claims about himself in Exod 4:10 "but I am heavy of speech and heavy of tongue."[1]

> Arithmetic, geometry, the lore of meter, rhythm, and harmony, and the whole subject of music ... were imparted to him by learned Egyptians. These further instructed him the philosophy conveyed in symbols.... He had Greeks to teach him the rest of the regular school course, and the inhabitants of the neighboring countries for Assyrian literature and the Chaldean science of the heavenly bodies. (Philo, *Life of Moses* 1.23)

> Pharaoh's daughter adopted him and brought him up as her own son, and Moses was educated in all the wisdom of Egypt, and he was powerful in his words and actions. (Acts 7:21–22)

While these readings make room for people like me and other trained readers[2] to find their place in the popular liberation struggles, the absence of any

---

1. James Kugel makes an interesting observation regarding this text that I quote at length that shows why ancient rabbinic exegesis (quoted below) tended to disassociate Moses from the uneducated, depriving semiliterate or under-educated people of an otherwise natural rapprochement with inarticulate Moses. "Eloquence in the ancient world was thought to be largely the result of schooling—and it was one of the most important things a person could possess. Was Moses thus saying that his education had been incomplete, and that this all-important trait was somehow lacking in him? This would have constituted a serious flaw in the eyes of ancient readers.... And in any case, the idea that Moses had not received a thorough education was certainly contradicted by the eloquent words he spoke throughout the Bible—and in particular by the book of Deuteronomy, which is, almost from the beginning to end, one long, highly eloquent speech uttered by Moses just before his death. For all such reasons, then, ancient interpreters were quick to supply what the book of Exodus had" (Kugel 1998:509).

2. In Jewish exegesis there is even room for viewing Moses more as an organic intellectual, whose training was homegrown. [The angel tells Moses] "Afterwards, when you had grown up, you were brought to the daughter of Pharaoh and you became her son. But Amram, your

signs of Moses having benefited by his life as Pharaoh's daughter makes room for people on the margins to identify with Moses.

> The guys look in their Bibles—someone dares to answer: "He was a murderer. It wasn't even an accident. He looked this way and that. He hid the body in the sand."

Moses indeed becomes an immigrant and a fugitive, working a minimum-wage job in the wilderness. His life did not yet have a place in God's project of liberation and life. Moses needed to do more than just "go out to see" oppression. Another kind of seeing was necessary for Moses to discover his new vocation. But this second "seeing" was not his own doing.

I point out to the men that the place of God's encounter supports this. The desert is the place where the rejected were cast (Hagar, Ishmael). It is also a place of revelation, of being set apart or to find your identity as God's people—and not just as Pharaoh's slaves. [3] Moses drives his flock "behind" the wilderness—a place of utter desolation. It's in this no-man's land that he comes to the mountain of God.

It is here that the Angel of YHWH appears/is seen to him. He sees a flame in a bush, a curious sight. The flame is approachable—it does not burn up the bush. He's drawn to contemplate. God calls him by name: Moses, Moses!

> "So what does this mean for us?" I ask the guys in my jail Bible study.

> "It's like God shows up where we work, man. He comes to the field, he comes to the factory. He appears right there," someone says. Another guy adds: "The desert is right here. This jail is the wilderness where we've been led. God appears to us here, when we've come to the end of our rope."

> When Moses is told he's in God's presence, a holy place, he hides his face in fear. "Why do you think he was afraid?" I asked the inmates.

> "He felt dirty. He felt ashamed to be in God's presence. Like he wasn't good enough," said one guy.

[Israelite] father, taught you writing. And after you completed three weeks [of years, that is, twenty-one years], he brought you into the royal court" (*Jub.* 47:9, quoted in Kugel 1998:510).

3. Sometimes I invite inmates to read together the places in Genesis and Exodus that support this (Gen 16:7; 21:14, 17, 20, 21; 37:22; Exod 4:27; 5:1, 3; 7:16; 8:27, 28; 13:18, 20; 14:3, 11, 12; 15:22, 22, 22; 16:1, 2, 3, 10, 14; 17:1; 18:5, 10; 19:1–2).

"He knew he was guilty of murder. He thought God would punish him, or take him in to Pharaoh," says someone else.

"So what *does* God do? Does he slap on the handcuffs and take him away? What does God say? Let's read the next verse," I suggest.

> I have seen the misery of my people who are in Egypt; I have heard their cry on account of their taskmasters. Indeed, I know their sufferings, and I have come down to deliver them from the Egyptians, and to bring them up out of that land to a good and broad land, a land flowing with milk and honey. (3:7–8)

The inmates can hardly believe it when they hear these words. It's like they're waiting for the hammer to fall, the bad news to be announced, but it just gets better and better. When I ask them what the people did in order for God to come down and save them, they smile with delight at the absence of religious-looking behaviors.

"They did nothing! They were in misery, they groaned, they cry out," someone says.

It surprises people that God says nothing to Moses about his murderous act. Someone else even observed that it was this same Moses who later was given the tablets of stone where God wrote with his very finger: "Thou shalt not kill." God shows surprising solidarity with Moses' first seeing. God too sees the oppression, and God has come down to do something about it. I ask the men at this point if God's knowledge of the people's condition differs from Moses.

We look together at a detail that speaks clearly to any would-be liberator. Moses does go out and sees the burdens and an Egyptian beating one of his people. In the Hebrew text YHWH speaks in the first person using the emphatic doubling of the verb "to see" that echoes Moses seeing. Gods seeing of the misery of his people is followed by two other verbs that suggest a deeper solidarity not yet experienced by Moses. YHWH continues:

> I have heard their cry on account of their taskmasters. Indeed,
> I know their sufferings.

YHWH's words to Moses are suggestive to any would-be liberator that a deeper solidarity is required that implies a descent into the condition of the oppressed. Hearing people's cries related to their taskmasters and knowing their suffering imply a shift in social location.

In addition, God's response differs markedly from Moses' murderous act. YHWH speaks in the first person about coming down to deliver them from the

Egyptians, and to bring them up out of that land to a good and broad land, a land flowing with milk and honey. This coming down, delivering and bring the people out implies a commitment to a liberation process on behalf of the entire people rather than a violent removal of a single perpetrator on behalf of one victim. The reader is left wondering at this point how God will accomplish such an ambitious project. A volunteer reads the next verse that clearly states God's surprising choice for the task.

> The cry of the Israelites has now come to me; I have also seen
> how the Egyptians oppress them. So come, I will send you to
> Pharaoh, to bring my people, the Israelites out of Egypt. (3:10)

God calls Moses and sends him back. This time armed with a staff and the word of YHWH. God uses Moses, the failed liberator, the reluctant savior. In response to Moses' repeated protests: "Who am I that I should go?" God says: "I will be with you." God assures Moses of his very presence along the way.

Moses is no hero figure and his task is not easy. He presents excuse after excuse to not go. "What if they don't believe that you appeared to me (4:1)?" "But I don't know how to speak," (4:10) and finally "O my Lord, please send someone else" (4:13). Moses' reluctance makes room for our excuses and fleeing. God's persistence and final victory over Moses shows us God's unwavering commitment to liberation—in spite of our resistance.

God is recruiting, calling people to lead others out of slavery and misery and into the promised land of freedom and abundance: a land flowing with milk and honey. God recruits unexpected people, common people. So how is this good news? Roger, a fellow American white male sums up by saying:

> "Moses, he's so unsure of himself. He's so human. This makes me realize, hey, I'm not alone. There's another really important guy in Israel's history who didn't feel cut out for this. Look, God used him. God can use me too."

Israel, a Mexican man serving two years in prison, sums it up this way:

> "This makes me very emotional because Moses was a sinful person. So God can use people like us. Yes, God is calling us. This jail is a desert. There is nothing that we can do. But God gives us a mission. Even though Moses is a sinner, God continues to call him, even though he was very rebellious."

Jose, too, says it in his own way: "God works through humble people, people who are rejected, people with vices, and he uses us to announce his kingdom and the good news to the world."

Toward the end of the Bible study I invite the men to read 1 Cor 1:26–29:

> "Consider your own call, brothers and sisters," Paul writes to the Corinthians. "Not many of you were wise by human standards, not many were powerful, not many were of noble birth. But God chose what is foolish in the world to shame the wise; God chose what is weak in the world to shame the strong; God chose what is low and despised in the world, things that are not, to reduce to nothing things that are, so that no one might boast in the presence of God. (1:26–29)

People are nearly always visibly delighted by God's surprising choice of the nobodies as God's mediators. To conclude this study I often ask people to try and summarize how their image of God has shifted or more specifically who they now perceive God to be according to our reading of this story.

GOD'S SHIFTING SOCIAL LOCATION AND HUMAN LIBERATION

Together with inmates we talk about a new image of God that counters the dominant theology. God's encounter with Moses shows YHWH as close and present in contrast to the distant, impersonal God of the dominant theology whose will is synonymous with the status quo. The God who meets Moses appears (literally is seen to) regardless of whether he was a murderer who was not even looking for God. God embraces Moses' past and identifies with his reaction to injustice. God reveals God's Self as one who sees, hears and fully knows human suffering. This radically contrasts with images of God as unapproachable, exclusive, angry, and punishing. In addition, this story suggests to careful readers:

✦ God may very well use people from the domination system such as Pharaoh's daughter as agents of liberation. These people may well be required to act as change agents at great personal risk. Moses name as in the words of Pharaoh's daughter "I have taken him out of the water" betray her very act of civil disobedience as Egyptians were required to throw Israelite baby boys into the water.

✦ God desires to bring people out of every kind misery and oppression into a place of abundance.

✦ God delivers the oppressed through enlisting the most unlikely mediators, fully identifying with people like Moses, with people like us—being willing to be associated with weakness, reluctance, failure. "I will be with you."

✦ In fact, becauseGod so fully identifies with mediators—the people often know God primarily through those mediators.

According to the Exodus story, God empowers us to do God's very work, enlisting us for the work of liberation. God calls us to bring people from every nation, ethnic group, city, village and family out of bondage and into a place of wholeness: the land flowing with milk and honey. God is doing this work and is continually recruiting—and recruiting recruiters to usher in the kingdom.

CONCLUSION

As I read this story with inmates, I experience with them a massive shifting of social locations that include the biblical characters (most notably Moses and God), myself as facilitator and them. Moses' social location has been on the way down from 2:11. By the end of the story, Moses has descended from privileged insider to criminal fugitive immigrant outsider shepherd who invites increasingly inclusive contemporary equivalents from among the marginalized. Meanwhile, my own role as sympathetic guide has revealed both my solidarity with the shifting biblical characters and, most importantly, the marginalized inmate readers. By the time we get to the burning bush, we have come to surprising place of common ground. At the very moment when our identification with Moses and each other becomes the easiest, God's social location shifts, making God absolutely approachable in the intriguing flames on a bush—a curiosity that brings Moses close. There before the burning bush, for an instant, we all stand as curious spectator equals before a yet to be revealed God with us. God's calling Moses by his name, Moses' fearful hiding of his face and God's gracious response reveal a God who loves and fully embraces Moses in his moment of greatest distance from his people and God there on the other side of the desert. Finally, God's calling of Moses, his insecurity, refusal, and ongoing reluctance, bring Moses and our humble circle of readers in the heart of the jail closer and closer as we face our common insecurities, fears and unbelief. God's belief in Moses, in spite of his transparent weakness, invites my own corresponding pastoral faith in my inmate brothers as I find myself finally agreeing with God in his call to us: Come, I will send you to Pharaoh that you will bring forth my people out of oppression.

"How Could He Ever Do That to Her?!" Or, How the Woman Who Anointed Jesus Became a Victim of Luke's Redactional and Theological Principles

Monika Ottermann

Introduction

For long years, I lived in the North Brazilian region Bico do Papagaio that is marked by violent land conflicts. Within the general frame of my pastoral activities, the Bible and the Women's Associations always held a special place. Many of the women organized in associations had lived and worked with, or at least known, Father Josimo Moraes Tavares, a young local priest who engaged himself in the struggles of the land conflicts. So did many other catholic priests, but not on the same side that Josimo chose: on the side of the poor and dispossessed campesinos. He was murdered, finally, on 10 May 1986, after months of serious threats and after a first attack on his life in April 1986—a classical case of an "announced death."

"Everybody knew ... he knew ... the babaçu palms knew ... and they feared and trembled and cried, but they staid"—as it is put in one of the many local poems. He chose to stay in the region, and many people, men and women, chose to stay near him, to protect him with the simple "arms" of being present close to him. They tried to protect him, but also to strengthen him, to comfort him with countless signs and gestures of love, friendship and solidarity. The protection part failed. He was murdered, and in the very special way of faith which is one of the few supports of these people, comparisons with Jesus, his option, the persecutions and the death he suffered, are abundant, even more because of the fact that Josimo, too, was murdered at the age of thirty-three.

Some years after Josimo's murder, the Bible team of the parish where he had worked had chosen to study the narrative of the woman that anointed Jesus, and had asked me to facilitate the study day with the women's association. They explained the choice of the text by the fact that it was time of Lent, and that this was a text more comforting and interesting, especially for women, than the passion announcements of Jesus or some persecution stories. Thus I prepared a Bible study process, some orientating questions, and a general scheme, according to the method of popular Bible reading practiced by CEBI, the Brazilian Bible Study Center. As usual, we would start with the words of our lives, pass to the Bible to see how its words meet ours, and leave the community center at the end of the day, going back to our daily lives with some inspirations born from this dialogue.

The Bible Study Process

In the beginning of our meeting, I made a short introduction to the anointing story in the Gospels, helping the women to remember what they knew well: that Jesus had lived persecuted because of his option for the poor, that his death had been "announced," the price fixed, and that the only question had been the "where" and "when," given the necessity to imprison him secretly. Then I mentioned (alluding to the Gospel of John) that one of his women friends, Mary of Bethany, had anointed him at the eve of his passion, thus comforting Jesus and announcing the murder plan. Then we passed to talk in little groups, raising facts and memories of our lives connected to this type of situation.

And here it happened in one of the small group discussions: Edna, a catechist, insisted with her group that it was Mary Magdalene, a prostitute, that approached Jesus with oil (and more dubious intentions, of course), and, remembering the label "sinner," someone else managed to find the chapter of Luke's anointing story. On reading Luke's narrative, the whole group had its discussion set upside down, discovering that there was nobody here called Mary wishing to comfort Jesus at the eve of his death, and that this was not an initiative of a concerned friend but of a repentant whore! When this small group came back to the plenary, it did not contribute in the discussion on their life situation, as is the practice, as did the others, but demanded an immediate and clear explication of the "facts" they had read in Luke.

At that time, I wasn't completely sure if Luke had modified the general tradition of the anointing, or if he was telling a second story without knowing the first. But some Synoptic comparisons I had made in preparation for the meeting, and a general suspicion concerning the treating of women in the Gospels, led me to the spontaneous answer that most probably it was the same story told with other accents. I tried to show that, very often, an evangelist modifies and adapts a story about Jesus according to the situation of his communities, the goal of his catechetical material, and so on. However, Raimunda interrupted at once: "This isn't just a story about Jesus; this is a story about Mary, too!" And another woman, a catechist, objected: "But I have always found Luke so gentle with women! He loves Our Lady, it is only he that tells us a bit of her life. It is he who wrote down her liberation song that is so important to us!"

I confess that I didn't know what to answer. In those days—in the late 1980s, rather cut off from any library or research center—I also still had the impression that at least Luke was an "evangelist of women and children" and that we—we women—could apply to him when searching for some texts fitting for us. Even so, I dared to answer, stressing that this was not yet proven, that he could have had his own reasons and interests in cutting that story from the passion circle and putting it into another context, of sin and love, of repentance and forgiveness. But with this consideration, the situation grew worse. One of my friends, Rita, a separated mother who gave birth to twins after some years of "living without a man," grew pale and with a voice nearly fainting, she said to me: "But Monika—how can you defend that! You know what one is suffering when one is judged a prostitute! You know what people say and what they do to us!" And very readily, some women recorded their persecution by land owners, politicians, police, judges (and a whole range of others), regarding their participation in the land-worker's union, the labor party, the base community. They shared how these accusations and defamations concentrated on their private life, labeling them as prostitutes and whores, and pointing to the smallest irregularity in their lives to say that this woman is worth nothing. One shouted: "It is very severe, dirtying a woman's image saying that she is a sinner—everybody will understand that she is a whore and exclude her!"

As I listened I heard about misogyny, standard male practices against women, and so on. I then suggested that they remember that women's sexuality is the common target for society, and that the easiest way to diminish her importance and the credibility is to cast doubt on her sexual morality. What I was trying to say was that this was an almost automatic reaction of a man with patriarchal attitudes. But now the situation nearly exploded, with the observation of Expedita, who cried out: "But listen! Here we are not talking about our enemies who always do all this to us! Were are talking about Luke! And Luke was a friend of Jesus! He went with him on his journeys, he was there when Mary anointed him! He knew, and he was a friend of Mary! How could he ever do this to her?"

This time, it didn't need *me* to answer. Nearly all the women present had had sad experiences of the contrary: fathers, brothers, friends, boyfriends, fiancés, lovers, husbands, and "companions" over and over again do precisely this to a woman when she acts out of the range of patriarchal expectations, when she makes an attempt to free herself, to contribute with the liberation of other people, and so on.

That day, we didn't study the anointing of Jesus by Mary as her gesture to comfort him before sure suffering and death. We studied our sufferings, our "deaths" provoked by patriarchal tactics to dirty the image of a woman who dares to do what she must do. And I had to promise that I would do some research to clarify if Luke really "did this to her" or not, and to clarify what possible motives might have led him to do this: "But, Jesus Christ, why? Why would he do that to her?!"

I fulfilled my promise in a simple but satisfactory manner soon after, but it was only in recent days that I had the opportunity to deepen my research. So let me now once again try to answer those desperate questions: "Did he really do this to her?!" and: "Why would he do that?!" The latter is the key question which will help us to judge Luke's narrative, to know if and why he "dirtied" the image of a woman who should have been his friend.

Answering the Question: "Did He Really Do It?"

A comparison of Luke 7:36–51 with Mark 14:3–9, Matt 26:6–13, and John 12:1–8 points to a double phenomenon that marks our pericope: First, there are many significant similarities between the Lukan and the Markan text, above all in its structure, but also differences that are no less significant. Second, the same is true for the relationship between the Lukan and the Johannine story. In the story of John, its dependence on Mark is obvious, but it is necessary to suppose a second substantial influence on the final text. This second influence should be viewed as being closely related to the text of Luke, because of common elements that do not derive from Mark.

The Relationship Between the Narratives of Mark and Luke

For the relationship between the pericopes of Mark and Luke, the few identical words (house, woman, alabastron flask of myrrh, Simon, to let) are key words that determine their content. It is highly unlikely that five identical constituent elements would occur in two different incidents. In addition, the host's identical name, Simon, cannot be explained as casual. Above all, the basic structure of the two narratives is identical. To explain these similarities, there is no better explanation than Synoptic dependence: Luke knew the pericope of Mark and integrated it into his Gospel, submitting it to modifications that are explained in the following by his redactional and theological principles.

First of all, we notice an extensive use of words typical of Luke only in the parts that do not have parallels in the Markan or Johannine story. This leads to the conclusion that the elements he borrowed from his sources were embedded in a special Lukan redaction that emphasizes the themes of Jesus as a prophet and a friend of sinners, and someone who forgives sins.[1]

Furthermore, the identification of Simon with a Pharisee is part of the general tendency in Luke to accentuate the conflict between Jesus and the Pharisees, and to emphasize their presence and their criticism of Jesus' attitude (in being a

---

1. Among these words, I emphasize, e.g., ἐρωτάω and κατακλίνω in v. 36; δάκρυον and βρέχειν in v. 38; προφήτης and ἁμαρτωλός in v. 39; διδάσκαλος in v. 40; χαρίζομαι in v. 42; and ἡ πίστις σου σέσωκέν σε· πορεύου εἰς εἰρήνην in v. 50.

friend of sinners). By avoiding the naming of the host at this moment (v. 36), and by describing him as "one of the Pharisees," Luke turns the individual man into a representative of the entire category.

In quantitative terms, Luke does not refer more to the Pharisees than the other Synoptics. But almost all of these references are quite accentuated by him, and Pharisees are also given prominence in his special material. Modifying the material met in Mark, Luke increases or accentuates the Pharisees among Jesus' opponents in three of five cases: 5:17, 21 (cf. Mark 2:6); 5:30 (cf. Mark 2:16); and 12:1 (cf. Mark 8:15).

In the Lukan use of the material deriving from Q, we notice the same principles, as in Luke 19:39 (cf. Matt 21:15) and Luke 11:37–54. While Luke narrates at the end of the latter speech that Pharisees *and scribes* began to persecute Jesus because of the accusations he made against them (v.54, a redactional observation without parallel in Matthew), his "woes" are directed exclusively against the Pharisees, while Matthew directs them against "scribes and Pharisees" (Matt 23:13–36). The modification of larger reach, however, we find in the redactional frame that Luke gives to this scene. In Matthew, the speech is directed to the crowds and the disciples, in a context of controversial speeches uttered in the temple after Jesus' entrance in Jerusalem (cf. Matt 21:23, 22:23, 24:1). This situation corresponds to the arrangement of Mark who, in spite of not having the material in question, also tells a series of controversies between Jesus and his opponents in this time and space, in other words, within the temple, soon before the passion (Mark 11:27–13:2). Luke, however, disconnects this speech from the eve of the passion and transports it to the phase of Jesus' journey to Jerusalem (9:51–19:28). Besides this, he creates a scene extremely similar to that of our pericope of the anointing: the invitation to supper by a Pharisee (11:37), followed directly by the speech of the "Woes" deriving from Q. It is apparent that Luke "invented" the invitation and the details of the situation in view of the message against the Pharisees that he had met in the traditional material, and that this setting has the function of scenic reinforcement and narrative embellishment, to show with more impact Jesus' critique of the Pharisees. To me, this analogous procedure reinforces the hypothesis that the details of the banquet of Luke 7:36–50 are also a creation of Luke.

In his special material, Luke focuses on the Pharisees in a very special way, and sometimes emphasizes clearly their rejection of tax collectors and sinners. In the immediate context of our periscope (7:29), Luke mentions explicitly the tax collectors and sinners among the people that accepted John's baptism and says, also explicitly, that the Pharisees and scribes rejected them; in 13:31, 14:1–6, and 15:1–3 we find something familiar in his introduction to the parables of the "lost," once again with stereotypes of Jesus' friendship with tax collectors and sinners, and of the Pharisees' criticism of this attitude); in 16:14 Luke refers to the Pharisees as "friends of the money"; and in 17:20 and 18:9–14 Luke includes the parable of the Pharisee and the tax collector in the temple, with the explicit observation that Jesus directed it to persons who considered themselves as just and who despised all others.

These observations, considered in their whole, show that the Pharisees, especially in their opposition against "sinners" and the nonorthodox attitudes of Jesus, are one of Luke's favorite themes, and that, for the benefit of this theme, he interprets and modifies quite freely the material he encounters in his sources.

The theme of sinners, intimately connected with that of the Pharisees, is a key theme of Luke's soteriology. This is shown statistically in his much elevated use of the word ἁμαρτωλός and in a more profound way in his special material dedicated to such people. Let us just remember the pericope previous to ours, 7:31–35, where Luke makes the Jesus mention the accusations against him, of being "friend of the tax collectors and sinners." It is interesting that Luke here does not take advantage of the opportunity to point out what is implied; he does not have the courage to call Jesus a "friend of prostitutes."

Thus, the context shows a first good reason for a dislocation and modification of the Markan story to this place in Luke's Gospel. The lack of Jesus' name in the beginning of our pericope, verse 36, indicates its close connection with the previous section, with what Jesus taught to the crowd. In this teaching, two key themes stand out: friend of tax collectors and sinners, but also the one of the prophet. In verse 26 Jesus affirms that John the Baptist was more than a prophet, but even so, he was just the one that prepared his way. This statement, in turn, is linked with the testimony of the crowd, who immediately before, in Nain, glorified God because of Jesus, saying "A great prophet rose in our midst" (v. 16). These two themes are recapitulated in our pericope; here, Luke thematizes and illustrates in a single way Jesus' friendship with a sinful person, insinuating that the woman of the anointing was sinful, and thematizing Jesus' being a prophet, showing that he was not just a real prophet, but more than a prophet, somebody who forgives sins.

Luke emphasizes the theme of sin and love, created by his characterization of the woman as a sinner[2] and his description of her acts, in 7:41–42, with the Parable of the Two Debtors. Without doubt, it is part of his special material and in which he wants to make us discover a proportional relationship concerning the size of the forgiveness received (literally what the debtor "gave in grace," gratuitously, ἐχαρίσατο) and the size of the love given in consequence. In the Gospels, the verb χαρίζομαι is used exclusively by Luke, twice in this parable, and a little earlier in 7:21, where Luke tells us that Jesus "gave in grace" sight to blind

---

2. Within the context of his time and society, the characterization of the woman as a sinner does not leave any doubt about its specific sense: Luke is declaring her a prostitute, the "local whore"; cf. his expression γυνὴ ἥτις ἦν ἐν τῇ πόλει ἁμαρτωλός, woman who was a sinner in the town

persons. Thus, Luke expresses the gratuity of Jesus' gifts (that ultimately are gifts of God): health, forgiveness and, finally, the gratuity of the salvation.

The same logic of the proportional relationship between having received and given, we find in another parable of Luke's special material, in 12:47–48. The servant who knew the will of his master and did not act in agreement with it, will receive many lashes, and the servant that did not know the will of the master and did not act in agreement with it, will receive few lashes, because to whom a lot was given, of him a lot will be demanded. In the same way, in the Parable of the Talents in 19:11–26, Luke presents a proportional relationship between the allocated amounts and the reward (ten coins—ten cities, five coins—five cities) that is not found in Matt 25:14–30 and that very probably stems from his redactional modification of the material met in Q. We can affirm, therefore, that this parable encapsulates a typical Lukan thought. To find a similar proportional relationship built into the narration of the anointing means that the woman of the anointing was characterized as sinner *by Luke*, in order to give an example of Jesus' free, gratuitous forgiveness, interpreting her many gestures of love as the consequence of her many sins that were forgiven.

In the continuation of his dialogue with Simon, we find Jesus turning to the woman and saying rhetorically to Simon "Do you see this woman?" With this hiatus between the direction of Jesus' movement and the direction of his speech, Luke indicates that, to him, it is the teaching to Simon that is in the center of his attention. Thus, Luke shows two men debating behaviors and attitudes, using the occasion of having encountered different behaviors and attitudes. Luke deletes any indication of Jesus' receiving attitude that, in the other narratives of the anointing, praises and thanks the "beautiful deed" of the woman and classifies it as a prophetic act (see Mark 14:6; Matt 26:10; John 12:8). In verse 47, Luke makes Jesus sum up the lesson of the comparison of Simon's behavior and the behavior of the woman: "Therefore, I tell you, forgiven are her many sins, because much she loved. To whom, however, is forgiven little, little loves." The sentence begins with the expression "therefore," which refers to the woman's actions previously narrated. Thus they are understood as the signs of the "loves a lot" because of which her many sins are forgiven. Such logic contradicts completely the logic established in the parable—here the forgiveness is a consequence of the love, there the love is a consequence of the forgiveness.

Luke's hermeneutic move here calls my attention to the fact that the verb ἀφίημι the basic meaning of which is simply "to let be," is used in two of the other narratives of the anointing, by Jesus, to defend the woman. In Mark 14:6 he says: ἄφετε αὐτήν ("Let her," imperative plural directed to the disciples), in John 12:7 he says: ἄφες αὐτήν ("Let her," imperative singular directed to Judas). This strongly suggests to me that the double sense of the verb, "to let, to leave (leave in peace)," and "to forgive," facilitated Luke's manipulation, preserving this verb in the mouth of Jesus but shifting its focus, here not to criticize other men and to defend the woman but to show him as the savior of a woman labeled as sinner.

In verse 48 Jesus suddenly turns to the woman and affirms that her sins are forgiven. It is another strange element in the whole of the pericope, because it repeats what was already affirmed in the previous verse, and it might be one more indication of its complex formation. This evaluation is reinforced by the following verse (v. 49), where some of those "at the table with him" begin the "to say among themselves" (cf. Simon's reaction in v. 39): "Who is this, who even forgives sins?" The two verses show such a close similarity with the passage of Mark 2:5–11 in the pericope of the paralytic's cure (see also Luke 5:20–24), that it is most probable that they are an adapted copy of these, possibly included here by some editor who felt the need for an explicit word of forgiveness uttered by Jesus.

Thus the analysis of the pericope's structure and its comparison with the anointing narrative of Mark show a good deal of incongruities and contradictions that confirm my suspicion that it is, in fact, a Lukan adaptation—sometimes a rather forced one—of a story he met in Mark, and not a different story of his own.

The Relationship between the Narratives of Luke and John/ John and Mark

Regarding the relationship between Luke and John, there is again the same basic structure and a high degree of agreement in the central action in terms of the content and of the words used. However, this agreement exists in opposition to the text of Mark.

The best interpretation of this phenomenon is the common dependence upon another written source, since oral traditions are unlikely to produce such accentuated similarities. A dependence of John's narrative upon Luke does not seem probable to me, since the coincidences are limited to elements not found in Mark, and which do not include material that would be typical of the Lukan narrative. Here we can draw upon the research of Tim Schramm, which showed that in cases like this we are dealing with "lateral sources" (Schramm 1971:207) used by Luke, which were also known by John. If it was this lateral source which preserved the woman's identity, or if her identification with Mary of Bethany was the work of the Johannine redactor, we cannot say with certainty. Even if the source had contained her name, it would have been impossible for Luke to reconcile his need for an image of a sinner with the person of the well-known leader Mary of Bethany, should he have found this name in his lateral source. This would be reason enough for omitting the name, given his overarching theological concerns.

For John, however, Martha's and Mary's special prominence in his narrative might have been inspired by this source or else might have motivated him to transfer the prophetic gesture of this woman in the source he shared with Luke, whose name had been lost, to his protagonist Mary. We cannot exclude this possibility, but we should remember the special interest that the women in the Jesus movement and in the first communities had in preserving their memories and histories. This interest shows up in many indications and tracks in the middle of androcentric and misogynist texts. Therefore, it might be more probable that women have preserved the name of the woman of the anointing in a source of theirs, a name that Luke deletes and that John appropriates.

Turning now to the relationship between the pericopes of John and Mark, we see that is determined by the identical structure and according to the following agreements:

Mark 14:3: μύρου νάρδου πιστικῆς πολυτελοῦς	John 12:3: μύρου νάρδου πιστικῆς πολυτίμου
Mark 14:5: πραθῆναι ἐπάνω δηναρίων τριακοσίων καὶ δοθῆναι τοῖς πτωχοῖς	John 12:5: ἐπράθη τριακοσίων δηναρίων καὶ ἐδόθη πτωχοῖς
Mark 14:6: ἄφετε αὐτήν	John 12:7: ἄφες αὐτήν
Mark 14:7: πάντοτε γὰρ τοὺς πτωχοὺς ἔχετε μεθ᾽ ἑαυτῶν	John 12:8: τοὺς πτωχοὺς γὰρ πάντοτε ἔχετε μεθ᾽ ἑαυτῶν
Mark 14:7: ἐμὲ δὲ οὐ πάντοτε ἔχετε	John 12:8: ἐμὲ δὲ οὐ πάντοτε ἔχετε
Mark 14:8: εἰς τὸν ἐνταφιασμόν	John 12:7: τοῦ ἐνταφιασμοῦ μου

This high degree of agreement that includes whole parts of sentences can only be explained as literary dependence of this Johannine pericope upon Mark. In spite of the open discussion on John's dependence upon the Synoptic Gospels, there exists a wide consensus on the hypothesis that John's passion narrative was elaborated with, at least, the knowledge of Mark's passion narrative. Although our pericope is not placed in the immediate context of John's passion narrative, theologically it shows a close connection with this, and in Mark it is encountered in this context.

Answering the Question: "Why Did He Do That?" The Redaction of Luke-Acts: Literary Techniques and Theological Principles

The first part of the Luke-Acts, the Gospel of Luke, is a work composed on the base of written sources, the main ones being the Gospel of Mark and Q, besides lateral sources—oral or literary—from which he drew his large amount of special material (cf. Schramm 1971). In making use of his main sources, Luke shows a great liberty. He maintains the general sketch of Mark, but re-arranges its parts to fit his own theological scheme, and omits what does not interest him or what scandalizes his theological principles. Within Luke's basic scheme, we find the mechanisms that explain the transformation of the anointing by a woman friend on the eve of Jesus suffering as an act of comfort into the anointing by a sinful woman, interpreted as a sign of her repentance.

Quantity versus Quality: The Increased Occurrence of Texts on Women in Luke-Acts

It has long been noticed that Luke-Acts pays special attention to women. This attitude is particularly noticeable in Luke's Gospel, where Synoptic comparison shows that the material of Luke contains many more pericopes that speak about women than the other canonical Gospels. Therefore, Luke is called by many the "Evangelist of the Women." Feminist exegesis of recent years, however, has identified this material as patriarchal and androcentric, showing that the simple fact of an abundance of texts about women does not mean anything regarding the patriarchal or liberating posture of Luke.[3] To the contrary, specialized studies show clearly the androcentric and patriarchal reasons and intentions that determine the presence and the form of the presentation of this material in Luke-Acts. Among the many feminist voices, I shall emphasize mainly that of Mary Rose D'Angelo, who in one of her studies analyzes Luke's redactional procedure of interest to this essay.

In her article "Women in Luke-Acts: The Redactional View" (D'Angelo 1990:441–61), D'Angelo bases her research in part on an article by Constance F. Parvey in which she analyzes Luke's "multiplication of stories about women" and his "tendency to pair stories about women with stories about men" (Parvey 1974:139–46). D'Angelo observes a tension here. While increasing the number of narratives about female figures and experiences, Luke depicts the roles of women as more limited by what was acceptable in the conventions of the Roman Empire's world of those times than do Mark and John. Drawing on the analysis of Parvey that showed the catechetical function of these masculine-feminine pairs (but see Schüssler Fiorenza 1992:65), D'Angelo interprets this as a tension between two socio-historical realities: the need of catechizing converted women who were of real political importance in the church of Luke's days, and the fear that an amplified role of women would cause the Christians to be seen as practicing "un-Roman activities." It is within this sociohistorical tension that Luke constructs for his readers a wide variety of feminine role models, but roles that reveal a very limited and conventional range of activities and that function, therefore, at the same time as a means of edification and of control.

Jesus, the Prophet Anointed by the Holy Spirit, versus Women in the Prophetic Ministry

D'Angelo also detects and analyzes another of Luke's theological interests and redactional techniques: the dispensation of the spirit and the role of feminine

---

3. For a general vision of that opinion and the authors who defend it, see Janssen and Lamb 1998:514–17.

figures in relation to this (see D'Angelo 1990:452–60). In Luke-Acts, one of the means of elaborating his Christology is the periodization of history oriented to Jesus Christ. In the era of "the law and the prophets," the spirit is given spontaneously in order to act accordingly to the objectives of God, and in this era women appear in prophetic roles. After Jesus' anointing with the spirit in Luke 4, however, exclusively Jesus' actions are associated with the manifestation of the spirit. Consequently, from now on Luke shows women functioning only as reinforcement of Jesus' image as a prophet. Similarly, individual men are also no longer presented as prophets. D'Angelo also identifies apologetic reasons for distancing women from prophecy and the ministry of the community. According to her, the portrayal of women in Luke-Acts is addressed both to detractors who see in women's spiritual leadership as a sign of social disorder, and to the women who practiced this prophetic ministry, with the intention of confining their participation within the limits of discreet behavior (461).

D'Angelo also shows how Luke's literary plan uses parallel masculine-feminine pairs to narrate Jesus' ministry in Galilee. Among other masculine-feminine pairs, the narrative of the banquet with the presence of the sinful woman without name constitutes the "feminine pair" of the narrative of the banquet with the presence of the sinful man Levi (5:27–32). Furthermore, because the focus in the section in which our periscope is located is on Jesus being a prophet, the question of John the Baptist as well as the action of the woman that anoints Jesus are not accorded their proper value, but primarily serve Luke's theological purpose of showing Jesus as the greatest of the prophets. It is also clear that this theological concern of Luke's, namely that after his anointing with the Holy Spirit, prophetic action passes exclusively through Jesus, does not allow him to preserve what is probably the original sense of the anointing, its prophetic character. Luke could not admit that the peak of Jesus' ministry, his passion and resurrection, was proclaimed by a woman, that a woman exercised a prophetic sign in preparation and interpretation of this peak, anointing him to be a suffering messiah. For Luke, the one who anointed Jesus was the Holy Spirit in the beginning of his messianic ministry of salvation, and not a woman on the eve of its end.

But it was not only the memory—the dangerous and subversive memory—of this prophetic gesture accomplished by that woman companion and friend of Jesus, of one of the leaders of the first group of men and women disciples, that inconvenienced Luke. It was also the fact that women companions and friends of Luke, leaders of the Lukan communities, preserved this memory as legitimation and empowerment of their own prophetic and ministerial activities. Luke deformed this memory of one of the first Christian woman leaders to control and to cut down women's leadership of his time. This androcentric, even misogynist, phenomenon can be observed in all Christian literature and with regard to all women leaders in the Jesus movement. Beside the distortions that the images of Mary Magdalene and Martha have suffered, (D'Angelo 1990:461), the woman of the anointing is another victim of this androcentric attitude, especially so if the Johannine version is historical, if she was in fact Mary of Bethany.

Jesus, the Savior, versus the Saving Acts of Women

One of the main characteristics of Luke's Gospel is the interest in poor and disfavored people, and in sinners. For example, Luke's narratives of meals show how Jesus scandalized the socio-religious sensibilities of his society. Furthermore, a great variety of Lukan narratives show "salvation as reversal" (Green 1995:15, 76–90), our pericope being the most clear example to illustrate this theological idea.

Because of this christological focus on Jesus as friend and savior of the "poor" (excluded) and sinful people, Luke made several changes to the narrative of the Anointing he met in Mark. First, he simply turned the excluded disciple Simon into a Pharisee. Luke did not "need" the leper because he had already integrated into his scheme the excluded disciple Levi, through the party in his house. Soon afterwards, Luke created and introduced the feminine "pair" of the sinner Levi and the anonymous sinful woman. This creation obeys the same logic: Luke did not "need" the prophetic anointing at the end of Jesus' ministry, related to his death, because all prophecy already concentrated exclusively on Jesus since he was anointed by the Holy Spirit at the beginning of his ministry. By being so eager to show that Jesus was a friend of sinners and that he criticized the Pharisees, Luke did what was totally against Jesus' attitude: he turned an honored woman into a despised sinner and a leprous disciple into an opponent Pharisee. Following the logic of his own theological interests, he neglected the vital principles of Jesus. So Luke did not take seriously what was central for Jesus: the participatory construction of the kingdom of God, of which the anointing accomplished by a woman was a symbol and for which the leadership of women was constituent.

For Luke, the center of attention was exclusively the divine savior Jesus, besides whom human actions, like saving love, lost their importance. Thus, Luke denies the importance of the attitudes and actions of men and women who, together with Jesus and as his followers, announced the kingdom of God and its salvation.

Jesus, the Autonomous Suffering Messiah, versus Comforting Women

In the other Gospels the narrative of the woman of the anointing is placed in a strategic position: it opens the cycle of the passion narratives. In Luke, it is placed in the middle of Jesus' Galilean ministry, for christological reasons. As Hans Conzelmann argues, this part of the Lukan scheme already shows Jesus' self-awareness as Suffering Messiah (Conzelmann 1961:52–58). This self-awareness is the reason for his ascent to Jerusalem (see 13:31ff.), and for Luke, his entrance into the city has one single objective: to take ownership of the temple. That explains his strong adaptation of the Markan narrative and still other omissions of Markan material, including the idea that Jesus does not accomplish any miracle in Jerusalem.

For Luke, nothing should obstruct the path of the Passion of which the teaching in the temple was part. Conzelmann affirms: "According to Luke, Jesus teaches "daily" in the Temple and goes each night to the Mount of Olives. There is neither place nor time for an anointing in Bethany" (77).

Thus we see that Luke had strong theological reasons to eliminate any "strange" element from the midst of the suffering Messiah's path, be this a secondary element or an element of larger significance, such as the anointing. Luke also showed Jesus as totally autonomous in facing his destiny. Therefore, Conzelmann considers it "unacceptable" to Luke that Jesus would "need" the human comfort of an anointing on the eve of his death, together with its eschatological significa- tion. According to Conzelmann, Luke was prepared to accept the gesture "as his variation in 7:36ff. only as a demonstration of love and as a sign of repentance. It is not a human being that strengthens Jesus for the hour of his death, but an angel. The body is evidently not to be anointed until after the death (23:53f.), and only by his own followers; but then the anointing is no longer necessary, because he is alive" (Conzelmann 1961:79).

Although I agree with the general interpretation of Conzelmann, I cannot help finding strange the words "only by his own followers." Luke 23:55–56 nar- rates that "the women who had followed him since Galilee followed Joseph; they looked at the grave and how his body was placed in it. Then they returned and prepared aromas and perfumes." Does Conzelmann want to insinuate that the woman of the anointing, who was present in Jerusalem in the days of that Pass- over, according to the other Gospels, was not a follower of Jesus? If this is the case, his observation would be one more of the many examples of how, in the history of interpretation, the figures of women are treated with disregard and superficiality and in many cases with contempt and misogyny. In the face of such postures it is not strange that traditional exegesis has not discovered, or at least has not analyzed, Luke's redactional maneuvers that have manipulated the memory of the woman of the anointing.

Final Considerations about the Initial Questions: Luke's Manipulation of the Memory of Women and of Jesus

Reinforcing previous studies, my analysis has shown that Lukan literary proce- dures are, in fact, androcentric, macho, and christocentric. His christocentrism was so intense that it diminished the importance and dignity of other people, so as to increase the importance and divinity of Jesus. Such a procedure has harmed Jesus' memory more than it has honored it. It is clearly against his prin- ciples and interests. In fact, it is against the project of his life for which he was murdered and resurrected. Still worse, Luke manipulated and thus annulled an unheard-of historical fact that bears in itself a singular liberation force regarding the sexuality of women and men, the devolution of dignity, and the liberation of women.

Luke dirtied the name of Simon, an excluded disciple with whom Jesus was in solidarity, turning him into a Pharisee hard of heart. Luke dirtied the memory and the good reputation of the woman of Bethany (who, maybe, was Mary), a prophetic leader whose attitude Jesus defended and praised expressly, turning her into a prostitute who needed salvation by Jesus. In this context of dirtying names and memories, the worst stereotype is passed on to the woman: instead of taking advantage of the leper's impurity to show that Jesus accepted contact with socially impure people, Luke projects the impurity onto the woman, and he turns the physical impurity of leprosy into the moral impurity of prostitution.

Luke dirtied the memory and the good reputation of a woman community leader, who should be a friend of his, precisely to diminish, to silence, and to hide the leadership of women. This is not as absurd as it seems, and much less is it an isolated case. The cry, "But why did they ever do this to us?" must have been uttered a million times, even and especially among the women who followed Jesus.

The interests shown in Luke's redaction and theology certainly do not correspond to Jesus' interests. It seems that Luke's misguided attempt to "save" the life of his community, threatened by Roman imperialism and a pervasive patriarchy, reveals his own lack of courage to face the danger of losing this life because of the kingdom of God. Thus, Luke did not do what Jesus ordered, and he knew it well, because he had Mark's Gospel on his desk, reading there Jesus' explicit order: to proclaim, wherever the Gospel was proclaimed in the whole world, what the woman of the anointing did, *in memory of her* (Mark 13:9). In *his* Gospel, Luke did not proclaim what she really did. According to his own theology (cf. 12:47–48), he made himself the first candidate to receive many lashes, because he knew the will of his Master and did not fulfill it. But it seems to me that this also is *his* theology and not the theology of Jesus.

Discovering all this, thus answering the questions that were the starting point of my research, certainly is not meant to comfort today's women concerning the violence and injustice they and their beloved ones suffer. To recover and restore these testimonies in their most faithful form is a debt of justice not only to the first Christians, women *and* men, and to Jesus himself, but especially to all women who demand respect and recognition of their gestures, struggles and ministries of transformation and love.

Bible and Citizenship

Valmor Da Silva
Translated by Timothy Deller

Introduction

The lack of a sense of citizenship is a constant reality in Brazil as well as in the whole of the Latin American continent. The acquiring of the rights of citizenship in a society like ours is still an unattainable dream for the great majority of the population. The door to fundamental human rights is firmly closed to the poor, and the so-called democracy is still the legalization of the rights of the privileged few who are at the top of the social pyramid, and this at the expense of the majority. On top of this there still exists the problem of marginalization by reason of color, gender, physical characteristics, accent and manner of dress, among many such prejudices.

The real picture shows a multitude of people who suffer exclusion. Shortcomings in education leave millions in ignorance who can neither read nor write, inadequacies in medical care result in long queues of sick and hopeless people. Lack of adequate housing multiplies the number of homeless thrown into despair. The high levels of unemployment increase constantly because those who are the leaders and the owners of modern technology have more interest in machines than in they have in people. The landless who live beneath canvas resist and struggle to reclaim their rights.

The Bible is considered a holy book, the word of God and the standard for life for multitudes, especially for those in greatest need. How can the sacred scriptures make a significant contribution to the yearning of the people of Latin America for greater citizenship? This question will be addressed in this essay.

The Bible is used to undergird a wide variety of political stances. It can even be used to defend opposing positions. Some recent examples from a variety of different contexts serve to illustrate this affirmation.

In Chile, Pinochet presented himself as a liberator like Moses. Ronald Regan launched an attack on Nicaragua in what he considered a godly cause. Ferdinand Marcos, of the Philippines, declared that he had not come to destroy the law but to complete it. In South Africa, the apartheid regime sought its justification in the Bible. In the Latin American dictatorships, those who governed were almost all daily readers of the Bible and regular in attendance at the Sunday mass. In the Brazilian National Congress, the Bible is kept in a central position as a permanent display. The churches, for their part, use the Bible to justify dogmas, to establish moral codes, to determine norms of sexuality, to support hierarchical position while excluding women from positions of leadership.

The poor, in their turn, appeal to the Bible in different ways. For the Pentecostals, the Bible is thought to solve all problems, whether religious, political, economic, medicinal, or emotional. Many of their illiterate learn to read by using the Bible and then use it in order to understand its teaching better. The Bible gives them a sense of security, of citizenship and a new way of life. By joining the Pentecostal church, the new believer takes on a new social status, he carries a book (in this case, a Bible) beneath his arm, uses a tie and jacket, plays an instrument and takes part economically in his community by paying his tithe. As this is a wide and very complex subject, I will not deal with it specifically in this presentation.

This analysis has as its focus the very poorest layer of our population, multitudes of the poor and marginalized who struggle for their place in society. This struggle finds expression in the base communities, in line with the theology of liberation. We shall seek to discover the viewpoint of the indigenous, the colored, the women, the children, the elderly, the immigrants, the handicapped, the homosexuals, the landless, the homeless, and the environmentalists, among others.

A GLANCE AT HISTORY

The continent known today as Latin America was occupied twenty thousand, or perhaps fifty thousand, years ago by people who lived in an entirely different form of social order that, nevertheless, followed a quite distinct model or pattern. In such a community, it is clear, the sense of citizenship was different but the social inclusion of the people was much greater. We are told that at the meeting of Latin American bishops in Medellín, some indigenous people were introduced and asked to make a pronouncement in the Quechua language. The whole assembly noticed two words that were constantly repeated—*oppression* and *marginalization*. In the debate that followed, it was pointed out that in the indigenous languages neither word existed.

Albert Samuel, a scholar and expert in the study of religions, describes very well the sense of citizenship among the indigenous peoples:

> In animism, the priority which is given to the community does not permit the hierarchy to transform itself into domination. The king or the chief are the servants of the order that the community needs. For this reason, power should never be given to those who seek it for itself. An ambitious person would serve himself rather than the community. Decisions should not be dictated by the

chief but should be in accordance with the traditions and customs of the community. They should result from a consensus of opinions with the chief being content to preside whilst giving the elders their right to speak. He should not even express a preference. By this means the leadership comes from the collective wisdom of the elders, inspired by experience and enshrining the traditions that underline their authority. Thus the social and religious orders are inseparable. (Samuel 1997:65–66)

The sense of citizenship among indigenous peoples is based, therefore, on a different model, on an integrated view of life in which humans are a part of a total universe. The barrier between the sacred and the secular is completely broken. For this reason, all the realities of life are submitted to the divine and find their expression in the form of myths, rituals, dances, and the like. Many of these have been turned into sacred texts and registered in codes of practice such as the *Popol Vuh* and the *Chilam Balam*. Others have been transmitted orally and are celebrated even today.

With European colonization, the Bible arrived and it was soon imposed as the only sacred book. Its use, however, throughout these five hundred years, has been ambiguous. It has often been used to justify discrimination and massacres, while at other times it has been the seen as a defense of the oppressed classes. Here are a few examples that illustrate the ambiguity in Bible usage with regard to Indians, coloreds, women, and children. These examples, derived from the Latin American context, are extracted from a study given by the author at a special conference in Ecuador (Silva 1994:26–59).

The use of the Bible with regard to the indigenous people was, in general, traumatic. This is well illustrated in the famous controversy of Valladolid. This was an assembly convened in 1550 to consider the attitude to be taken with regard to the Indian communities in the New World. Two widely opposing mindsets were observed, two opposite positions, two biblical arguments, that of Juan Ginés de Sepúlveda and the other of Bartolomé de las Casas.

Sepúlveda defended the thesis of domination over the Indians. He appealed to various arguments in support of his position. Just as the Hebrews conquered the promised land, so the colonialists should possess the new land. Surely it was God who ordered the destruction of pagan temples (Deut 12:2) and also ordered the taking of booty as the fruits of warfare (Deut 20:13–14). The floodwaters destroyed the wicked (Gen 6–8). Abraham went to war against the four kings who had offended Lot and his friends (Gen 14). Later, fire and brimstone destroyed the iniquitous cities of Sodom and Gomorrah (Gen 19). It is a brotherly obligation to set free barbarians threatened by death, as in the story of the Good Samaritan in the Gospel (Luke 10:29–37). The argument from silence is used to support the idea that the Bible never mentions Indians by name, whereas the Spanish are mentioned in Rom 15:24, 28.

In his turn, Las Casas raised a counterargument. The Bible should be read from a spiritual point of view that overrides the literal and cannot contain anything false. The one who gives meaning to the Bible is the Holy Spirit, and it is not open to individual interpretation. Examples taken from the Old Testament, while they can be admired, should not necessarily be imitated. In the conquest of Canaan, for example, the booty was only to be taken from the idolatrous Canaanites. Las Casas denounced the oppressors as the blind and deaf of the gospel and accused the conquistadors and those who sent them as idolaters because of their *auri sacra fames*. The oppressed Indians he saw as the whipped Christ of these lands. A golden text for him was that which states that "the bread of the beggars is as the life of the poor and whoever takes the life of the poor is a murderer" (Eccl 34:21).

As concerns the so-called *indigenous children*, two opposing and contradictory positions were held. On the one hand, that of a childlike and innocent Indian and, on the other, the Indian seen as idolatrous and evil. In order that they should be called for catechism, appeal was made to *compelle eos intrare* "make them come in" (Luke 14:23). On the positive side the work of mission is to invite them to the eschatological banquet (Matt 22), where their places are already prepared (John 14:2–3). The catechism used representations of biblical scenes that, for their part, became the precursors of the Brazilian theater.

With regard to black Africans, it was argued that slavery was justified as a divine punishment and that toil should be with "the sweat of your brow" (Gen 3:19). The Africans should be considered, it was said, as the descendants of Canaan who was cursed for uncovering the nakedness of his father, Noah (Gen 9:25–27). Joseph was sold as a slave to the Midianites by his own brothers (Gen 37:27–28). The journey of slaves from Africa to Brazil has been compared to the transmigration from Egypt to the promised land (Exod 15). It would be an act of Christian charity to provide freedom for the slaves. Thus, rather perversely, was it argued that the Africans should be released from the sin of Africa (hell) via a provisional redemption in Brazil (purgatory) to complete freedom in heaven (paradise). More directly, the Bible has much to say: "For the ass, food, a whip and a heavy load; for the slave there is bread, discipline and work (Eccl 33:25). Slaves are required always to obey their masters (Col 3:22–24, Eph 6:5–9, 1 Pet 2:18–21). "Happy are those servants whom the master finds watching" (Luke 12:37). "Carry each other's burdens" (Gal 6:2).

The case presented for the defense of the slaves was, on the other hand, very weak as regards biblical sources. In Guinea, it was stated, the Jesuits applied the law of the sabbatical year, which offered freedom after six years (Lev 25). As Rebekah diverted the blessing of Isaac from Esau to Jacob (Gen 25), the Virgin Mary can divert the blessing from the heirs to the slaves. From this came the custom of using a rosary around the neck.

With regard to women, many applications have been found in the Bible. The dangers presented by women and the virtues of marriage received lengthy consideration. The myth of Eve (Gen 3) maintained the image of the temptress, Satan's instrument. Oppression of women was justified by such expressions as that the husband should "rule over her" (Gen 3:16) and "wives submit to your husbands"

(Eph 5:22). By contrast, the image of woman was idealized as virgin and mother in the pattern of Mary. In practice, however, women have always stood out as educators and catechists. Mothers have been seen as responsible for the transmission of the faith and society values from the beginning of time until now.

As a conclusion to this part it may be said the use of the Bible throughout these five hundred years of evangelization has more reasons for *mea culpa* than for *Gloria tibi domine*.

In recent times and linked to the ideas emanating from liberation theology, the Bible is now being read through different eyes. Bible reading is being done within the context of the hermeneutical triangle: text, reality and community. The conflicts that lie behind the written text gain importance. The sociohistorical method gains ground seeking ideas that lie behind the text. Reading between the lines, it is possible to discover people who are discriminated against because of their social class, their ethnicity, gender, and other characteristics. Some of these features of a new approach to the sacred text will now be outlined.

THE BIBLE LINKED TO THE LIFE IN COMMUNITY

There is seen to be a complete integration between the sacred text as shown and the reality in which people live day to day. For this reason, when we interpret the Bible, it is necessary to be faithful both to the biblical text and the life that people lead. Beyond this, it is important to emphasize the value of communal readings of the Bible. It was written to establish life in community and it comes from that community life. Its journey only ends when it comes into contact with today's communities. In other words, it previews inclusiveness and citizenship. The hermeneutic circle can only be complete, therefore, in the daily life of today's communities. The logical outcome of such a reading of the text is that it becomes militant, engaged and fully involved in the fight for justice. The objective is not simply to get to know the past history but to form a new society.

THE BIBLE AS A SECOND BOOK

The first book is life, history, and the difficulties faced in the daily life. It is written in nature and is being written ever since the first day of creation. The Bible is the second book, not as a substitute for the first but to enable it to be interpreted. This concept, presented by Carlos Mesters (1983:26), is developed in the various strands of Latin American hermeneutics. It states that the Bible contains the word of God but does not exhaust it, because the divine word goes much further than the limits of one book. Consequently, the history of indigenous and African populations contained the word of God long before the arrival of the Christian

scriptures. For this reason also, the correct way to read the Bible will involve dialogue and ecumenism. The point of reference moves from institutional support to
the struggle for justice.

THE BIBLE READ SOCIOHISTORICALLY

This method seeks to discover that which lies behind the written text in terms of
the communities found therein. Various aspects of a particular biblical passage
are examined such as social, political, economic, and ideological strands. Often
the search for the conflict that first produced the text helps in our understanding
of what is being read. Apart from considering and giving value to other methods
of approaching the biblical text, the sociological method seeks to go one step
further with the aim of discovering the context of the biblical people. It seeks
also to analyze the daily life of such people by looking at the whole micro-system
of relationships.

THE BIBLE READ BY FOCUSING ON NEW SUBJECTS

By this approach the sacred book is considered from other angles giving emphasis to people who are anonymous or obscure in the original text. In the first place,
this way of approaching the text highlights a particular class, according to a
socioeconomic viewpoint, and especially the poorest layer of society. Other social
categories are also identified and strengthened by the word of God. One could
speak, for example, of an indigenous reading of the Bible emphasizing the point
of view of ethnicity. The same ethnic key would enable a reading from the standpoint of color, while equally important would be a reading from with a feminist
or gender focus.

Yet other social categories find strength and affirmation in the Bible: children, as a group receiving God's special favor; the elderly, as those imbued
with wisdom, experience and fullness of life; foreigners and ethnic minorities
as forming part of the rich variety of the people of God; the disabled, as those
bereft of health and full participation in society; homosexuals, who are not discriminated by God nor by the Bible; the landless and homeless, who read the
Bible both as an example and as a partner in their fight; environmentalists, who
find in the sacred pages support for their defense of the natural world—and
many other categories.

Bible Reading from an Indigenous Viewpoint

It is possible to argue that our so-called civilization is not able to enter into
dialogue with indigenous cultures, nor is it able to meet the needs of Indian communities. This has been true within our continent for the last five hundred years.
The political powers, by and large, do nothing except for a few legal protections,

while the church in general continues missionary practices that both alienate and prejudice the native populations.

Recently the indigenous culture and its values have been affirmed, but from an entirely different model from ours. Within this cultural context, religion occupies a prominent position. This new approach is seen in courses, encounters, congresses, documents, and action plans, not to mention marches, manifestations, and protests—all within the context of what has been happening for five hundred years.

In order to be heard, having been silent for so long, indigenous groups have begun to be more articulate. Theologians and biblical scholars are well to the front in support of this movement. An Indian theology is beginning to be developed, coupled with a reading of the Bible through indigenous eyes. In an evaluation of this emerging trend Peley Chourío (1993:24) has written an article that emphasizes three fundamental perceptions of this new hermeneutic. Briefly, God reveals himself in the indigenous peoples just as he revealed himself in the people of Israel. This is confirmed in myths of creation, in a variety of covenants, and in the dream of a land without evil, among other similarities. Second, the indigenous communities cease to be the objects of a religion and become the subjects of their own religion. Their own particular culture generates life, faith, and theology. Third, indigenous traditions help us to read the Bible better in the same was as the Bible helps us to a better understanding of the indigenous traditions. This process recognizes the dignity of the Indians, shows us their particular values when set against other cultural traditions, and helps to affirm indigenous citizenship. Various elements in the Bible resonate with the indigenous culture. We only need to appreciate the relationship with mother earth, the *pachamama*, to verify this harmony as expressed in the following psalm to Mother Earth.

> Beloved land, you are sacred,
> Holy mother, you are the mother of life,
> For you are the guardian of wisdom,
> For this reason, your Indian children love you,
> We, therefore, care for you, and you enable us to eat and drink at your breast.
> (quoted by Carrasco 1996:33)

From this, we deduce an ecological and sacred respect for nature and an ample sense of the land as being the property of God on loan to humankind (Lev 25:23). The indigenous ethic could very well be linked with the commandments: do not steal, do not be idle, do not lie.

Fundamental to the cultural and religious affirmations of indigenous people has been the paradigm of the exodus. In that epic, the slaves take over their own destiny and seek a land that flows with milk and honey, a mirror image of indigenous utopias. The leadership of Moses is fundamental, as one who assumes an entirely new posture, different from his roots, and confronts the clutching hands of Pharaoh (López Hernández 1996:16–24).

Bible Reading from an African or Colored Viewpoint

As we have seen with the indigenous population, so too with the African where, especially in Brazil, we see clearly the marks of social discrimination. The document issued by the Catholic Church for the Campaign for Brotherhood in 1988, the centenary year of the so-called liberation of the slaves, judging the reality of the situation in the light of the Bible, declared: "The description of the reality of the Negro peoples in the history of Brazil yesterday and today, evokes the situation of the captivity of Israel in Egypt and the liberating activity of God, which demonstrates the condemnation of any and every form of human oppression" (CNBB 1988:64).

The Ecumenical Association of Third World Theologians (ASETT 1986), in its consultation concerning African culture and theology in Latin America, asked for a "negrification of the theologian," that is, that the battles and struggles, the cultural heritage, the religious practices, and other aspects of the African tradition should be taken into account.

The Second Ecumenical Consultation of Afro-American-Caribbean culture and theology, in November 1994, in São Paulo, elaborated a document regarding the Bible and African communities in which it drew out some of the presuppositions for an Africa hermeneutic. Criticizing the absolutist view of the Bible as the supreme "Word of God," and, considering it rather as the "Second Word," it affirmed:

> The Bible declares the manifestation of God as liberator in the daily life of all oppressed people irrespective of the ethnicity, but only taking into account their existential situation of oppression and exclusion. It reveals a God who hears and acts with and for them in the transformation of history (Exod 3:7–10), and who is in no way in favor of their being marginalized and excluded. (Andrade et al. 1994:2)

Other consultations followed these and also courses, studies, reflections and testimonies. Beyond this there was direct action against racism, protests and proposals to change the actual situation. A part of the resistance strategy of the African cultures in Brazil was the process of acculturation that assimilated Christian symbols and integrated them in African religiosity. From this arose what can only be described as syncretism or Afro-Brazilian religion.

The issue here revolves round the "right to be different" (Mattos 1994:16). People have difficulty living harmoniously with those who are different. Because of this, they discriminate against anyone who has any distinctive characteristic whether of belief, religion, language, thought or color.

A reading of the Bible that seeks to hand back citizenship to African cultures has much to offer. In the first place, it asks for a clearly argued position from all who would use the reading of scripture to condemn the African population and support slavery. Second, it would cause the scriptures to be read as a normative text to affirm the equality of all brothers and sisters and hence to prohibit all attempts to enslave them. The condemnation of the evil treatment inflicted on the Hebrew in Egypt and the subsequent liberating activity of God, are firm arguments in support of the liberation of all enslaved people (Exod 3:7–10). This truth remained firmly in the memory of the people of the Bible, demanding a Sabbath rest for the slaves (Deut 5:12–15), denouncing the oppression of the poor, the orphan, the foreigner and the widow (Isa 1:15–17). Zephaniah, the so-called African prophet, proclaimed, "From the other side of the rivers of Ethiopia, my worshippers, my scattered people, will bring me an offering" (Zeph 3:10; cf. Isa 18:7). The queen of Sheba visited Solomon and made a covenant with him (1 Kgs 10:1–13).

At the outset of the Christian communities, the Africans had a strong participation, as can be seen in the case of Simon of Cyrene, the first disciple to carry the cross of Jesus (Mark 15:21), by the presence of people from Libya at Pentecost (Acts 2:10), by those participating in the synagogue worship in Jerusalem (Acts 6:9; 11:20), and by the Africans integrated into the Christian community in Antioch (Acts 11:20; 13:1). The letter of Paul to Philemon, above all else, can be seen as a tract in support of the liberation of slaves.

Bible Reading from a Feminist Viewpoint

Feminist theology, specifically a feminist stance toward the Bible, has raised entirely new considerations. It no longer places the starting point in the centrality of reason but in the reality of the body. The real desire is to break away from rationalism, androcentrism and all forms of philosophy and practices that discriminate against women. The objective is to recover the use of senses, desire, taste, pleasure, pain and the mystery of life. It is a point of view which seeks to reflect with the body, that is, with sensitivity, with sexuality and, finally, with the story of the body itself. This is seen in the words of Ivone Gebara:

> My option is for the body, the human body, alive, and the centre of all relationships. A body from which come all problems and towards which all solutions converge. A body that is affirmed by its beauty whilst, at the same time, being a handicap for the divine which may be considered as pure spirit. Such a body experiences ecstasy and oppression, love and hate. It shows both the symbols of the Kingdom and also of the resurrection. (1988:201)

Throughout history, there have been many forms of prejudice about the human body. Both in theology and Bible reading, God is depicted as bearded, as the savior of humankind, as a man, and the way to authenticity as a Christian is to be celibate.

One of the first steps in a feminist reading of scripture was to recover the female presence within the biblical texts. Many books and articles have sought to rediscover this memory as, for example, Navia Velasco 1991. Eve, the mother of all living persons, is depicted more as being a wise person than as a temptress. Matriarchs such as Sarah, Rebecca and Leah were no less important than the patriarchs. The exodus, and the liberation from Egypt were articulated by women, by midwives and mothers. Rahab made possible the taking of the land of promise by the people of God. Deborah and Jael had a decisive part in the process of Israel's formation and the beginning of prophecy. Huldah was the prophet who mediated a great reform in Israel. Ruth, Judith and Esther upheld the strength of God's people. The young lover, with all her forthrightness in the Song of Songs, proclaimed the erotic power of love.

In the Jesus movement, there were women among the band of disciples who followed him from Galilee. They were also present at the cross and were the first witnesses to the resurrection. The genealogy of Jesus includes women considered sinful. There are women associated with the word, like Mary Magdalene as well as Mary and Martha of Bethany. There are women who are cured and even restored to the office of deacon, such as the mother-in-law of Peter. Other women who were cured included the woman with the issue of blood, the daughter of Jairus and the woman with dropsy. There are women evangelists like the Samaritan woman and the Syro-Phoenician woman. In the Christian communities, there are women who are involved in worship and prophecy such as those in the Corinthian church. It would even be possible to mention others, such as, Priscilla, Lydia, Phoebe, Mary, and many more.

There is, however, an even more challenging subject raised by a feminist approach to the scripture. That is the whole question of the silent or absent women in the Bible. Here we encounter a deeply suspicious problem. Why is it that of the 1,426 proper names in the Hebrew Bible, there are only 111 women? Where are the others? There could have been innumerable texts produced and transmitted by women that went on to be written by men. Many passages hint at an uneven distribution of power and the possibility of domination of the forgotten women. For this reason, it is essential to deconstruct the texts. This process of deconstruction presupposes the unmaking of the corrupt processes that produced the text. It calls for a reading between the lines in an analytical way in order to discover what lies behind the written word. The monarchy, for example, was a mechanism that destroyed women. How can we recover these women and rediscover their forgotten lives?

Having broken down the text, it becomes necessary to rebuild it with new gender relationships. In this way we will be able to discover how it is possible for women and men, for women and women, and also for men and men to build a new way of life. This reconstruction of the text implies the search for new paradigms and the discovery of new messages from the newly formed text (Pereira 1996:7–9).

Children, For Theirs Is the Kingdom of God

The situation in which many of our children live is nothing short of alarming. Violence, drugs, and death have taken over the headlines in the media. All this without mentioning the hunger, sickness, lack of schooling and the manipulation of the little ones. There has also been a theological amnesia with regard to children. As we awake from our forgetfulness, the children begin to appear and become visible, and this is especially so in the Bible where we read "theirs is the kingdom of God" (Mark 10:14).

I now, therefore, turn to explore the world of children as we take a walk through the Hebrew Bible. We gather together some examples from a work of Mesters (1997:9–20). The exodus began with four women defending the threatened lives of children (Exod 1:15–22; 2:1–10). When Pharaoh ordered the newly born babies to be thrown into the river, the womenfolk, Shiphrah and Puah, Jocabed and Miriam began to resist and rebel against the orders of Pharaoh. They feared God and for this reason received his blessing.

Hagar wandered hopelessly through the wilderness, with Ishmael in her arms (Gen 21:8–21). The angel of the Lord consoled her and said, "What is the matter, Hagar? Do not be afraid, God has heard the boy crying as he lies there" (Gen 21:17). After this, "God opened the eyes of Hagar and she saw a well of water" (Gen 21:19). Hagar fed the child and he grew up in the desert until he became a strong nation.

Criticism of child sacrifices is made in the order given to Abraham, "Do not lay a and on the boy" (Gen 22:12). The Covenant Code decrees: "do not take advantage of a widow or an orphan" (Exod 22:22). From the Decalogue, we can still hear today, "Honor your father and your mother" (Exod 20:12), a command that was given to preserve in the family clan an ideal environment for children. In Hosea, the children are symbols of divine mercy: "I will show compassion to the child 'Not cared for'" (Hos 2:25). Isaiah introduces us to the child Messiah, "Emmanuel, God with us" (Isa 7:14).

In the New Testament the examples are multiplied, as argued by Silva (1997:58–70). The Messiah who was to save humankind was a child born in one of the poor regions of Galilee in the difficult context of the Roman Empire. Jesus kept a special place in his heart for children. He healed them (Mark 5:21–43; 9:14–29) and used them as a very special model for his teaching. He said, "Whoever welcomes one of these little children in my name, welcomes me" (Mark 9:37). He threatened that anyone who offended one of these little ones would be deserving of the death penalty. Who would believe it! "It would be better for him to be thrown into the sea with a large millstone tied around his neck" (Mark 9:42). On one very significant occasion, while blessing and embracing the children, he called to task his own disciples who were holding them back and said: "Let the little children come to me, and do not hinder them, for the Kingdom of God belongs to such as these" (Mark 10:14). In the book of Revelation, the new communities are represented as the children of a woman in childbirth (Rev. 12:1–6).

These examples of Bible readings through the eyes of a child are but a small part of the many ways in which the scriptures both defend and promote the place of children.

Wisdom Belongs to the Elderly

It appears to be true that our modern society does not know how to respect the elderly. Senior citizens often constitute one of the categories most marginalized in society. They should, however, be the most appreciated of all. The Biblical culture, on the other hand, holds the elders in very special regard. They are the ones who, in the patriarchal system, presided over the family. Most towns and cities were governed by a council formed by elders.

The commandment "honor your father and your mother" is accompanied by the promise "that you may live long in the land that the Lord your God is giving you" (Exod 20:12). Job states: "Is not wisdom found among the aged? Does not long life bring understanding?" (Job 12:12). The book of Proverbs repeats many injunctions such as: "Listen, my sons, to a father's instruction" (Prov 4:1), and "A wise son brings joy to his father" (Prov 10:1). Counsel comes from the wise (Jer18:18; Ezek 7:26) and this counsel often carries the sense of legal authority. The prophet dreams of a paradise, with a long life, and in which "Once again men and women of ripe old age will sit in the streets of Jerusalem, each with a cane in hand" (Zech 8:4). Rehoboam, the successor to Solomon, is criticized for not having followed the counsel of the elders and to this fact is attributed all the weakness of his government (1 Kgs 12:8–13).

The New Testament reflects very well the important position given to the elders in the Christian community. This is clearly expressed in the letter written to Timothy: "Do not rebuke an elder" (1 Tim 5:1). In the book of Revelation the twenty-four elders constitute the divine counsel (Rev 4:4–10).

Love the Stranger, For You Were Foreigners in Egypt

Difficulties caused by living close to people who are different have always generated some form of discrimination. For this reason there have always been problems, both historically and today, that result in the rejection of foreigners or those of an ethnic minority. This is known today as xenophobia, or the rejection of strangers.

The principle is always the same, and it was this that caused the Roman Empire to use the word *barbarian* for those of a different race and culture and, later, the words *pagan* and *idolaters* for those who do not profess the Christian faith and to call common or rabble those who are not of noble birth. It goes without saying that the conflicts of an ethnic and racial nature that we witness today are a stain on the global map and a cause of shame to humanity. There is still a long way to go in terms of full acceptance of all foreigners in our communities.

The Bible is a great help in the search for inclusion. The very formation of the people of the Bible was the result of the integration of the twelve tribes or, as one might say, of various groups with diverse origins and cultures. The ancient list of tribes such as we find in Judg 5 outlines very well this reality. As the Hebrews left Egypt it was reported that "Many other people went up with them, as well as large droves of livestock, both flocks and herds" (Exod 12:38). Even the one God, Yahweh, can be thought of in terms of a foreign deity, perhaps being brought into the community by a foreign group which was integrated into the confederation of ancient Israel, perhaps from Midian (Exod 3:1–6). Biblical legislation clearly ordained, "Do not deprive the alien" (Deut 24:17), coupled with the warning: "Remember that you were slaves in Egypt" (Deut 24:18). The abiding presence of this recommendation, in the Hebrew memory, is in the motivation to redeem the land in the year of Jubilee: "The land must not be sold permanently, because the land is mine and you are but aliens and my tenants" (Lev 25:23).

The attitude of Jesus to foreigners is shown in a variety of ways. It is seen in the healing of the daughter of the Syro-Phoenician woman (Mark 7:24–30), in the story of the Good Samaritan (Luke 10:29–37), in the dialogue with the Samaritan woman (John 4), and in the universality of his message. The apostle Paul directed his entire mission to foreigners and made great efforts to reach those considered pagans and gentiles. The first letter of Peter is written to those described as "aliens and strangers" from the interior of Asia Minor (1 Pet 2:11). The same could no doubt be said of the community addressed in the letter to the Hebrews (Heb 11:13). The exhortation to treat foreigners well is found also in the recommendation given to Gaius (3 John 5). The list of the chosen in the book of Revelation includes, after mentioning the 144,000, "A great multitude that no one could count, from every nation, tribe, people and language" (Rev 7:9).

The Disabled, Take Up Your Bed and Walk!

Problems of ill-health were considerable in biblical times, as they are today. Despite the tremendous advances made in medicine, access to the best resources is still the privilege of the few.

The Hebrew Bible, in general, reflects an out of date view of medicine for obvious reasons. In the first place, biblical people, by and large, were strong and healthy. They lived in the country districts in the greater part and many were former slaves accustomed to manual labor. Besides this, medicine was closely linked to religion and magic, being exercised by priests with no concept of specialization. It could be argued that many taboos impeded the advance of medical care, such as the order not to touch cadavers, the aversion to touching blood and the widespread nature of diseases linked with leprosy. However, health was always seen as the greatest of all sacred gifts, a symbol of a life lived in dependency on God (Ps 139:13–16). Cures were in general attributed to God (Ps 41), and all medical care should be given only after prayer (Sir 38:1–15).

In the time of Jesus, the situation was much worse. The blind, the lame and the disabled populated the towns and cities. A great number of skin diseases were classified as leprosy and this marginalized many sick people. Prejudices and taboos created innumerable laws to distinguish the pure from the impure, which weighed particularly heavily against women. A lack of knowledge of psychology and psychiatry decreed that mental illness was almost always considered to be demon possession.

In this situation, Jesus was seen as an exorcist and healer. He achieved fame by his miracles. He was extremely attentive to the afflicted, to children, prostitutes, the blind, lame, leprous and many others. The gospel writings are clearly in sympathy with these and this is shown by the stories they tell. Jesus presented a new vision of healing and separated sickness from its traditional links with sin (Luke 13:2; John 9:3). A large part of his activities was concentrated on caring for the whole person and the desire to give complete health to the people he touched. It was with this in mind that he cured the paralytic (Mark 2:1–12), exorcised the demoniac in the region of the Gerasenes (Mark 5:1–20), cured the woman with a flux of blood (Mark 5:25–34), made the deaf mute speak (Mark 7:31–37), reintegrated the demoniac epileptic (Mark 9:14–29) and opened the eyes of blind Bartimaeus (Mark 10:46–52), to cite but a few examples.

Homosexuals, Friendships More Wonderful Than the Love of Women

The discrimination of homosexuals and lesbians is still violent in our society. The prejudices are many, and homosexual people are prone to suffer jokes, scorn, and worse. The churches in general have contributed to this discrimination, as has theology and the reading of scriptures. In spite of this we have news of opposing doctrinal positions from the first centuries. One tradition states that the apostles Philip and Bartholomew formed a couple, as did the martyrs Baco and Sergio during Maximum's reign, as well as the Byzantine Bail and Michael III.

The actual Bible could be reread from another more favorable position toward homosexuals and lesbians. In the words of Onaldo Pereira:

> The Bible does not have much to say about homosexuality. In the language that the texts were written no such word exists. The practice of homosexuality is briefly, and always mentioned, in negative contexts, as is adultery, unfaithfulness, violence and idolatry. The condemning attitude of Christians is often a result of ignorance of the contexts in which homosexuality is mentioned. (1998: A36)

In the same article he rereads classic texts that condemn homosexuality and argues that a good reading would reveal other facets of the question. The sin in Sodom and Gomorrah (Gen 19) was not homosexuality but lack of hospitality and violence against the foreigner, as other texts such as Isa 13; Ezek 16:49–50, Luke 10:10–12 bear out without mentioning homosexuality. In addition, the texts in Leviticus that prohibit homosexuality (Lev 18:22, 20:13) are part of the laws that will distinguish the Israelites from the other nations. Quoting Paul, in Rom 1:26–27, he affirms that all have sinned and are therefore absent from the glory of God, so we are all tainted with the sin of idolatry and promiscuity.

A rereading of the Bible from a homosexual standpoint would lead us to rethink some of the great friendships in the Bible such as Ruth and Naomi, Jonathan and a David who sings: "I grieve for you, my brother Jonathan; how dear have you been to me! Your love for me was more wonderful, even more than the love of women" (2 Sam 1:26). What might we ask was the young man who fled naked in Mark's account of Jesus in Gethsemane doing (Mark 14:51–52)? Many gnostic traditions attribute this text to a homosexual group of Christians.

Landless, but the Land Is a Gift from God

The unjust distribution of land is a central problem in Latin America, especially in Brazil. We have inherited from colonial times, as a chronic plague, the concentration of this vital resource in the hands of a small minority of people. Generous estimates calculate that 93.8 percent of the land is in the hands of 7 percent of the population.

However, new convictions are being established in the minds of many communities influenced by cultural, theological, and biblical considerations. "The land is a gift from God" (Lev 25:23) and as such should be cared for. The land is the ground of culture, is synonymous of life and has an almost mystical significance. In our context the land has become a seedbed for martyrs as a consequence of the struggle for land rights. In our struggle for the land, the Bible has become our greatest ally (Souza 1983). The entrance into Canaan, the Promised Land, becomes a mirror for landless groups who organize themselves for the "conquest" of their own land. Biblical laws such as the Sabbath Year and the Year of Jubilee (Lev 25) provide an instantaneous motivation in the proposals for agrarian reforms. The fight for justice in the prophetic books, carries condemnation of the landowner as well as incentives to the landless. The incentives are easily applied to our own days: "Have you not murdered a man and seized his property?" (1 Kgs 21:19), said Elijah to Ahab after the latter had stolen the vineyard belonging to Naboth. "Woe to you who add house to house and join field to field" (Isa 5:8). Micah is equally scathing in his condemnation of those who steal houses and lands to make themselves rich (Mic 2:1–2). "Woe to him who builds his palace by unrighteousness," declares Jeremiah (Jer 22:13). All of this finds an echo in the words of Jesus: "Woe to you who are rich, for you have already received you reward" (Luke 6:24). It also reverberates in the condemnation made by James: "Now, you rich, weep and wail, your wealth has rotted and the moths have eaten your fine clothes" (Jas 5:1–2).

Jesus, as a poor countryman from Galilee, called disciples and headed up a movement initially formed mainly by country people, even though it later grew and expanded. The language of the Gospels is the language of the countryside embracing plowing and reaping, seeds and flowers of the field, birds of the air, and so forth. In one of the key texts of the Gospel, Jesus himself said, "Blessed are the meek, for they shall inherit the earth" (Matt 5:4).

Ecology: Nature Cries Out with the Pains of Childbirth

Humanity has arrived at a position of tension with the environment. The created universe, built like a house, is in danger of collapse. For this reason, facing the danger of destroying its own dwelling, humanity is rethinking its relationship with the environment. The Bible strongly supports these endeavors to recover the basic human function, namely, to care for the land. For this it is necessary to read and interpret the text correctly because false readings have manipulated the teaching of the Bible and caused environmental catastrophes.

A very wise and ancient biblical law proposed a rest for the land every seven years (Lev 25). The Jubilee tradition, for example, was taken up in the year 2000, reinforcing the proposal to cancel the debts of the poorest countries (Reimer and Reimer 1999). The prophet Hosea takes us back to the beginning of creation with a reiteration of the divine promise: "In that day I will make a covenant for them with the beasts of the field and the birds of the air and the creatures that move along the ground. Bow and sword and battle I will abolish from the land" (Hos 2:20). He goes on to propose a fertile dialogue between heaven, earth and the people (2:23–25). In this concept of complete integration, the creation responds in accordance with the use made of it by those who dwell there.

As in the days of the apostle Paul, so today, "the whole creation has been groaning as in the pains of childbirth" (Rom 8:22), awaiting its deliverance. This dream of humankind runs throughout the Bible and finds its final expression in the creation of "a new heaven and a new earth" (Rev 21:1), and it will be called "the home of righteousness" (2 Pet 3:13).

Conclusion

In all these areas the Bible has provided us with valuable resources for changing our world. Read with the resources of common people, the Bible speaks directly into our contexts, not as the first word, but as the second word. Our realities are the first word that we bring to the Bible, inviting the Bible to illuminate our realities and allowing our realities to interpret it.

The Bible in British Urban Theology:
An Analysis by a Finnish Companion

Kari Latvus

From Latin American to British Liberation Theology

One of the main innovations of liberation theology in its Latin American version was a new way of reading the Bible connected to everyday issues. Reading the Bible in its social context has colored liberation theology so deeply that it has even been called "a movement of Bible reading" (Schürger 1997:166). Its starting point is that the reality of current social and cultural context is brought into mutual interaction with the Bible. Essential to the dialogue between the Bible and reality is its locality in a particular community and by people of a particular social sector. Liberation theology has underlined the preferential option for the poor both as a core content of the biblical message and as a method of hermeneutics: the primary interpreters are the poor and oppressed (Mesters 1989; Rowland 1999:1–16).

In the 1980s, Latin American liberation theology shifted from its golden period, a shift that was due to opposition from the Roman Catholic hierarchy as well as changes in global economic and political systems—not forgetting the growing challenge of Pentecostal movements in Latin America. At about the same time, liberation theology had started to create a new form in a European context, in Britain.

---

   * During previous decades Finland has been labeled as a Scandinavian welfare society belonging to the most equal, democratic, and socially balanced part of the Europe, now part of the European Union. The success stories of the modern paper industry and mobile technologies have been shadowed since 1990s by growing inequality in the social and welfare sector due to changed global/local politics and local economic recession. This has caused a growing need to learn from different ways of doing socially oriented contextual theology. The first version of this paper was read in the Institute for British Liberation Theology in Sheffield at the Urban Theology Unit in 2001. This essay is part of a larger Finnish-speaking research project published in 2002. Warm thanks for these (and many other) comments to Paul Skirrow, Tony Addy, and Tim Corringe.

Starting in the 1970s and deepening in the middle of the 1980s Britain faced severe economic and political challenges that hit first and foremost the inner-city areas. A weakened economic situation connected with ideological changes in politics led in many areas to large-scale, long-term unemployment joined with social, political, and racial problems. Changes in British society forced the churches to react because the fourth world had entered into the midst of the world of European social welfare.

British liberation theology has long indigenous roots in the movement of social Christianity, but the expression of an explicitly articulated British liberation theology was effected by Latin and North American experiments. The main concern of this essay is to reflect on how a new contextual model of Bible reading was used in the European context, specifically in the British theological movement that has been labeled liberation theology or urban theology. The analysis is focused on the literary material published in a process that started with *Faith in the City* (1985), *Theology in the City* (1989), *God in the City* (1995), and *Urban Theology* (1998), but is supplemented by the publications in the British Liberation Theology series (ed. J. Vincent and C. Rowland) and some other studies written by Laurie Green, Christopher Rowland and Mark Corner, Andrew Davey, and John Vincent.

Analysis based on these written materials was supplemented with interviews and participatory observations during several visits to Manchester and Sheffield during the years 1996–2001. My methodological perspective is that an adequate analysis of modes of reading the Bible or creating hermeneutical models is not possible without experimental learning from among the grassroots. I am painfully aware that this study does not cover all existing material, but I am convinced that the sources I have used are able to give a solid and adequate enough overview of recent British contextual theology and its way of using the Bible.

FAITH IN THE CITY PROCESS

FIRST PERIOD, 1985–1989

Faith in the City (FITC 1985) was written by an Anglican multidisciplinary commission. FITC is a remarkable document pointing out the critical condition of British society and introducing new theological innovations. The strength of the work lies in its well argued view of the reality of poverty and the marginalization experienced by a large section of the population in the beginning of the 1980s (FITC 1985:3–26). Being confronted with the realities of where and how people lived the commission gave many recommendations directed to the church and to the nation. The severe situation convinced the commission to consider new ways of doing theology at the grassroots and at street level. There is a clear intention to introduce liberation theology both into practical work in the church and into theological education.

Today, there are factors which again call into question the appropriateness of traditional theological methods. Lay people are learning, not just *about* the Bible, but how to *use* the Bible to reflect on their own experience. Young [*sic*] clergy must have the confidence and skill to help them in this. (FITC 1985:63–65, quote 120)

However, when FITC begins to give practical proposals, there is less clarity than one might expect. Concrete proposals are given, but at a rather general level. For example, it is pointed out that there is a need to financially support parishes located in deprived inner-city areas (which led to the establishment of the Church Urban Fund) and to encourage them to develop parish life, especially worship, to became more participatory and "incarnational." Striking, however, is the fact that, unlike in Latin American liberation theology, use of the Bible does not have central position, and is only mentioned on a few occasions (FITC 1985:73–165).

Retrospectively, it is easy to say that theologically *Faith in the City* was excellent in making a diagnosis, good in encouraging the finding of new directions and solutions and rather modest in writing the prescription. Using the terms of Carlos Mesters, there is a solid attention to the social context, the pre-text and also interest in encouraging communities to use participatory methods in order to empower people, but the missing element is methodology in general and Bible reading methodology in particular.

Already the name of the subsequent document, *Theology in the City* (TITC; Harvey 1989), pointed to the growing need to clarify the theological profile of the process. However, practically only one text, written by Andrew Kirk, really tried to enter into the methodological issues related to the Bible. Even in this case the chosen position is rather abstract because at that time, according to his view, "there are no real examples yet of genuinely local theologies to discuss." The model Kirk introduced, namely, to read the Bible connected to the social world of local communities, was directly copied from Latin America. In the text no special attention is paid to the British situation, culture or any local issues (Kirk 1989:15–31, quote 23).

In many ways the document followed the direction given earlier by FITC. TITC was still speaking about liberation theology and social analysis at a structural level, using the terminology of FITC. This trend was strongly affected by the collapse of communism, which was symbolically evident in the fall of Berlin wall in 1989, just a few months after the publication of TITC. Those liberation theologies that had socialist sympathies or that were using Marxist tools or even just Marxist terminology faced a severe challenge to reorient their fundamental views. Even those who had not been directly connected to these changes were also forced to reprocess their social analysis. In British urban theology the effect can be seen by noticing the differing stance that *God in the City* (Sedgwick 1995) and *Urban Theology* (Northcott 1998) took in their position and practice toward social analysis. In general terms there is a different approach toward social and especially toward political issues.

Ten years after publishing FITC, a group of professional theologians, parish work-ers, and laypeople was established as an Urban Theology Group. Their work, *God in the City* (GITC; Sedgwick 1995), contains a model to do theology in the context of urban deprivation. It was soon followed by *Urban Theology: A Reader* (UrTh; Northcott 1998), which provides a fairly comprehensive documentation of the British voices related to urban theology. In these publications certain aspects that were missing in earlier forms are now present. An especially strong place is given to the stories of individual people who live in deprived areas, so that the authentic voices and experiences of the oppressed and poor now replace official statistics and facts about poverty. Social analysis is no longer used in the earlier sense. GITC underlines and uses the stories of individuals (Sedgwick 1995:27–51).

Another interesting point is the growing interest in creating local contextual spirituality. An illuminating example of this is given by M. Northcott when he criticizes liberation theologians for marketing Marxist tools to do social analy-sis: "At the same time the liberation theologians were often blind to the spiritual riches of the religious and indigenous cultures of the poor whom they claimed to speak for" (Northcott 1998:5). In the same direction, Gill Moody is worried that the church is so concerned about social and political issues that it forgets its task: "Is the Church so tied up with social programs, that it forgets the most important reason for its existence, to nurture faith in community?" (Moody 1995:11).

This different approach underlines the need of spirituality as an essential part of urban theology. It is worth noticing that the growing interest in spiritual-ity is not only focused on local worship and liturgy but also, to some extent, on the Bible. However, whoever takes GITC and UrTh in their hands will see that in British contextual theology the Bible is mostly marginal and if mentioned is not related to praxis. The Bible as a tool to do contextual theology is mentioned by Laurie Green in introducing the hermeneutic circle (Green 1995:91; 1998:11–16), by Margaret Walsh in telling a story from Wolverhampton (Walsh 1995:67), and by Andrew Davey in telling a story from Peckham (Davey 1998:8–11). How-ever, the Bible or biblical hermeneutics is not a topic of any larger chapter or main section.

The first reason for this stems from the problem-oriented agenda. Issues of social reality are the natural starting point in liberation theology. GITC and UrTh follow this pattern and choose a reasonable number of their headings from inner-city issues: poverty in the city, power in the city, work in the city, crime and violence. Both documents, however, do also concentrate on church-oriented issues, dedicating several chapters to the ministry and worship, so one might expect some focus on the Bible.

There is, indeed, a symbolic location given to the Bible. Symbolic of the use of the Bible in the whole FITC process is the way UrTh always opens a chapter with a lengthy quote from the Bible. However, there is not sustained interaction between the text and reality. This working method is really quite different from, even opposite to, the Latin American use the Bible. Though UrTh grants the Bible a very prominent symbolic position, there are no real connections to the context. Does this, perhaps, reflect something about British social and cultural reality more generally? Unlike their Latin American forerunners, urban theologians have mostly ignored the possibility of using the Bible successfully in context. Among urban theologians there is little attention given to issues on how to use the Bible in a European city-context and how to create adequate structures and methods to empower people to interpret the Bible. With a few exceptions there seemed to be only a minor interest or trust in creating forums and methods to create an appropriate British biblical hermeneutics.

Perhaps urban theologians considered Latin American models to be too precritical, fundamentalist, or too naive (see Harvey 1989:10). Intrinsically, the difficulty is probably not in a lack of spirituality generally, because, as I have indicated, this theme is discussed widely and practiced in various ways. It seemed to be easier to find a place for urban prayer or worship done in everyday language touching the issues of ordinary people than to use a highly respected ancient book among the urban poor. This may reflect local cultural traditions toward books. Unlike earlier centuries, in current Britain book reading in general and Bible reading especially is a phenomenon belonging to the middle and upper class, and to clergy, and when it is read this is done largely within church walls.

It is also possible to ask if the tradition of a charity culture was unconsciously transferred into the sphere of spirituality. Poor people should be helped because they can not manage and because they need help. The Bible may be recommended to them and may also be interpreted for them. Perhaps this doing-things-for-other-people tradition was stronger than the empowering trend in liberation theology. One further answer might be that the Anglican tradition in Britain is more concentrated on liturgy than on the Word. There are plenty of examples of how Anglican liturgical resources have been successfully used and applied in the context of urban theology.

URBAN THEOLOGY UNIT

Finally, in British urban theology there is direction that cannot be ignored. It is the work done in the Urban Theology Unit in Sheffield. A remarkable finding is that nearly all the names associated with the Bible in the documents discussed above were connected to the Urban Theology Unit, Sheffield (UTU), which seems to be the innovation center concerning a British contextual approach to the Bible. UTU is a Methodist organization in its background but operates ecumenically.

The main documents representing the views of the UTU are contained in a short booklet, *Crucibles: Creating Theology at UTU* (2000), edited by I. K. Duffield, C. Jones, and J. Vincent; and the British Liberation Theology series and studies by Laurie Green (an Anglican bishop who has a close connection with

UTU), Andrew Davey (an Anglican priest with a doctoral thesis through UTU), and John Vincent (a former director of UTU). In these resources one finds plenty of examples of grassroots work being done in a variety of contexts. Although it is not possible here to provide a detailed analysis of the biblical hermeneutics of this group of writings and their authors, there are some significant similarities.

A major connecting feature is that all the writers construct their hermeneutics on the "See-Judge-Act" method originally pioneered by the Belgian priest Joseph Cardijn in the early twentieth century. A more developed version of this hermeneutic model is articulated by Laurie Green. In his model the following steps create an interpretative circle: Experience—Exploration—Reflection—Response—New Situation/Experience. Green underlines the decisive role of our own experiences and the need to be more aware about this in the process of doing theology (L. Green 1996:24–41). To connect Bible reading to the hermeneutic circle, Green turns to those methods that can empower the group and connect personal experience to the text. Green seems to have an ambiguous relationship with formal biblical studies exegesis because, on the other hand, he introduces scientific methods as appropriate working tools but, on other hand, he is aware that this kind of sociohistorical biblical exegesis has created a gap between the present and the past—or at least made us aware of a gap. To bridge the gap, Green supports methods that he calls "participatory methods" or what he calls "bibliodrama," a term he uses to embrace a whole range of creative and experimental approaches (77–91).

A similar hermeneutical process is described in *Crucibles: Creating Theology at UTU*. Experimental learning in the streets and the Bible are directly linked in a dialogical process that includes the streets, the academy, experience, and the church. In this case, it is possible to see how a more traditional use of the "See-Judge-Act" method forms the backbone of the approach. The streets are a synonym for "See," group reflection around the Bible is a form of "Judge," which then leads to collaborative action, "Act." Other ways of creating a dialogue between the street and the Bible can be found in John Vincent's book *Hope from the City* (Vincent 2000:43–168). Here Vincent looks at the similarities between his present context and biblical texts, sandwiching these different layers into one new product. Vincent establishes a fusion of horizons through finding correspondence between our experiences and Bible stories.

A Way Forward

Analyzing the hermeneutics of the urban theology process leaves one somewhat perplexed. Although "a mild form of Liberation Theology became common currency" (Hastings 2001:xx) in Britain, at least at some level, there are very few documented examples of a liberative use of the Bible. One explanation for this is that there are undocumented street level experiments but nobody has been able or motivated enough to document them. This, however, cannot be the whole truth, because there are few signs of this undocumented reality. Proposals and calls to create participatory interpretation methods are confined to only a few writers. Lonely voices that make a call to "liberate exegesis" (Rowland and Corner 1991) and hermeneutics have largely gone unanswered with concrete responses that address grassroots British reality.

In comparing the reading of the Bible contextually in community in its Latin American forms with British urban theology, it is clear that the latter has chosen a rather different road, concentrating mostly on connecting social reality and spirituality—not the Bible. A few isolated writings alongside this mainstream emphasis do however show a contribution to a contextual biblical hermeneutics from the urban theology movement. This is most apparent in the work of the UTU. Their image of a crucible which contains "gospel bits" and "situation bits" and the related work of Green which emphasizes the need to develop more participatory methods are good examples of this contribution.

Is an empowering European hermeneutics possible after all? Cultural barriers and obstacles rising from local traditions deserve to be analyzed in more detail than I have done here. Whatever the barriers, however, there is a continuing need to develop empowering ways of reading the Bible which take the current social situation seriously and show a strong interest in the community's need and right to read the Bible for themselves. Among the approaches proposed, special attention should be given, in my view, to bibliodrama.[2] Bibliodrama is a group process with a trained facilitator. Its basic methodological framework is derived from the soil of socio- and psycho-drama. Bibliodrama uses body movement, role-play, and other creative tools to study the roles or positions in the text of narrators, characters and addressees. Key to bibliodrama is identification with certain aspects of the text which overcome the historic gap between current interpreter and ancient text.

Bibliodrama touches both sides of the interpretive process, the reader and the text. There are many examples of how bibliodrama can easily move in the direction of therapeutic forms, particularly if the facilitator has had training. Bibliodrama also allows opportunity to work with exegetical issues as well. This becomes evident when bibliodrama is done in co-operation with or by biblical scholars. An example of this is the Finnish bibliodrama tradition, where there is an overt engagement with biblical scholarship (see Räisänen 1989:235–40).[3] However, there is also a need to develop bibliodrama along the lines of a more socially oriented Bible reading.

The task that lies ahead of us, I would argue, is not only theoretical but also very practical. Those of us committed to grassroots forms of contextual biblical

---

2. Two recent works concerning bibliodrama are Pitzele 1998; Martin 2001.

3. Räisänen 1989 gives a critical but positive description of his experiences as an exegete participating in bibliodrama.

hermeneutics need to develop and test new forms of participatory hermeneutics like bibliodrama.

POSTSCRIPT

A consultation on developing a European contextual theology related to urban mission, held in Liverpool in 2002, confirmed many views presented above but also provided the impulse for one or two additional comments by way of a postscript. First, there are signs of contextual biblical interpretation in certain settings in local urban parishes. The most common form of this and place for this is the sermon in Sunday services. Here local issues *can* be shared and studied in dialogue with the congregation. In these moments social reality is brought into dialogue with the Bible by pastors and by the congregation.

Second, there seems to be clear distinction between those who *do* contextual biblical interpretation at a grassroots level and those who *write* about contextual theology. Experiments and experiences "at street and sermon level" are not usually documented and shared with a wider audience, and when they are, it takes a long time for these grassroots-derived distillations to find their way into academic writings.

Reading Other-wise

Naveen Rao

Introduction

This is an interesting and stimulating collection of essays written on and around the theme of "Reading the Bible Other-wise," appropriating the Bible from various locations (social and other) such as indigenous, jail inmates, Asian, African, women, children, elderly people, and so on. Some of the essays I have found to be more engaging and reflective. Here I would like to submit my reflections, reactions, dialoguing with and on these essays.

Valmor Da Silva, Bible and Citizenship

This paper explores a new methodological position in the area of reading the Bible from different social locations in terms of race, color, and gender, as well as different social categories such as children, the elderly, foreigners, ethnic minorities, homosexuals, landless and homeless and ecological parties. In proposing a new approach to the Bible the author mentions the following points:

- ✦ Bible linked to the life in community (first book-life experiences);
- ✦ Bible as a second book;
- ✦ Bible reading from an indigenous, African or colored, feminist viewpoint;
- ✦ children, for theirs is the kingdom of God;
- ✦ wisdom belongs to the elderly;
- ✦ love the stranger, for you were foreigners in Egypt;
- ✦ disabled, take up your bed and walk;
- ✦ homosexuals, friendships more wonderful than the love of women;
- ✦ landless, but the land is a gift from God;
- ✦ ecology: nature cries out with the pains of childbirth.

Finally in the conclusion of the paper, it is said that "the Bible speaks directly into our contexts, not as the first word, but as the second word. Our realities are the first word that we bring to the Bible, inviting the Bible to illuminate our realities and allowing our realities to interpret it."

COMMENTS

The author seems to place a lot of emphasis on the "social location" of the reader— glorified, romanticized, and glamorized. Therefore my first comment would be on "social location" itself. How is a social location allocated: is it an imposed given-ness or self-acclaimed? Are the social locations watertight compartments, fixed and fatal? Is there any space for a movement, shift, growth, liberation from a self-acclaimed or imposed social location? Bob Ekblad in his article suggests that during the Bible study a shift in social location takes place.

   Second, the author, very remarkably, shows that this way of reading the Bible has a flow and a movement from text to context and vice versa, a two-way process, a symbiosis. This aspect of the article needs to be developed further.

   Third, an issue can be picked up on how much significance we are willing to give to the "experience," as the author takes experience to be "the first book" and the Bible second.

BOB EKBLAD, JOURNEYING WITH MOSES TOWARD TRUE SOLIDARITY:
SHIFTING SOCIAL AND NARRATIVE LOCATIONS OF THE OPPRESSED
AND THEIR LIBERATORS IN EXODUS 2–3

This paper is a reflection-report on Bible studies (on the text Exod 2:11–3:12) conducted in Skagit County jail in Washington state with "incarcerated Latino immigrants." The basic premise of the "facilitator" is "that oppressive interpretations can be subverted by careful reading of the narrative itself. This best happens when guided by such a facilitation that directly questions assumptions and invites unexpected identifications." The method of the Bible study is that the first-glance assumption of the biblical character's social location is a prejudiced (shaped by his or her own place in the world) reading of the story. "These biased interpretations of biblical stories are often alienating, reinforcing people's feelings of powerlessness or exclusion." But the author is sure that this "oppressive interpretation can be subverted by careful reading of the narrative itself." The study reflects a process of locating, identifying oneself in the narrative with the characters (situation of oppression, exile, abandonment) and along with them moving out of it (into liberation and empowerment as agents of transformation and change) with them.

   In the study, the first impression is of abused Israelites fighting with each other and Moses killing a taskmaster and running away from the scene of oppression; not only Moses but God is also absent from the scene. But as the study develops and deepens, new identifications become evident with a shift in location. Interestingly, the paper shows "God's shifting social location"; from an unapproachable, exclusive, angry, punishing, distant, impersonal God of the dominant theology (of the status quo), God shifts social location and comes to meet Moses in wilderness, embraces Moses' past, and identifies with his reaction to injustice. God comes in the wilderness to meet, embrace, and commission Moses as an agent of empowerment and liberation in the moments of his isolation and distance from his people. Along with Moses and God, the inmates also begin to identify with the shift in their social location from jail inmates (isolation, oppression, abused) to agents of empowerment and liberation.

COMMENTS

First, the Bible study shows a very remarkable feature of a movement, a flow, a growth, and a transformation at all the three levels: in the textual characters (Moses), in theology (God), and also in the participants (jail inmates) of the Bible study. Moreover, it shows that there is a possibility, scope, and space for liberation, empowerment, and transformation, no matter how bleak the present situation is.

Second, although the Bible study begins with identification of the present realities (social location) of the participants, no matter how depressing these are, the study has the potential to move beyond it.

Third, the choice of place or location (jail inmates) for Bible study is outstanding and praiseworthy, as it liberates the Bible from the confines of the centrally located churches to the outskirts and margins where these jails and correction houses are located. The move from the center to the margins is both metaphorical and literal, geographical and social.

GERALD WEST, (AC)CLAIMING THE (EXTRA)ORDINARY AFRICAN "READER" OF THE BIBLE

This essay begins with a question: What constitutes "ordinary" African biblical interpretation? This question emerges from the studies (mostly empirical) that have shown that "Africans adopted a variety of strategies in dealing with an ambiguous Bible, including rejecting it" (Mofokeng 1988:40).

The essay takes up three (extra)ordinary interpreters of the Bible, spanning two hundred years of biblical interpretation in South Africa: Queen Mmahutu (early 1800s), senior wife of Mothibi, chief of the BaTlhaping people (Tswana); Isaiah Shembe (late 1800s), the leader of a Christian sect who emphasized virginity and sexual purity; and Trevor Makhoba (late 1900s), an artist with extensive work on the religious themes that have impacted both African (traditional) religion and Christianity.

In conclusion, after having traced and discussed the genealogy of biblical interpretation in Africa, Gerald West offers a call "bracket—but not abandon—the prescriptive/interventionist paradigm; it is time to listen rather than to proclaim." It is a call for a descriptive paradigm, "to observe and analyze the manner in which African Christians 'read' and view the Bible" (Maluleke 1996:15). This will help one to understand the genealogy of Bible reading realities, to become precise about the analytical categories being employed, and beyond the concerns of cultural studies, by paying attention to these African interpreters, the African biblical scholars will be helped to discern the contours of their task.

COMMENTS

The choice of these three interpreters for the study is commendable, namely, a queen (a female, a mother, a leader, not a male patriarch), a cult figure (a non-mission person, a nonconformist, a charismatic leader, not a mainline renowned preacher or a missionary), and an artist (quiet, making use of traditional art forms and metaphors, not a great preacher and orator, one who is using expressions rather than vocal words).

The author proposes to reverse the process of learning—who should teach and who should learn—by saying that now the time has come for African biblical scholars to learn from the African interpreters such as the queen, the cult leader, and the artist, who come from outside the scholarly circle. The first question that arises is: Will it be possible, because it sounds too good to be true? Will scholars let go of their power and monopoly over the Bible, its study, and its "valid" (in their own eyes) interpretation? It is indeed a commendable feat of the author to even propose such a thing that allows space for biblical interpretations coming from the nonformal (theological and academic) quarters. It will liberate Bible from the clutches of the powerful academicians and church hierarchy so that the Bible may come within the reach of the ordinary readers, where it truly belongs.

How far can one go ahead with these interpreters in an uncritical learning mode? Will there be a time when these interpreters will be allowed to interact and dialogue with other interpretations of recent times?

NICOLE M. SIMOPOULOS, WHO WAS HAGAR? MISTRESS, DIVORCEE, EXILE, OR EXPLOITED WORKER: AN ANALYSIS OF CONTEMPORARY GRASSROOTS READINGS OF GENESIS 16 BY CAUCASIAN, LATINA, AND BLACK SOUTH AFRICAN WOMEN

The paper has a twofold objective: to explore the validity of the readings offered by the three groups; and to advocate for the establishment of a dialogical interpretive interface between ordinary readers and academicians. A Bible study on the text of Gen 16 brings out varied interpretations, identifications, and responses (three), and the author hopes "each interpretation is valid, valid simply because the interpretations speak meaningfully to the reader's specific context."

✦ White, middle- to upper-class Catholic and Protestant women living in northern California, the majority of whom had been divorced by adulterous husbands when they found new mistresses, identified with Sarah's jealous rage toward Hagar; during their divorces they also identified with Hagar's loneliness and desperation in the desert.

✦ Latina Presbyterian immigrants and refugees from Mexico and Central America living in northern California identified with Hagar as an exilee from her native country, as an outsider and outcast living in a foreign and hostile land.

✦ Black South African Protestant women from both rural and urban South African townships enrolled in theological training program identified with Hagar's exploitation as a slave or worker under her master's oppression.

In conclusion, the author expresses her anguish that "I do not assume that they [these three interpretations] are valid in the sense that they stand in accordance with traditional, established historical-critical methods and conclusions.... I am compelled to state that validity needs boundaries, especially if we are to safeguard against oppressive interpretations." She contends that the interpretation needs to be liberative and redemptive message of hope, and it is most valuable when it is relevant to life and one's search for transformation and meaning. She advocates for the articulation of the voices of ordinary readers in determining meaning in the biblical text as the academic discipline of biblical studies traditionally had little or no place for ordinary, untrained readers of the Bible.

COMMENTS

The plea of the author seeking validation for these three interpretations coming from three groups of women is moving, sincere, and genuine. But at the same time it is reflective of the monopoly that has been created and imposed by the traditional, male, historical-critical scholarship, so much so that when women do dare to interpret the Bible they have to plead for validation for their interpretation. It is a pathetic and sickening state of affairs as far as the equal participation and freedom of women is concerned in the field of biblical interpretation.

On the other side, the women interpreters are being too naïve and modest in seeking validity, I do not know from whom and why. To think that someone "OTHER" holds the authority to grant "validity" to women's interpretation of the Bible is a state of mental-colonialism, and it needs to be challenged, broken down, and gotten rid of—*Talitha Kumi*.

MONIKA OTTERMANN, "HOW COULD HE EVER DO THAT TO HER?!"
OR, HOW THE WOMAN WHO ANOINTED JESUS TURNED INTO A VICTIM
OF LUKE'S REDACTIONAL AND THEOLOGICAL PRINCIPLES.

This paper is a good example of making use of the historical-critical methods for reading "otherwise," and it produces a feminist, liberative reading of the story in Luke. It brings out the issue that historical-critical methods need not be labeled "oppressive" *en toto*. By making use of these same methods, a liberative interpretation can also be brought out, as this essay has done.

Another point that this paper brings out is how the biblical writers make use of the "raw-material" in their borrowing, selection, and application for the formulation of a "Gospel" for a particular community (Lukan, in this case). This essay brings out wonderfully that at times this process of the formulation of "gospel" while attempting to be "politically correct" with the status quo of its time can be oppressive for the "Other."

Therefore, "Reading Other-wise" is not an option but a necessity for Bible readers to continue and perpetuate the prophetic proclamation in every age and place.

Growing Together: Challenges and Chances in the Encounter of Critical and Intuitive Interpreters of the Bible

Werner Kahl

"Some people claim to know the Bible, but the Bible doesn't know them" (Ghanaian preacher).

Introduction

A few months ago, a new Bible translation was published in Germany: The People's Bible (Volxbibel). The translator radically rendered the New Testament in the contemporary German as it is spoken by German teenagers, most of whom reject church and would never touch a Bible. With the publication of the Volxbibel, the unexpected has happened: quite a good number of these teenagers, "cool" and "bad" as they are, have discovered this Bible as *their* Bible. For the first time, they begin reading the New Testament, and many just cannot stop until they have reached the last chapter of Revelation. Jesus and all the other characters of the New Testament speak *their* language, and what is written speaks to them directly. In John 20:19, for example, revealing himself as the risen Christ to his disciples, Jesus does not greet them with a solemn "Peace be with you," but with the German equivalent to "Hi guys, what's up?" This is not meant to be funny. The translator or rather transformator took seriously the most likely assumption that Jesus and his followers communicated in the colloquial language of their time and location, and not in an antiquated manner. The writings of the second- to the fourth-generation Christians that are collected in the New Testament canon are written in Koine Greek, which gives support to this assumption (see also Paul in Phil 3:8).

The Volxbibel has become a bestseller within a very short period of time. Some Christians in Germany who hold the Bible in high esteem, that is, the version that goes back to Luther's translation (cf. in the English-speaking world the King James Version and its revisions), have expressed grief about this latest version; it would—metaphorically—drag the Bible into the dirt of the street. Of course we know that Jesus and his followers preferred to be exactly there: close to people who were forced to live in dirt or who were regarded as such (see Luke 7:34; 1 Cor 1:26–29).

It is commendable from the perspective of the New Testament that some of "the wise of this world," some trained philosophers or theologians (see 1 Cor 1:19–21), have begun to turn their attention to the formerly unheard or ridiculed voices of people who have *not* been regarded as important readers of, or listeners to, the Bible in the past. The essays collected in the present volume cover quite a wide range of grassroots interpretations of Scripture from the margins of the centers of economic power. What should be the function of the academically trained reader, the theologian, when he or she comes into contact with so-called ordinary interpreters who, more often than not, offer extra-ordinary interpretations of Scripture? And who profits most from this encounter? Who takes the initiative in establishing the contact? Who needs whom, and for what purpose (maybe to get a thesis done, as in my case when doing field research in Ghana)? What are the—at time conflicting—expectations on either side? What are the challenges and chances of the encounter, for everyone involved in the process? These are some of the questions that need critical reflection, if the project of a cooperation between these two types of interpreters of the Bible should yield any meaningful fruit, as it should. In what follows, I intend to clarify some of the issues involved in this project. Even though I will focus my observations on sub-Saharan Africa, I will make reference to all the papers collected here.

Critical and Intuitive Interpreters

First a word about the designation "trained or scholarly" versus "ordinary or popular" readers: I suggest to rather use "critical" versus "intuitive" *interpreters*. Of course, by far not all Christians in Africa are able to *read* the Bible. Some simply *listen* to readings from the Bible, and they might know these stories and sayings by heart. "Ordinary" or "popular" are attributes that carry some problematic connotations. I prefer the designation *intuitive interpreters* for the following reasons. It is by intuition, that is, by relying on common sense and an inner feeling of what is true, that these interpreters arrive at certain interpretations that, to them, seem to be self-evident. In addition, as members of a church they commonly derive meaning from the Bible with the understanding that God directs their mind spiritually to a proper appropriation of a passage within a given life situation. Spiritual insight is a prerequisite to understanding the Word of God. And the Bible is revered as Word of God. It is Holy Scripture. God as Spirit—this is the emic view—talks to them directly when reading Scripture. The meaning-generating process involves Scripture, the spiritual direction of God, and the preparedness of the interpreters to carefully listen to the divine voice. Therefore, Bible studies in Africa are commonly framed by songs and prayers. This has the function of inviting the Spirit of God into their midst. So intuitive interpreters tend to have a direct access to the Bible. They easily identify with the narrative addressees of biblical speakers such as Moses, Jesus, or Paul. From the perspective of the Gospels, for example, this is *not* a problematic procedure. On the contrary, such intuitive readers and listeners were expected as ideal recipients of these writings. It can be shown, for example, that Mark intentionally involves his readers when he has Jesus narrate the parables (Mark 4). And in the Gospel of John the addressees of Jesus' speeches on the syntagmatic plane are conflated with the addressees of the Gospel: both should believe that Jesus is the Messiah in order to have everlasting life (see John 3:36; 20:31).

Academically trained theologians or exegetes, on the other hand, are expected to be *critical* readers of the Bible, which they are not supposed to interpret as the direct Word of God. *Critical*—which is derived from the Greek *krinō*, to distinguish, differentiate, judge after careful consideration of all aspects of a matter—should be understood here in a double sense. First of all, theologians should employ literary and historical tools of analysis that allow for an understanding of a given biblical text within the parameters of its original setting. Second, they should be able to *reflect* on their own life-contexts, intentions, preunderstandings, and methods employed for analysis.

The following chart illustrates the proposed critical interpretation of a biblical text. It is an attempt at taking into consideration a critical analysis of both the text in its original contexts and the contexts of the interpreters, in order to arrive at an interpretation that is textually adequate as well as meaningful and relevant to the interpreters.

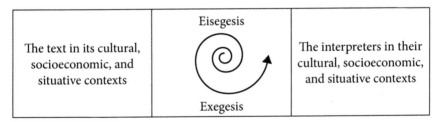

The text in its cultural, socioeconomic, and situative contexts	Eisegesis Exegesis	The interpreters in their cultural, socioeconomic, and situative contexts

This model also applies to intuitive interpretations, with the difference that the interpreters representing such an approach commonly do not reflect critically on either the textual or the interpretative context. Every interpretative act is bound to a certain perspective. This perspective—be it a particular interpretive community among exegetes or church members—informs the questions put to the text, the methods employed to access the text, and so forth. It determines to a certain degree already the outcome of an interpretation. Exegesis and eisegesis are mingled up in the process. *Ideally*, however, this meaning generating process should not describe a hermeneutical circle but rather a *hermeneutical spiral*. Previously undetected aspects of meaning can be discovered if interpreters with different perspectives read a biblical text together. By so doing, blind spots as well as problematic interpretations of all the partners involved could be brought out. This allows for a fresh view of the same text, and new discoveries can be made.

Critical analysis is supposed to do justice to the text by exposing ethnocentric or anachronistic projections onto the text. Also, trained readers are not free from reading preconceived positions into a given passage, as the history of biblical interpretation indicates. A case in point is the contribution of Mônica Ottermann. In her feminist reading of Luke 7:36–50 she accuses Luke of an "androcentric, macho, and christocentric" redactional procedure, by means of which he "dirtied the memory and the good reputation of the woman of Bethany." His turning the memory of this woman, whose real character came to expression in Mark 14:3–9; Matt 26:6–13; and especially in John 12:1–8, allegedly into a prostitute, revealed Luke's agenda of embracing "Roman imperialism and a pervasive patriarchy."

I would like to point out a few problematic constructions by the author of this paper. While she has made plausible that Luke 7:36–50 is Luke's invention based on Mark 14:3–9, and while it is not to be contested that Luke did not challenge the patriarchal system of Mediterranean antiquity (but who did among Christians in the first centuries?!), she projects her own value system onto the Gospel text. This is problematic, since it leads to distortions of the passage and effects a caricature of the Gospel of Luke. In addition, Ottermann identifies her position with Jesus'. How she arrived at a solid knowledge of Jesus' attitude toward women remains clouded. Reference to Mark 14:3–9 and similar passages in the Gospels will not suffice in establishing Jesus' position reliably. What seems to be beyond doubt, however, is that his inner circle of twelve followers consisted of men only. It is methodologically unsound to select Gospel passages that seem to agree with our own predilections and declare them to be a memory of what Jesus *really* did. It should be rather acknowledged that we do not have direct access to the historical Jesus, and only a few historical data of his life can be established reliably. The life of Jesus research from the nineteenth century to the present times, however, has been the history of anachronistic reconstructions. In claiming to present Jesus' position in her feminist critique of Luke, Ottermann actually leaves her critical competence behind and becomes an intuitive reader. And this reader does no longer takes seriously the signals of the biblical text that disturb her preconceived notion of the passage. First of all, in the passage, the woman is *not* called explicitly a prostitute (*pornē*, cf. Luke 15:30), but "a sinner (in the city)." While it is possible that Luke alludes here to prostitution, we cannot be sure if this was his or the projected addressees' strongest connotation. In fact, Luke leaves open the concrete denotation. This space is being filled with "prostitute" not by Luke but by Ottermann. So, strictly speaking, it is her, not Luke, who turns this woman into "a local whore."

Furthermore, she criticizes Luke for not having "the courage to call Jesus a 'friend of prostitutes,'" referring to the expression "friend of the tax collectors and sinners" (Luke 7:34b) in the immediately preceding passage (7:24–35). By implication, however, Jesus is actually presented in 7:36–50 as a "friend" of this woman, who is called a sinner, whatever might have qualified her as such in the eyes of the narrator and the character of the Pharisee (note that *Luke* does not have Jesus address, or refer to, the woman as sinner!). In fact, while in Luke 7:29 tax collectors are being presented as endorsing Jesus' message, 7:36–50 can be understood as an exemplary story by means of which Luke wanted to exemplify Jesus' concern not only for tax collectors but also for sinners, challenging the position of the Pharisees, who in the Gospel of Luke are regularly exposed as those who claim to be without sin, that is, without the need of having their sins forgiven.

We must acknowledge that all we have are, at times very differing, *interpretations* of what Jesus was all about—and these interpretations, as they are collected in the New Testament, have been written in particular situations by men, none of whom questioned the existing patriarchal structure of their societies or of their communities. While some Christ-believing women did challenge certain male-dominated aspects of their church gatherings (see 1 Cor 14:33b–36), it is quite unlikely that they questioned the patriarchal structure of their society, community, and church on a *fundamental* level.

The critical exegete must attempt to function as defendant of the ancient text; in this function he or she must reject interpretations that are distortions of textual meaning. By saying this, I do not favor an understanding of text that presupposes a one-dimensional meaning generating process. In fact, semiotics has taught us that texts do have a *meaning potential*. But while it is possible that different interpretations of one text can be equally valid, I would like to emphasize that false interpretations do occur. And they can be identified. For example, one of the most attractive biblical verses among Christians in West Africa is Matt 6:33, "But seek you first the kingdom of God and his righteousness, and all these things shall be added onto you." This verse, however, is commonly memorized in the following way—by preachers and church folk alike: "Seek you first the kingdom of God and his righteousness, and *everything* will be added onto you." The expectation that God will bless true believers with everything they wish for, and especially material riches—an understanding of divine intervention that is informed by African traditional religion as well as by values of the modern world—is read into the passage. This interpretation necessitates, however, the prior decontextualization of the verse, for the literary context does not allow for such an understanding. It rather has "all these things" refer unambiguously solely to food, drink, and clothing. And the message of the pericope Matt 6:25–34 within the context of the Sermon on the Mount is clearly that the addressees of this speech of Jesus should not worry about securing their lives but should trust that God will provide for their daily needs while they should fully devote their lives to doing the will of God.

When critical and intuitive interpreters meet—for example, at the occasion of a joint Bible study—they should do so with the understanding that their interpretations are equally important even though their accesses to the Bible as well as their objectives are different. If a group of intuitive interpreters—for example, in a church—claim to give *textually* adequate interpretations, they should be open to have their interpretations checked and challenged by the trained experts of textual criticism.

By means of the following diagram I try to differentiate various levels of interpretation or contexts within which a given motif could acquire different aspects of meaning.

HIERARCHY OF MOTIFIC FUNCTIONS

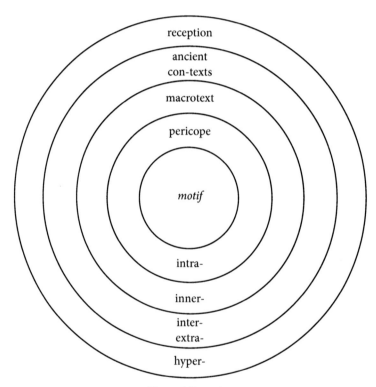

Textual Functions

The diagram might help exegetes who read biblical texts together with intuitive interpreters to locate a particular interpretation on a certain level and to identify contexts that might not have been considered by a given interpretive community. It should be noted that the reconstruction activity of the interpreters increases the further the interpretative contexts are removed from the center. At the same time, the certainty of textual adequacy of an interpretation decreases.

The critical interpreters should reckon with the possibility that their partners open up dimensions of textual meaning that might be unheard of in the academic discourse but that nevertheless might be adequate. Living conditions and the conceptualization of the world in most of sub-Saharan Africa are much less removed from antiquity than respective experiences and dominant worldviews in the West. However, a closer proximity to ancient culture and the realities of life among most Africans does not mean that they have a hermeneutical advantage per se over against academically trained readers. Nevertheless, the former might grasp by intuition meaning dimensions and implications of a given passage that are hidden to readers who share a modern worldview and who enjoy the securities of the Western world. For example, the insight that the seen world and human existence are embedded in an unseen spiritual world is shared by most if not all African ethnic groups as well as the peoples of Mediterranean antiquity. This cosmology is in sharp contrast to the understanding of the world as it prevails in the West, including the church. Here the existence of a realm besides the visible world is commonly denied or—as in the church—reserved for life after death, that is, the beyond, and is thought of being almost disconnected to life.

Translations of another prominent verse among West African Christians illustrate the issue. Some English Bible versions translate the last two words of John 3:16 with "eternal life" (Luther's translation: "ewiges Leben"). This connotes life of the soul beyond, after death. The King James Version, however, reads "everlasting life." And the Twi version (an Akan language in Ghana) emphasizes the aspect of an everlasting, never-ending life even stronger, for it renders the Greek *zōēn aiōnion* as *daa nkwa*, that is, "life from day to day"—a translation that comes very close to the Greek, since *aiōnion* is derived from *aei*, always. The implication in the Gospel of John is indeed that God is concerned about the *whole life* of the believer, including both the present and the future, the body and the soul: the believer has been connected to God, the source of life, and he or she cannot fall out of God. The Western tradition, however, has favored a spiritualized understanding of Christianity where God is basically concerned with the souls after life. Grounded in an African worldview and in a respective experience of life, Africans in this instance understand immediately—by intuition—and correctly what John meant.

Academic readers and especially exegetes, however, should also be able to discover aspects of meaning in a given passage by means of literary analysis, historical research, and careful comparison with other ancient texts. Intuitive and critical interpreters need one another to come to a broader and deeper, that is, a more adequate understanding of the biblical text, *if this is their common objective.* If they allow their respective interpretations to be challenged and if they are open to learn from one another—the criterion should be the parameters and literary contexts of a chosen biblical passage—while at the same time an atmosphere of mutual respect prevails, the precondition is set for an exciting development, that is, that intuitive and critical interpreters *grow together*—in the double sense of the expression. By means of this procedure, the problematic tendencies of both an uncritical *listening to* (by the exegete or by a church group) the respective other and a paternalistic *interpreting for* (e.g., by the exegete or by a prophetic spokesperson of a church group) the respective other might be suppressed if not avoided. What is needed is a community of intuitive and critical interpreters both of whom understand and appreciate that they come to the biblical texts from different perspectives that are equally valid. While it is true and also desirable that academic readers be challenged "by their conversations with peripheral readers" (Masoga), I would like to point out the necessity that intuitive interpretations are likewise to be challenged. Certainly, up until very recently interpretations at the grassroots level all too often have not been taken seriously by trained theologians, with the latter attempting to impose their readings onto the people. However, as the contributions by Gerald West, Mosamme Alpheus Masoga, Nicole M. Simopoulos, and Stephen C. A. Jennings suggest, these attempts have proved futile. The same applies, by the way, for the missionary attempts from Europe to "evangelize" West Africa in the nineteenth and twentieth centuries. *Spiritually* the European missionaries could never reach their missionary objects, who turned out to be subjects who undermined the Western strategies. Now, it would be naïve and counterproductive if theologians today shifted from the tendency of theological export and domination to an uncritical import, that is, servile acceptance of theological positions from the grassroots level. These positions indeed do need to be heard and taken seriously. They are not taken seriously, however, if they are being endorsed uncritically.

For a biblical interpretation to become meaningful within a particular community of interpreters, it needs to be both culturally plausible and relevant in a given life context or situation. Those theologians who do not share the same conceptualization of reality and the life conditions of a group of intuitive interpreters of the Bible should by all means refrain from applying a textual meaning to the situation of their partners. The responsibility and ability to do so lie solely with the intuitive interpreters.

THE BIBLE AND ITS INTERPRETERS: WHO IS THE SUBJECT?

The quotation of a Ghanaian Neo-Pentecostal preacher in the heading of this response points to a fundamental challenge of the (Western) critical interpreter when he or she engages in a joint Bible study with intuitive interpreters in, or from, sub-Saharan Africa. The Bible as Holy Scripture can be regarded as active subject in the meaning-generating process, and the readers are being subjected to its activity. Presupposed here is a fundamental difference in worldview to most critical readers, which for most Christians in, or from, sub-Saharan Africa is grounded in traditional conceptualizations of reality. As already stated above, among most if not all ethnic groups in sub-Saharan Africa it is presupposed that the material, seen world is embedded in the wider context of the invisible spiritual world, whose agents are regarded as more powerful than the ordinary human being. What happens within the visible world might have been caused by a spirit, be it an ancestor or a local divinity. These spiritual forces of traditional Africa are often identified, from a charismatic Christian perspective, with demons or Satan. In fact, from this perspective it is essential that human beings act in accordance with the plans of these powers, or to be protected against their influence, in order to avoid hardship in life.

SPIRITUAL WORLDVIEW IN SUB-SAHARAN AFRICA

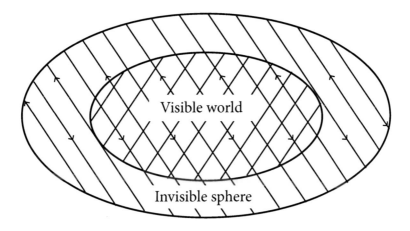

People in general understand themselves not as being independent subjects, but they are rather subject to wider communities, spiritually and socially (extended family, ethnic group). What is important in the context of this paper is the recognition of the fact that this self-understanding of many Africans in general, and of African Christians in particular *contradicts* the self-understanding of at least the common academician who has been trained in a Western-oriented institution informed by the philosophies from the Enlightenment until postmodernism, which share the notion that the human being is, or rather should be, the master of his or her own destiny, without any recourse to the activity of supernatural beings. In fact, the belief in these is generally held in despise. This fundamental contradiction in worldview is not to be neglected when trained theologians read the Bible together with church groups in Africa. The same holds true for large populations in Latin America and Asia. Eric Anum's observation that the recourse to the involvement of the Spirit among members of a Bible study group in Botswana is meant to undermine attempts of an academician at dominating the discussion makes sense in the context of the described worldview. The experience and expectation among intuitive interpreters of the Bible in Africa, that "God is in control" even as "they read" the Bible, actually empowers them.

The academically trained theologian has no choice but to accept this fundamental difference, if he or she intends to continue the exercise. It might be helpful for him or her to realize that this notion of an essential subjection of human beings to spiritual powers, including God, was certainly shared by the historical Jesus, his followers, and the early Christians. The most powerful active subjects according to the biblical narratives are God, his Spirit, and Jesus Christ. So at least the critical interpreter has the chance of learning something new of fundamental importance about the Bible. In addition, in the process of the encounter with intuitive interpreters, he or she might accept the challenge and reflect critically on his or her self-awareness of a self-reliant, active subject shaping his or her life independently and in self-control. This notion might be part of a powerful myth of Western civilization since the Enlightenment.

TRANSFORMING THE GOSPEL

I have emphasized above the need of critically checking the textual adequacy of biblical interpretations by intuitive readers or listeners, as the responsibility of the trained theologian. This, however, applies only if the intuitive interpreters allow for such critical reflection and if they *claim* to present interpretations that were *textually* valid. Such an understanding of biblical interpretation is still informed by the Protestant principle of *sola scriptura*. This principle, however, has been undermined to a certain degree by the widespread claim and experience among many grassroots-level Christians in Africa, Asia, and Latin-America, that it is the *Holy Spirit* who interprets Scripture for them, while they simply need to be prepared to receive divine revelations on the meaning of the gospel. Charismatic or Neo-Pentecostal Christians presuppose that the direction given by the Spirit might open up the real meaning of a difficult passage and even override the literary meaning of a biblical passage. This spiritually informed meaning-generating process, of course, is analogous to the procedure followed by the early Christians in interpreting their Scripture, that is, the Christian Old Testament, as well as the meaning of Christ or the will of God (cf. the functions of the Paraclete in the Gospel of John; the role of the Spirit in Acts; 2 Cor 3). In the same way the early Christians relied on divine guidance for understanding, a growing number of Christians at the grassroots level today interpret the Bible, the meaning of the gospel, and their world and existence.

Yet the Bible as the Word of God or Holy Scripture is held in high esteem, and more often than not these interpreters ascribe a timeless validity to—selected!— New Testament instructions without recognizing that these instructions are context- and culture-bound actualizations of the meaning of the gospel in particular situations of the past. Within the parameters of such an understanding, it could become the function of an academically trained theologian to encourage the interpretive community to live up to their divinely bestowed potential to become true custodians of the gospel, appealing to their experience with divine revelation and spiritual guidance. In this perspective, the canon still remains valid as a collection of early Christian writings that document in an exemplary manner the freedom and the responsibility of early Christians to bring to expression what the gospel meant to them in particular situations. Present Christians could be encouraged to emulate these interpretive activities. In pointing out the fact of the variety among the New Testament writings in content and style, the trained theologian might succeed in making plausible the *possibility* as well as the *necessity* of the ongoing process of translating or rather transforming the gospel, so that it might become meaningful in a particular situation of a particular community, in other words, culturally plausible and contextually relevant. Intuitive interpreters might realize that meaningful continuity with the early Christian experience as documented in the New Testament can only be achieved in the process of an ever-evolving and ongoing transformation of the gospel. In this process, the dimension of spiritual revelation is as important as is critical analysis of biblical passages as well as of the interpretive situation, in order to arrive at actualizations of the *gospel* that are in *continuity* (not identical) with early Christian understandings of the gospel and that are relevant and meaningful to a particular community today (see the chart below). What "gospel"—the good message from God—meant among the early Christians can be described in general terms only in a very unspecific way: God has come close to his people with good intentions and to have his will established everywhere on earth. The implications of this act of God are actualized in a variety of ways in the New Testament writings, such as the kingdom of God will bring about divine justice and peace; believers will gain life in its fullness; God shows a predilection for those marginalized in society; untimely death and illness can be overcome; life-threatening spiritual powers have been subjugated; belonging to his people transcends ethnic origin; people are spiritually empowered to spread the gospel courageously; there is trust of being gathered with God and Christ eternally after death.

Some of the papers collected in this volume suggest what gospel could mean in particular situations of particular communities today: it is a "life-giving resource" (West); it implies the eradication of discrimination against marginalized people (Da Silva); it overcomes oppression of incarcerated Latino immigrants in the United States of America (Ekblad); it allows for "empowering ways of reading the Bible" at the grassroots level and makes possible a participatory hermeneutics (Latvus); it empowers Jamaicans at the grassroots level to "resist and counter" oppressive effects of globalization (Jennings); it brings freedom, liberation, and hope to marginalized women (Sinopoulos); and it helps in transforming society on behalf of the oppressed (Lees). In how far these actualizations are, or can become, meaningful to intuitive interpreters at the grassroots level, many of whom have turned charismatic, is a matter of an ongoing negotiation that challenges preconceived notions of all partners involved in the process. At the same time, however, it bears the chance for new developments: academically, personally, in church, and in society.

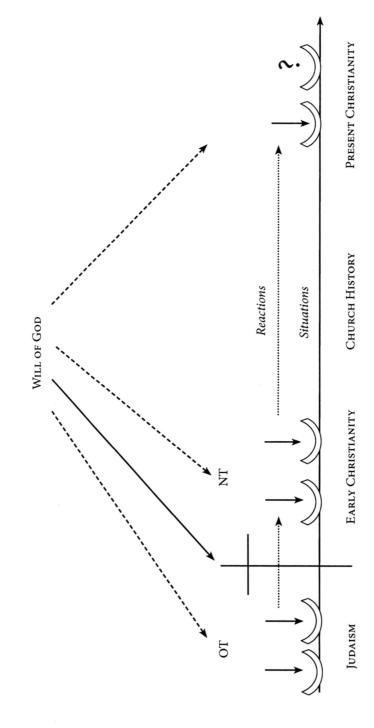

THE CHRISTIAN INTERPRETIVE COMMUNITY BETWEEN TRADITION, REVELATION, AND SITUATION

WILL OF GOD

OT

NT

Reactions

Situations

JUDAISM

EARLY CHRISTIANITY

CHURCH HISTORY

PRESENT CHRISTIANITY

(W. Kahl)

WORKS CITED

Adamo, David Tuesday. 1999. African Cultural Hermeneutics. Pages 66–90 in *Vernacular Hermeneutics*. Edited by R. S. Sugirtharajah. Sheffield: Sheffield Academic Press.

———. 2000. The Use of Psalms in African Indigenous Churches in Nigeria. Pages 336–49 in West and Dube 2000.

Amin, Samir. 1997. *Capitalism in the Age of Globalization: The Management of Contemporary Society*. Cape Town: Institute for Policy and Social Research; London: Zed Books.

Andrade, Ezequiel Luiz de, et. al. 1994. *Biblia y comunidades negras*. Second Consultation of Afro-American-Caribean Culture and Theology. São Paulo: Polycopy.

ASETT [Associação Ecumênica de Teólogos do Terceiro Mundo]. 1986. *Identidade negra e religião—Consulta sobre cultura negra e teologia na América Latina*. Rio de Janeiro: Centro Ecumênico de Documentação e Informação (CEDI); São Bernardo do Campo: Edições Liberdade.

Barron, Bruce. 1986. *The Health and Wealth Gospel*. Downer's Grove, Ill.: InterVarsity Press.

———. 1992. *Heaven on Earth? The Social and Political Agendas of Dominion Theology*. Grand Rapids: Zondervan.

Barrow, Steve. 1993. *Songs and Liner Notes: Tougher Than Tough*. Birmingham: Island Records.

Barrow, Steve, and Peter Dalton. 1997. *Reggae: The Rough Guide*. London: Rough Guides.

Bediako, Kwame. 1995. *Christianity in Africa: The Renewal of a Non-western Religion*. Edinburgh: Edinburgh University Press; Maryknoll, N.Y.: Orbis.

Benn, Denis, and Kenneth Hall, eds. 2000a. *Contending with Destiny*. Kingston: Ian Randle.

———. 2000b. *Globalization: A Calculus of Inequality—Perspectives from the South*. Kingston: Ian Randle.

Bible and Culture Collective. 1995. *The Postmodern Bible*. New Haven: Yale University Press.

Botha, J. 1994. How Do We Read the Context? *Neot* 28:291–307.

Brathwaite, Kamau. 1982. The Slavery Rebellion in the Great River Valley 1831/2. *Jamaican Historical Review* 8:11–20.

Brown, Duncan. 1998. *Voicing the Text: South African Oral Poetry and Performance*. Cape Town: Oxford University Press.

Brueggemann, Walter. 1993. Trajectories in Old Testament Literature and the Sociology of Ancient Israel. Pages 201–26 in *The Bible and Liberation: Political and Social Hermeneutics*. Edited by Norman K Gottwald and Richard A Horsley. Maryknoll, N.Y.: Orbis.

Bryan, Patrick. 1991. *The Jamaican People 1880–1902*. London: Macmillan.

Burchell, William J. 1824. *Travels in the Interior of Southern Africa*. Vol. 2. London: Longman, Hurst, Rees, Orme, Brown, & Green. Repr., Cape Town: Struik, 1967.

Burkett, Randall. 1978. *Garveyism as a Religious Movement*. ATLA Monograph Series 13. Metuchen, N.J.: Scarecrow.

Buthelezi, Manas. 1973. The Theological Meaning of True Humanity. Pages 93–103 in *Black Theology: The South African Voice*. Edited by Basil More. London: Hurst.

Campbell, John. 1815. *Travels in South Africa: Undertaken at the Request of the Missionary Society*. London: Black, Parry & Co. Repr., Cape Town: Struik, 1974.

Carrasco A., Victoria. 1996. Antropologia indígena e bíblica. *Revista de Interpretação Bíblica Latino-Americana* 26:25–47.

Chambers, W. Val. 1993. Ethiopia Shall Soon Stretch Out Her Hands to God: "The African-Caribbean Context." *Caribbean Journal of Religious Studies* 14:41–48.

Chang, Kevin O'Brien, and Wayne Chen. 1998. *Reggae Routes*. Kingston: Ian Randle.

Chevannes, Barry. 1993. *Rastafari: Roots and Ideology*. Barbados: University of the West Indies Press.

CNBB [Conferência Nacional dos Bispos do Brasil]. 1988. *Ouvi o clamor deste povo: Campanha da Fraternidade 1988—Manual*. Brasília: CNBB.

Comaroff, Jean, and Comaroff, John L. 1991. *Of Revelation and Revolution: Christianity, Colonialism and Consciousness in South Africa*. Chicago: University of Chicago Press.

———. 1997. *Of Revelation and Revolution: The Dialectics of Modernity on a South African Frontier*. Chicago: University of Chicago Press.

Conzelmann, Hans. 1961. *The Theology of Luke*. New York: Harper & Row.

Curtin, Philip. 1990. *The Rise and Fall of the Plantation Complex: Essays in Atlantic History*. Cambridge: Cambridge University Press.

D'Angelo, Mary Rose. 1990. Women in Luke-Acts: A Redactional View. *JBL* 109:441–61.

Davey, Andrew. 1998. Liberation Theology in Peckham. Pages 8–11 in Northcott 1998.

Draper, Jonathan A. 1994. Jesus and the Renewal of Local Community in Galilee. *JTSA* 87:29–42.

———. 1996. Confessional Western Text-Centered Biblical Interpretation and Oral Residual Text. *Semeia* 73:59–77.

———. 2002. "Less Literate are Safer": The Politics of Orality and Literacy in Biblical Interpretation. *AThR* 84:303–18.

———. 2003. The Closed Text and the Heavenly Telephone: The Role of the *Bricoleur* in Oral Mediation of Sacred Text in the Case of George Khambule and the Gospel of John. Pages 57–89 in *Orality, Literacy and Colonialism in Southern Africa*. Edited by Jonathan A. Draper. SemeiaSt 46. Atlanta: Society of Biblical Literature; Pietermaritzburg: Cluster; Leiden: Brill.

———. 2004. George Khambule and the Book of Revelation: Prophet of the Open Heaven. *Neot* 38:250–74.

Draper, Jonathan A., and Gerald O. West. 1989. Anglicans and Scripture in South Africa. Pages 30–52 in *Bounty in Bondage*. Edited by F. England and T. J. M. Paterson. Johannesburg: Ravan.

Dube, J. L. 1936. *UShembe*. Pietermaritzburg: Shuter & Shooter.

Dube, Musa W. 1996. Readings of *Semoya*: Batswana Women's Interpretations of Matt. 15:21–28. *Semeia* 73:111–29.

———. 2000. *Postcolonial Feminist Interpretation of the Bible*. St. Louis: Chalice.

Duffield, Ian K., Christine Jones, and John Vincent. 2000. *Crucibles: Creating Theology at UTU*. Sheffield: Urban Theology Unit.

Felder, Cain. 1989a. *Stony the Road We Trod: African American Biblical Interpretation.* Minneapolis: Fortress.

———, ed. 1989b. *The Study Guide to Dr Cain Hope Felder's Troubling Biblical Waters: Race, Class and Family.* Morriscontown, N.J.: Aaron.

Fisher, Humphrey J. 1973. Conversion Reconsidered: Some Historical Aspects of Religious Conversion in Black Africa. *Africa* 43:27–40.

———. 1985. The Juggernaut's Apologia: Conversion to Islam in Black Africa. *Africa* 55:153–73.

FITC. 1985. *Faith in the City: A Call for Action by Church and Nation.* A Report of the Archbishop of Canterbury's Commission on Urban Priority Areas. London: Church House Publishing.

Foucault, Michel. 1980. *Power/Knowledge: Selected Writings and other Interviews 1972–1977.* New York: Pantheon.

Fowl, Stephen E. 1998. *Engaging Scripture: A Model for Theological Interpretation.* Oxford: Blackwell.

Fowler, Robert M. 1992. *Let the Reader Understand: Reader-Response Criticism and the Gospel of Mark.* Minneapolis: Fortress.

Freire, Paulo. 1973. *Pedagogy of the Oppressed.* Harmondsworth, U.K.: Penguin.

Gayle, Clement. 1982. *George Liele: Pioneer Missionary to Jamaica.* Kingston: Jamaica Baptist Union.

Gebara, Ivone. 1988. A mulher, contribuição à teologia moral na América Latina. Pages 195–209 in *Temas latino-americanos de ética.* Edited by Márcio Fabri dos Anjos. Aparecida: Santuário.

Gottwald, Norman K. 1995. Framing Biblical Interpretation at New York Theological Seminary: A Student Self-Inventory on Biblical Hermeneutics. Pages 251–61 in *Reading from This Place: Social Location and Biblical Interpretation in the United States.* Edited by Fernando F. Segovia and Mary Ann Tolbert. Minneapolis: Fortress.

Gramsci, Antonio. 1971. *Selections from the Prison Notebooks.* Edited and translated by Quinten Hoare and Geoffrey Nowell Smith. London: Lawrence & Wishart.

Green, Joel B. 1995. *The Theology of the Gospel of Luke.* New York: Cambridge University Press.

Green, Laurie. 1995. Blowing Bubbles: Poplar. Pages 72–92 in Sedgwick 1995.

———. 1996. *Let's Do Theology. A Pastoral Cycle Resource Book.* London: Mowbray. [Orig. 1990]

———. 1998. Why Do Theological Reflection? Pages 11–23 in Northcott 1998.

Gunner, Elizabeth. 1986. The Word, the Book and the Zulu Church of Nazareth. Pages 179–88 in *Oral Tradition and Literacy: Changing Visions of the World.* Edited by Richard A. Whitaker and Edgard R. Sienaert. Durban: Natal University Oral Documentation and Research Center.

———. 2002. *The Man of Heaven and the Beautiful Ones of God: Writings from Ibandla lamaNazaretha, a South African Church.* Leiden: Brill.

Harvey, Anthony, ed. 1989. *Theology in the City: A Theological Response to "Faith in the City."* London: SPCK.

Hastings, Adrian. 2001. *A History of English Christianity 1920–2000.* 4th ed. London: SCM.

Henkett, Holger. 2000. *Between Self-Determination and Dependency: Jamaica's Foreign Relations 1972–1989.* Barbados: University of the West Indies Press.

Hermanson, Eric A. 2002. A Brief Overview of Bible Translation in South Africa. *Acta Theologica Supplementum* 2:6–17.

Herzog, William R. 1994. *Parables as Subversive Speech: Jesus as a Pedagogue of the Oppressed*. Louisville: Westminster John Knox.

Heuman, Gad. 1991. *"The Killing Time": The Morant Bay Rebellion in Jamaica*. London: Macmillan.

Hinga, Teresa M. 1996. "Reading with": An Exploration of the Interface between "Critical" and "Ordinary" Readings of the Bible: A Response. *Semeia* 73:277–84.

Holt, Thomas. 1989. *The Problem of Freedom: Race, Labor and Politics in Jamaica and Britain, 1832–1938*. Kingston: Ian Randle.

Horton, Robin. 1971. African Conversion. *Africa* 41:85–108.

———. 1975. On the Rationality of Conversion. *Africa* 45:219–35, 373–99.

Hutton, Clinton. 1992. "Color for Color: Skin for Skin": The Ideological Foundations of Post-Slavery Society 1838–1865: The Jamaican Case. Ph.D. diss. University of the West Indies.

James, Winston. 1998. *Holding Aloft the Banner of Ethiopia: Caribbean Radicalism in Early Twentieth-Century America*. London: Verso.

Janssen, Claudia, and Regene Lamb. 1998. Das Evangelium nach Lukas. Pages 514–17 in *Kompendium Feministische Bibelauslegung*. Edited by Luise Schottroff and Marie-Theres Wacker. Gütersloh: Christian Kaiser/Gütersloher Verlagshaus.

Jobling, David. 1995. Structuralist Criticism: The Text's World of Meaning. Pages 91–118 in *Judges and Method: New Approaches in Biblical Studies*. Edited by Gale A. Yee. Minneapolis: Fortress.

———. 1998. *1 Samuel*. Berit Olam. Collegeville, Minn.: Liturgical Press.

King, Anthony, ed. 1997. *Culture, Globalization and the World-System*. Minneapolis: University of Minnesota Press.

King, Fergus J. 2000. Nyimbo za vijana: Biblical Interpretation in Contemporary Hymns from Tanzania. Pages 360–73 in West and Dube 2000.

Kirk, Andrew. 1989. A Different Task: Liberation Theology and Local Theologies. Pages 15–31 in Harvey 1989.

Klak, Thomas, ed. 1998. *Globalization and Neoliberalism: The Caribbean Context*. Lanham: Rowman & Littlefield.

Kock, Leon de. 1993. Postcolonial Analysis and the Question of Critical Disablement. *Current Writing* 5:44–69.

Kramer-Dahl, Anneliese. 1995. Reconsidering the Notions of Voice and Experience in Critical Pedagogy. Pages 242–62 in *Feminisms and Pedagogies of Everyday Life*. Edited by Carmen Luke. Albany: State University of New York Press

Kugel, James L. 1998. *Traditions of the Bible: A Guide to the Bible as It Was at the Start of the Common Era*. Cambridge: Harvard University Press.

Lampe, Armando. 2000. *Christianity in the Caribbean: Essays on Church History*. Barbados: University of the West Indies Press.

Lategan, Bernard. 1996. Scholar and Ordinary Reader—More than a Simple Interface. *Semeia* 73:243–55.

Ledwith, Margaret. 2001. Community Work as Critical Pedagogy: Re-envisioning Friere and Gramsci. *Community Development Journal* 36:171–82.

Leeb-du Toit, Juliette C. 1993. *Spiritual Art of Natal*. Pietermaritzburg: Tatham Art Gallery.

———. 2003. Contextualizing the Use of Biblically Derived and Metaphysical Imagery in the Work of Black Artists from KwaZulu-Natal: c1930–2002. Ph.D. diss. School of Language, Culture and Communication, University of Natal.

Lees, Janet A. 1997. Interpreting the Bible with People with Communication Difficulties. M.Th. thesis. University of Natal, Pietermaritzburg, South Africa.

Leigh, Valerie T. L. 2002. Aspects of Identity in KwaZulu-Natal Art 1980–2000 with Special Reference to the Complexity of Influences Shaping the Work of Andries Botha, Jinny Heath, Derek Leigh and Trevor Makhoba, School of Language, Culture and Communication. M.A. thesis. University of Natal, South Africa.

Lewis, Rupert. 1987a. *Garvey's Forerunner*. Love and Bechward: Race & Class.

———. 1987b. *Marcus Garvey: Anti-Colonial Champion*. London: Karia

Lewis, Rupert, and Patrick Bryan, eds. 1986. *Garvey: His Work and His Impact*. Kingston: Institute of Social and Economic Research and the Department of Extra-Mural Studies, University of the West Indies.

Lewis, Rupert, and Maureen Warner-Lewis, eds. 1994. *Garvey: Africa, Europe, the Americas*. Trenton, N.J.: Africa World.

Long, Tim. 1996. A Real Reader Reading Revelation. *Semeia* 73:79–107.

López Hernández, Eleazar. 1996. Povos da Bíblia e povos índios hoje. *Revista de Interpretação Bíblica Latino-Americana* 26:16–24.

Maddix, Renford. 1986. Toward a Theology of Marcus Garvey. M.A. thesis. University of the West Indies.

Mafu, Hezekiel. 2000. The Impact of the Bible on Traditional Rain-Making Institutions in Western Zimbabwe. Pages 400–411 in West and Dube 2000.

Maluleke, Tinyiko S. 1996. Black and African Theologies in the New World Order: A Time to Drink from Our Own Wells. *JTSA* 96:3–19.

———. 2000. The Rediscovery of the Agency of Africans: An Emerging Paradigm of Postcold War and Post-apartheid Black and African Theology. *JTSA* 108:19–37.

———. 2004. African Christianity as African Religion: Beyond the Contextualization Paradigm. Pages 181–91 in *African Christian Theologies in Transformation*. Edited by Ernst M. Conradie. Stellenbosch: EFSA.

Martin, Gerhard Marcel. 2001. *Sachbuch Bibliodrama: Praxis und Theorie*. 2nd ed. Stuttgart: Kohlhammer.

Masoga, Mogomme Alpheus. 2000. *Weeping City, Shanty Town Jesus: Introduction to Controversational Theology*. Cape Town: Salty Print.

———. 2001. Re-defining Power: Reading the Bible in Africa from the Peripheral and Central Positions. Pages 133–47 in *Towards an Agenda for Contextual Theology*. Edited by McGlory T. Speckman and Larry T. Kaufmann. Pietermaritzburg: Cluster.

Mattos, Paulo Ayres. 1994. O direito de ser diferente (Lucas 9:51–56). *Revista de Interpretação Bíblica Latino-Americana* 19:16–22.

Meeks, Brian, and Folke Lindahl, eds. 2001. *New Caribbean Thought: A Reader*. Barbados: University of the West Indies Press.

Mesters, Carlos. 1983. *Flor sem defesa—Uma explicação da Bíblia a partir do povo*. Petrópolis: Vozes.

———. 1989. *Defenseless Flower: A New Reading of the Bible*. Maryknoll, N.Y.: Orbis. [Orig. 1983]

———. 1997. Criança não é problema! Ela é a solução! *EstBíb* 54:9–20.

Meyer, Wilhelm H. 2002. Reading Mark 4:35–41: A Study of Student Discourses in the School of Theology, the University of Natal, Pietermaritzburg. Ph.D. diss. School of Theology, University of Natal, Pietermaritzburg.

Mijoga, Hilary B. P. 2000. *Separate but Same Gospel: Preaching in African Instituted Churches in Southern Malawi*. Blantyre: Kachere.

———. 2001. Interpreting the Bible in African Sermons. Pages 123–44 in *Interpreting the New Testament in Africa*. Edited by Mary Getui, Tinyiko S. Maluleke, and Justin S. Ukpong. Nairobi: Acton.

Moffat, Robert. 1842. *Missionary Labors and Scenes in Southern Africa*. London: John Snow. Repr., New York: Johnson, 1969.

Mofokeng, Takatso. 1988. Black Christians, the Bible and Liberation. *Journal of Black Theology in South Africa* 2/1:34–42.

Moholo. Solly. 2000. *Ba Mmitsa Tsotsi*. Johannesburg: CCP Record Company.

Moody, Gill. 1995. Life in the City. Pages 9–15 in Sedgwick 1995.

Mosala, Itumeleng J. 1986. The Use of Bible in Black Theology. Pages 175–99 in *The Unquestionable Right to Be Free: Essays in Black Theology*. Edited by Itumeleng J. Mosala and Buti Tlhagale. Johannesburg: Skotaville; Maryknoll, N.Y.: Orbis.

———. 1991. Land, Class and the Bible in South Africa Today. *Journal of Black Theology in South Africa* 5/2:40–45.

———. 1996. Race, Class, Gender as Hermeneutical Factors in African Independent Churches' Appropriation of the Bible. *Semeia* 73:43–57.

Mudimbe, V. Y. 1988. *The Invention of Africa*: Bloomington: Indiana University Press.

Muller, Carol Ann. 1999. Rituals of Fertility and the Sacrifice of Desire: Nazarite Women's Performance in South Africa. Chicago: University of Chicago Press.

———. 2003. Making the Book, Performing the Words of *Izihlabelelo ZamaNazaretha*. Pages 91–110 in *Orality, Literacy and Colonialism in Southern Africa*. Edited by Jonathan A. Draper. SemeiaSt 46. Atlanta: Society of Biblical Literature; Pietermaritzburg: Cluster; Leiden: Brill.

Murrell, Nathaniel, Spencer William, and Adrian McFarlane. 1998. *Chanting Down Babylon*. Philadelphia: Temple University Press.

Naude, Piet. 1996. Theology with a New Voice: The Case for an Oral Theology in the Southern Context. *JTSA* 96:18–31.

Navia Velasco, Carmiña. 1991. *La mujer en la Bíblia: Opresión y liberación*. Bogotá: Indo American Press.

Ndung'u, Nahashon. W. 1997. The Bible in an African Independent Church. Pages 58–67 in *The Bible in African Christianity*. Edited by Hannah W. Kinoti and John M. Waliggo. Nairobi: Acton.

———. 2000. The Role of the Bible in the Rise of African Instituted Churches: The Case of the Akurinu Churches of Kenya. Pages 236–47 in West and Dube 2000.

Nkwoka, Anthony O. 2000. The Role of the Bible in the Igbo Christianity of Nigeria. Pages 326–35 in West and Dube 2000.

Nolan, Albert. 1996. Work, the Bible, Workers and Theologians: Elements of a "Workers" Theology. *Semeia* 73:213–20.

Northcott, Michael, ed. 1998. *Urban Theology. A Reader*. For the Archbishop of Canterbury's UrbanTheology Group. London: Cassell.

Nthamburi, Zablon, and Douglas Waruta. 1997. Biblical Hermeneutics in African Instituted Churches. Pages 40–57 in *The Bible in African Christianity*. Edited by Hannah W. Kinoti and John M. Waliggo. Nairobi: Acton.

Okure, Teresa. 1993. Feminist Interpretation in Africa. Pages 76–85 in *Searching the Scriptures: A Feminist Introduction*. Edited by Elisabeth Schüssler-Fiorenza. New York: Crossroads.

Patte, Daniel. 1996. Biblical Scholars at the Interface between Critical and Ordinary Readings: A Response. *Semeia* 73:263–76.

Parvey, Constance F. 1974. The Theology and Leadership of Women in the New Testament. Pages 117–49 in *Religion and Sexism*. Edited by Rosemary Radford Ruether. New York: Simon & Schuster.

Peel, J. D. Y. 2000. *Religious Encounter and the Making of the Yoruba*. Bloomington: Indiana University Press.

Peley Chourío, Marcos.1993. Leitura indígena. Pages 23–36 in *Bibliografia Bíblica Latino-Americana 5, 1992*. Edited by Milton Schwantes. Petrópolis: Vozes.

Perdue, Leo G. 1991. *Wisdom in Revolt: Metaphorical Theology in the Book of Job*. Sheffield: Almond.

Pereira, Nancy Cardoso. 1996. Mas nós mulheres dizemos. *Revista de Interpretação Bíblica Latino-Americana* 25:5–10.

Pereira, Onaldo Alves. 1998. A Bíblia e o homossexualismo. *Jornal Opção* 3–9 May:A36–A38.

Philpott, Graham. 1993. *Jesus Is Tricky and God Is Undemocratic: The Kindom of God in Amaoti*. Pietermaritzburg: Cluster.

Pierson, Roscoe. 1969. Alexander Bedward and the Jamaica Native Baptist Free Church. *LTQ* 4:66–76.

Pitzele, Peter. 1998. *Scripture Windows: Towards a Practice of Bibliodrama*. Los Angeles: Torah Aura.

Pobee, John S. 1996. Bible Study in Africa: A Passover of Language. *Semeia* 73:161–79.

Räisänen, Heikki. 1989. Bibliodrama ja Raamattu. [Bibliodrama and the Bible] *TAik* 94:235–40.

Ramm, Bernard. 1970. *Protestant Biblical Interpretation*. 3rd ed. Grand Rapids: Baker.

Ranger, Terence. 1986. Religious Movements and Politics in Sub-Saharan Africa. *African Studies Review* 29:1–69.

Reid, Clarence. 1983. *Samuel Sharpe: From Slave to National Hero*. Kingston: Bustamante Institute of Public Affairs.

Reimer, Haroldo, and Ivoni Richter Reimer. 1999. *Tempos de graça: O jubileu e as tradições jubilares na Bíblia*. São Leopoldo: CEBI/Paulus/Sinodal.

Riches, John K. 1996. Interpreting the Bible in African Contexts: Glasgow Consultation. *Semeia* 73:181–88.

Roberts, Esther. 1936. Shembe: The Man and His Work. M.A. thesis. University of the Witwatersrand, South Africa.

Roberts, Peter. 1997. *From Oral to Literate Culture: Colonial Experience in the English West Indies*. Barbados: University of the West Indies Press.

Rowland, Christopher. 1999. Introduction: The Theology of Liberation. Pages 1–16 in *The Cambridge Companion to Liberation Theology*. Edited by Christopher Rowland. Cambridge: Cambridge University Press.

Rowland, Christopher, and Mark Corner. 1991 *Liberating Exegesis: The Challenge of the Liberation Theology to Biblical Studies*. Cambridge: SPCK.

Rowland, Christopher, and John Vincent, eds. 2001. *Bible and Practice: British Liberation Theology.* Vol. 4. Sheffield: Urban Theology Unit.

Russell, Horace. 1989. *Foundations and Anticipations: The Jamaica Baptist Story 1783–1892.* Columbus, Ga.: Brentwood Christian.

Samuel, Albert. 1997. *As religiões hoje.* Translated from *Les religions aujourd'hui.* São Paulo: Paulus.

Sanneh, Lamin. 1989. *Translating the Message: The Missionary Impact on Culture.* Maryknoll, N.Y.: Orbis.

———. 1990. *West African Christianity: The Religious Impact.* Maryknoll, N.Y.: Orbis.

Schiller, Mimi. 1998. *Democracy after Slavery: Black Publics and Peasant Radicalism in Haiti and Jamaica.* London: Macmillan.

Schramm, Tim. 1971. *Der Markus-Stoff bei Lukas: Eine literarkritische und redaktionsgeschichtliche Untersuchung.* SNTSMS 14. Cambridge: Cambridge University Press.

Schürger, Wolfgang. 1997. Raamatuntulkinta vapautuksen näkökulmasta: Vapautuksen teologian haaste eurooppalaiselle hermeneutiikalle [Hermeneutics from a Liberation Point of View: The Challenge of Liberation Theology to the European Hermeneutics]. Pages 166–80 in *Raamatuntutkimuksen uudet tuulet.* Edited by R. Hakola and P. Merenlahti. Helsinki: Yliopistopaino.

Schüssler Fiorenza, Elisabeth. 1992. *But She Said: Feminist Practices of Biblical Interpretation.* Boston: Beacon.

Scott, David. 1998. *Refashioning Futures: Criticism after Postcoloniality.* Princeton: Princeton University Press.

Scott, James C. 1990. *Domination and the Arts of Resistance: Hidden Transcripts.* New Haven: Yale University Press.

Sedgwick, Peter, ed. 1995. *God in the City: Essays and Reflections from the Archbishop's Urban Theology Group.* London: Mowbray.

Segal, Ronald. 1989. *The Black Diaspora.* London: Faber & Faber.

Segovia, Fernando F. 1995. Two Places and No Place on Which to Stand: Mixture and Otherness in Hispanic American Theology. Pages 29–43 in *Mestizo Christianity: Theology from the Latino Perspective.* Maryknoll, N.Y.: Orbis.

Segovia, Fernando F., and Mary Ann Tolbert, eds. 1995. *Reading from This Place: Social Location and Biblical Interpretation in the United States.* Minneapolis: Fortress.

Serbin, Andres. 1998. *Sunset over the Islands: The Caribbean in an Age of Global and Regional Challenges.* London: Macmillan.

Shepherd, Verene, Bridget Brereton, and Barbara Bailey, eds. 1989. *Engendering History: Caribbean Women in Historical Perspective.* Kingston: Ian Randle.

Sherlock, Philip, and Hazel Bennett. 1998. *The Story of the Jamaican People.* Kingston: Ian Randle; Princeton: Marcus Wiener.

Sibisi, Paul. 1996. *Uma ngisaphila: As Long as I Live.* Grahamstown: Standard Bank National Arts Festival.

Silva, Valmor da. 1994. Historia de la lectura de la Biblia en América Latina. *La Palabra Hoy* 19:26–59.

———. 1997. Crianças no Novo Testamento. *EstBíb* 54:58–70.

Simopoulos, Nicole M. 1998a. Black South African Women's Reflections on Genesis Chapter 16. Bible study facilitated by the author. Tape recording, South Africa.

———. 1998b. Caucasian Women's Reflections on Genesis Chapter 16. Bible study facilitated by the author. Tape recording, California.

———. 1998c. Latina Women's Reflections on Genesis Chapter 16. Bible study facilitated by the author. Tape recording, California.

———. 2000. Caucasian Women's 2000 Reflections on Genesis Chapter 16. Bible study facilitated by the author. Tape recording, California.

Smit, Johannes. 2004. J. T. van der Kemp's Interpretation of the New Testament on the Frontier (1799–1801). Pages 129–56 in *Text and Context in New Testament Hermeneutics*. Edited by Jesse N. K. Mugambi. Nairobi: Acton.

Smith, Michael. 2001. *Transitional Urbanism: Locating Globalization*. Malden, Mass.: Blackwell.

Souza, Marcelo de Barros. 1983. *A Bíblia e a luta pela terra*. Petrópolis: Vozes.

Stackhouse, Max, and Peter Paris, eds. 2000. *God and Globalization: Religion and the Powers of the Common Life*. Pennsylvania: Trinity.

Steiner, George. 1979. Critic/Reader. *New Literary History* 10:423–52.

Sundkler, Bengt G. M. 1976. *Zulu Zion and Some Swazi Zionists*. Oxford: Oxford University Press.

Taylor, Paul V. 1993. *The Texts of Paulo Freire.*: Buckingham: Open University Press

Terreblanche, Sampie. 2002. *A History of Inequality in South Africa, 1652–2002*. Pietermaritzburg: University of Natal Press.

Tomlinson, John. 1999. *Globalization and Culture*. Chicago: University of Chicago Press.

Tshehla, Maarman Sam. 2003. Translation and the Vernacular Bible in the Debate between my "Traditional" and Academic Worldviews. Pages 171–87 in *Orality, Literacy and Colonialism in Southern Africa*. Edited by Jonathan A. Draper. SemeiaSt 46. Atlanta: Society of Biblical Literature; Pietermaritzburg: Cluster; Leiden: Brill.

Ukpong, Justin S. 1996. The Parable of the Shrewd Manager (Luke 16:1–13): An Essay in Inculturation Biblical Hermeneutic. *Semeia* 73:189–210.

———. 2000a. Developments in Biblical Interpretation in Africa: Historical and Hermeneutical Directions. *JTSA* 108:3–18.

———. 2000b. Developments in Biblical Interpretation in Africa: Historical and Hermeneutical Directions. Pages 11–28 in West and Dube 2000.

———. 2000c. Popular Readings of the Bible in Africa and Implications for Academic Readings: Report on the Field Research Carried Out on Oral Interpretations of the Bible in Port Harcourt Metropolis, Nigeria under the Auspices of the Bible in Africa Project, 1991–94. Pages 582–94 in West and Dube 2000.

Vincent, John. 2000. *Hope from the City*. London: Epworth.

Walsh, Margaret. 1995. Here's Hoping: The Hope Community, Wolverhampton. Pages 52–71 in Sedgwick 1995.

Wavlin, James. 1989. *Questioning Slavery*. Kingston: Ian Randle.

Weems, Renita J. 1996. Response to "Reading with": An Exploration of the Interface between Critical and Ordinary Readings of the Bible. *Semeia* 73:257–61.

West, Gerald O. 1991. *Biblical Hermeneutics of Liberation: Modes of Reading the Bible in the South African Context*. Pietermaritzburg: Cluster; Maryknoll, N.Y.: Orbis.

———. 1993. The Interface between Trained Readers and Ordinary Readers in Liberation Hermeneutics: A Case Study: Mark 10:17–22. *Neot* 27:165–80.

———. 1995a. *Biblical Hermeneutics of Liberation: Modes of Reading the Bible in the South African Context*. 2nd ed. Maryknoll, N.Y.: Orbis; Pietermaritzburg: Cluster.

———. 1995b. Constructing Critical and Contextual Readings with Ordinary Readers: Mark 5:21–6:1. *JTSA* 92:60–69.

————. 1996. Reading the Bible Differently: Giving Shape to the Discourses of the Dominated. *Semeia* 73:21–41.

————. 1999. *The Academy of the Poor: Towards a Dialogical Reading of the Bible*. Sheffield: Sheffield Academic Press.

————. 2000. Mapping African Biblical Interpretation: A Tentative Sketch. Pages 29–53 in West and Dube 2000.

————. 2002. Indigenous Exegesis: Exploring the Interface between Missionary Methods and the Rhetorical Rhythms of Africa: Locating Local Reading Resources in the Academy. *Neot* 36:147–62.

————. 2003a. *The Academy of the Poor: Towards a Dialogical Reading of the Bible*. Pietermaritzburg: Cluster. [Orig. 1999]

————. 2003b. Redirecting the Direction of Travel: Discerning Signs of a Neo-indigenous Southern African Biblical Hermeneutics. Pages 201–25 in *Redirected Travel: Alternative Journeys and Places in Biblical Studies*. Edited by Roland Boer and Ed Conrad. Sheffield: Sheffield Academic Press.

————. 2004a. Early Encounters with the Bible among the BaTlhaping: Historical and Hermeneutical Signs. *BibInt* 12:251–81.

————. 2004b. The Open and Closed Bible: The Bible in African Theologies. Pages 162–80 in *African Christian Theologies in Transformation*. Edited by Ernst M. Conradie. Stellenbosch: EFSA.

————. 2005. Shifting Perspectives on the Comparative Paradigm In (South) African Biblical Scholarship. *Religion and Theology* 12:48–72.

————. 2006a. Contextualised Reading of the Bible. *Analecta Bruxellensia* 11:131–48.

————. 2006b. Reading Shembe "Re-membering" the Bible: Isaiah Shembe's Instructions on Adultery. *Neot* 40: 157–84.

————. 2006c. The Vocation of an African Biblical Scholar on the Margins of Biblical Scholarship. *OTE* 19 (1):307–36.

West, Gerald O., and Musa W. Dube. 1996a. An Introduction: How We Have Come to "Read With." *Semeia* 73:7–17.

————, eds. 1996b. *"Reading With": An Exploration of the Interface between Critical and Ordinary Readings of the Bible: African Overtures. Semeia* 73.

————, eds. 2000. *The Bible in Africa: Transactions, Trajectories and Trends*. Leiden: Brill.

West, Gerald O., and Bongi Zengele. 2004. Reading Job "Positively" in the Context of HIV/AIDS in South Africa. *Concilium* 4:112–24.

————. 2006. The Medicine of God's Word: What People Living with HIV and AIDS Want (and Get) from the Bible. *JTSA* 125:51–63.

Wimbush, Vincent L. 1991. The Bible and African Americans: An Outline of an Interpretative History. Pages 81–97 in *Stony the Road We Trod: African American Biblical Interpretation*. Edited by Cain Hope Felder. Minneapolis: Fortress.

————. 1993. Reading Texts through Worlds, Worlds through Texts. *Semeia* 62:129–40.

————, ed. 2000. *African Americans and the Bible: Sacred Texts and Social Textures*. New York: Continuum.

Wittenberg, Gunther H. 1996. Old Testament Theology, For Whom? *Semeia* 73:221–40.

Yorke, Gosnell L. O. R. 1995. Biblical Hermeneutics: An Afrocentric Perspective. *Journal of Religious Thought* 52:1–13.

CONTRIBUTORS

Eric B. Anum is a New Testament lecturer in the Department of Religion and HumanValues at the University of Cape Coast, Ghana. He can be reached at eanum55@yahoo.com.

Valmor da Silva is a lecturer in the Postgraduate Program in Religious Studies in the Catholic University of Goiás, Goiânia, Brasil, where he also teaches courses in history, society, and biblical literature. He can be reached at lesil@terra.com.br.

Bob Ekblad is the Executive Director of Tierra Nueva and The People's Seminary in Burlington, Washington, U.S.A. He is also a minister in the Presbyterian church. He can be reached at bob@bobekblad.com.

Stephen C. A. Jennings is a minister of the Jamaica Baptist Union and currently serves as one of its vice-presidents and as pastor of the Mona-Mammee River Circuit of Baptist Churches in Kingston, Jamaica. He is president-elect of the Jamaica Baptist Union. He is also a part-time Baptist tutor of the United Theological College of the West Indies. He can be reached at didaphen@yahoo.com

Werner Kahl taught for some time in the field of New Testament at the University of Ghana, Legon. He was Professor of New Testament at the University of Kassel, before his current position as Head of Studies at the Academy of Mission at the University of Hamburg, Germany. At the same time, he is also Privatdozent for New Testament at the University of Frankfurt, Germany. He can be reached at werner.kahl@missionsakademie.de.

Kari Latvus is a Principal Lecturer at the Diaconia University of Applied Sciences, Finland. He is also an adjunct professor (Old Testament exegesis) at the Helsinki University and Visiting Professor of Diaconia at the Theological Institute (Tallinn). Before his current positions he worked at the Lutheran Theological Seminary in Hong Kong as Old Testament Professor. He can be reached at kari.latvus@diak.fi.

Janet Lees is a speech therapist and an ordained minister of the United Reformed Church in England. She is also a Research Associate in the Department of Sociological Studies of the University of Sheffield for a project called Religion and Family Life. She can be reached at J.A.Lees@sheffield.ac.uk.

Mogomme A. Masoga is Dean of the Pretoria Circuit, Central Diocese, Evangelical Lutheran Church of South Africa, and Research Fellow at the University of South Africa in the Human Ecology Department. He can be reached at dithobela@webmail.co.za.

Monika Ottermann works with CEBI, the Brazilian base-community Bible movement, is partner of Inter Editora publishing house, and works with several others publishers translating exegetical literature from German and English into Portugese. She can be reached at monicacebi@directnet.com.br.

Naveen Rao is an ordained minister in the Methodist Church in India and is Dean of the School of Theology and Registrar of Leonard Theological College, Jabalpur, India. He can be reached at nerao2003@yahoo.com.

Nicole Simopoulos is an Episcopal priest in the Diocese of Oregon and chaplain and religion teacher at Oregon Episcopal School in Portland, Oregon, U.S.A. She can be reached at simopoulosn@oes.edu

Gerald O. West is Professor of Old Testament/Hebrew Bible and Biblical Hermeneutics and the Director of Ujamaa Centre for Community Development and Research in the School of Religion and Theology at the University of KwaZulu-Natal, Pietermaritzburg, South Africa. He can be reached at west@ukzn.ac.za.

Printed in the United States
200032BV00004B/259-528/A

9 781589 832732